D1527731

# THE
# LEADERSHIP
# GENIUS OF
# ALFRED P. SLOAN

# THE LEADERSHIP GENIUS OF ALFRED P. SLOAN

Invaluable Lessons on Business, Management, and Leadership for Today's Manager

Allyn Freeman

**McGraw-Hill**

New York   Chicago   San Francisco   Lisbon   London   Madrid   Mexico City
Milan   New Delhi   San Juan   Seoul   Singapore   Sydney   Toronto

The *McGraw-Hill* Companies

1 2 3 4 5 6 7 8 9 0 DOC/DOC 0 9 8 7 6 5

ISBN 0-07-145796-8

This publication is designed to provide accurate and authoritative information in regard to the subject matter covered. It is sold with the understanding that the publisher is not engaged in rendering legal, accounting, or other professional service. If legal advice or other expert assistance is required, the services of a competent professional person should be sought.

> —*From a declaration of principles jointly adopted by a committee of the American Bar Association and a committee of publishers.*

McGraw-Hill books are available at special quantity discounts to use as premiums and sales promotions, or for use in corporate training programs. For more information, please write to the Director of Special Sales, McGraw-Hill Professional, Two Penn Plaza, New York, NY 10121-2298. Or contact your local bookstore.

This book is printed on recycled, acid-free paper containing a minimum of 50% recycled, de-inked fiber.

# Contents

# Preface

> Too often we fail to recognize and pay tribute to the creative spirit.
>
> *Alfred P. Sloan, Jr.*

At the completion of a television program on the Public Broadcasting System, the credit states: "Sponsored by the Alfred P. Sloan Foundation." Who is this Alfred P. Sloan who amassed such large sums that he, along with well-known wealthy families like the Rockefellers and Carnegies, could fund an entire PBS documentary?

To answer that question you might go to the www.sloan.org Web site to discover that the foundation started in 1934 and its philanthropic work covers a range of science, economic, educational, and cultural areas. At the end of 2003, the current value of its assets totaled an astounding $1.3 billion.

More research indicates that Sloan cofounded the Memorial Sloan-Kettering Cancer Center in New York City in 1946, one of the world's leading cancer care and research centers. He is the same man who endowed the prestigious Sloan School of Management at the Massachusetts Institute of Technology. Finally, the list ends with the Alfred P. Sloan Museum—Flint, Michigan's center for historic automobiles and regional history.

In the Web site's biographical section, it is revealed that Alfred P. Sloan, Jr., generated all his money as an employee while serving as president and chief executive officer of General Motors Corporation during most of six decades at GM, His accomplishments are universally considered the pinnacle of managerial and leadership achievements, a corporate career success unparalleled in the twentieth century of American business.

The elemental truth is that when Alfred P. Sloan, Jr., took the reins of General Motors, he transformed the concept of the modern corporate organization fosrever.

## FORMAT OF THIS BOOK

This work is composed of two elements: the managerial intelligence of Alfred P. Sloan, Jr., arranged in distinct chapters, and numerous examples of other companies and organizations, large and small, that have demonstrated the wisdom of his instructive and innovative practices.

Sloan's leadership and managerial lessons—derived from his two autobiographies and from other writings, most notably, by management guru Peter Drucker—provide a history of the first successful applications of the modern American corporation. These are basic, commonsense Sloan solutions to general and specific organizational and business situations of the past that can be applied today.

The case histories come from a wide range of diverse companies and organizations that reinforce or highlight some aspect of Sloan's particular business lesson. These actual cases demonstrate the success of adhering to one of Sloan's business concepts. Further, a few of these examples illustrate what happened when the Sloan principle was ignored.

Alfred P. Sloan, Jr., provided a dynamic new vision of how to lead and operate the modern corporation; and he did it with insights and rare good judgment. This book's contention is that a look at the historical Sloan GM experience represents a study in practical and logical thinking that can instruct a manager on the path to success.

*Allyn I. Freeman*

# Acknowledgments

The writing of this book could not have been accomplished without the valuable input and assistance of friends and colleagues. To that end, I am indebted to: Ruth Marzano, Arie Kopelman, Maria and Bill Brisk, Ezra Mager, Lawrence M. Small, Michael Herman, Peter Thompson, Richard and Susan Lewis, Carrie and William Rosenthal, Janice Lee, Steven Rhodes, Elissa Moses, Arthur Anderson, Robert E. Gorman, Joie Smith, Steven Berkenfeld, Pat Barry, Douglas Fielding, Cynthia Jenner, Ruth Mills, Peter Kiers, Jo-Ann Wasserman, Marian and Edward Last, Pat and Charles Clarkson, Sean Murphy, Kieran Murphy, Kathy Roeder, Hunan Pan, Ed Reilly, Three Lives Book Store, and Marcia Shrock.

Thanks to Jeanne Glasser, Senior Editor at McGraw-Hill, for suggesting the topic and hiring me to write the book. Lara Murphy at McGraw-Hill was also helpful with comments. Pattie Amoroso shepherded the manuscript to its completion.

# THE
# LEADERSHIP
# GENIUS OF
# ALFRED P. SLOAN

# THE GREAT ACCOMPLISHMENT: THE SLOAN SYSTEM

**A**LFRED **P.** S**LOAN**, J**R.** (1875–1965) changed the manufacturing methods, organizational structure, marketing, sales, distribution, financing, and advertising used in the automotive industry—in short, every aspect of U.S. automobile manufacture and production. Moreover, in this dramatic conversion, this complete industry makeover, he also revolutionized the world of the American corporation like no one had done before him or may ever do again.

In the beginning of his second autobiography, *My Years with General Motors*, published in 1963, in the chapter "The Great Opportunity—I," Sloan wrote about the two men who invented the American system of automobile marketing and car manufacture: "Mr. Durant [GM] and Mr. Ford had unusual vision, courage, daring imagination, and foresight. . . .They injected their personalities . . . without the discipline of management by method and objective facts.[1]"

The essence of Sloan's future transformation of the corporate world was the need for discipline, method, and facts. He was ready when the opportunity occurred to put into effect the "Sloan system." When he assumed the presidency of General Motors in 1923, he stated that "it was clear to me long before this time there was a real opportunity for great accomplishment."[2]

The story of Alfred P. Sloan, Jr., of General Motors is the story of leadership and managerial skill unsurpassed in the annals of American business.

## MEETING SLOAN

The team that Sloan captained for more than 42 years was the General Motors Corporation. He had come to work at GM after the company purchased the Hyatt Roller Bearing Company (Newark, New Jersey) in 1916, where Sloan was president and a major stockholder. The General Motors president at that time, William Crapo Durant, appointed Sloan to be the president of a newly formed GM corporate entity called United Motors Company, composed of automobile accessory manufacturers in the GM fold.

When Sloan moved from being head of United Motors to vice president of operations at General Motors in 1920 under Pierre du Pont's presidency, the corporation was a loosely formed assemblage of car divisions in organizational and financial disarray. In 1921, total production of GM cars from all of its five divisions generated a small 12 percent share of the U.S. automobile market compared to the Ford Motor Company's dominance at 60 percent. (GM was the second-ranking U.S. car manufacturing company.)

Historically, Henry Ford had been so successful with his Model-T assembly-line operation—mass production, fair wages, high volume to justify a low sales price—that the term "Fordism" was used worldwide to signify successful mass production and full employment. Even the leaders of the Russian Revolution used this odd catchword.

The Ford Company's stunning sales and production success in the 1910 to 1920 decade had been a boon for Sloan's Hyatt Roller Bearing Company. Ford Motor Company purchased annually almost 50 percent of the New Jersey-based company's ball bearing production. In effect, the future irony was that Alfred P. Sloan, Jr., rose to automobile prominence and riches partially on the coattails of Henry Ford's Model-T.

Probably to any one else but Alfred P. Sloan, Jr., the Ford Motor Company's dominant market supremacy in the early 1920s would have seemed an insurmountable challenge. Nevertheless, Sloan perceived that Ford was an overblown leviathan, a shaky monolith that if it could not be toppled could at least be challenged. He would be able to test this theory when he assumed the role of director of operations at GM in 1920 and when he became GM's president three years later.

GM's ascendancy was helped by Henry Ford's refusal to realize that the American automobile purchaser desired choices in color, style, and models. His infamous dictatorial remark characterized the reluctance to change when he said: "People can have a Model-T in any color they want, as long as it's black."

By the end of 1923, Ford Motor Company's market share had dropped from 60 percent to 52 percent of U.S. car sales. The steady decline would continue year after year with a brief, two-year Ford share resurgence when the Model-A came out in 1929.

By 1936, General Motors' share had climbed to 43 percent of the domestic market, Chrysler Company held 25 percent, and Ford Motors had dropped to a mere 22 percent, a spectacular 38-point market share drop from its 1923 high of 60 percent.

In those 13 years, Alfred P. Sloan, Jr., had brought about one of the most massive shifts of market share ever experienced in a major U.S. industry at great profit to General Motors and its shareholders and with great prestige for himself. In this time period, he had put into place ideas and concepts about the corporation that he had been considering for many years, and General Motors' unbroken years of profit and success confirmed the wisdom of his successful reorganization strategy.

## THE SLOAN SYSTEM—AN OVERVIEW

General Motors' dramatic rise to unprecedented growth, profitability, and unparalleled industry dominance occurred as a direct result of Sloan's managerial stewardship, beginning in 1920 as vice-president of operations and continuing until his retirement as CEO in 1946 and his retirement as chairman of the board in 1956. (He retained the title of honorary chairman of the board until his death in 1966.)

In Sloan's case, the right idea was not an invention or revolutionary discovery like Henry Ford's automobile assembly-line Model -T car or Bill Gates's Microsoft DOS computer operating system. Sloan's idea was a groundbreaking practice of corporate organization, a workable and democratic method to create an effective and decentralized system with centralized authority to run a large, diverse corporation efficiently. He wrote of that early period: "In those days when the industry was new and expanding explosively, its future was shaped by a small number of individuals who took leading positions; as often is not, the capital went to these men rather than the men to the capital."[3]

When Sloan retired as chairman of the GM board in 1956, General Motors had grown exponentially to become one of the largest corporations in the world. Its five manufacturing divisions (Chevrolet, Oldsmobile, Pontiac, Buick, and Cadillac) dominated the American market. General Motors also manufactured GMC trucks and, from 1927 to 1940, a semi-luxury car, the La Salle. Sloan's understanding of the automobile market and of the American consumer had led him to put forward the memorable and successfully simple concept: "A car for every price and purpose."

Sloan's General Motors success stretched beyond automobiles into refrigerators, locomotives, trucks, busses, auto components, and car accessories. And finally, the innovation of the General Motors-owned and -operated financing division GMAC, which, by assisting consumers in the financing of car purchases, has reaped enormous profits and generated billions of dollars for GM.

During World War II, the highly organized General Motors operation produced war materiel in massive volume. The output of tanks, trucks, and other vehicles must be considered one of the main reasons why the nation's war effort proceeded so efficiently. After the war, Japanese industrialists studied General Motors' organizational and production system, realizing that the automotive company could serve as the most useful model to copy in order to rejuvenate the defeated nation's economy. Forty-some years later, the successful Japanese car invasion would bequeath a bitter mockery to General Motors and to all American car manufacturers.

## THE NEW BREED OF CORPORATE MANAGER

Alfred P. Sloan, Jr., is one of the nation's first corporate executive success stories, an individual who amassed millions of dollars by earning a high salary and receiving stock options. Before Sloan, the only way to achieve great individual wealth in America (other than through finance on Wall Street like J. P. Morgan or by family inheritance like the Rockefellers) was by inventing a product or process. The nation's early history speaks to these inventor/innovator magnates like Andrew Carnegie, Thomas Edison, and Henry Ford.

In addition, Sloan was the one of the first of the university graduates (M.I.T. class of 1895), a small but up-and-coming group of college-educated men who would start the twentieth-century tradition that only people with a college degree demonstrated the intelligence to be a corporate executive. Ironically, in the 1920s and 1930s the automobile industry in general, and General Motors specifically, frowned upon hiring these college boys, insisting that only men who had worked with their hands on chassis and brakes were qualified to become automotive men in the manner of Henry Leyland (Cadillac), the Dodge Brothers, or Walter P. Chrysler.

Sloan studied electrical engineering at M.I.T., and his general thinking was organized along the logical lines of an engineering project. This systematic thinking process, which would flower and realize itself in the coherent plan for restructuring General Motors, was a definite educational corollary to Sloan's masterpiece, the "Organization Study," written in 1919, and discussed in this book in greater detail.

Sloan perceived himself as being a new breed of manager in the growing category of self-made, educated men. However, Sloan—whose father was a successful coffee and tea merchant who provided an upper-middle-class existence for the family in New Haven and later, in Brooklyn, New York—never tried to peddle his rise to riches as a poor boy's Horatio Alger tale.

Alfred P. Sloan Jr.'s belief in professional management as an organized system that could be taught and replicated was witnessed by his donating $5 millions to his alma mater for the creation of the M.I.T. School of Industrial Management. In 1965, the university's trustees changed the school's name to the M.I.T. Sloan School of Management to honor its founder. In addition to the executives he had educated in his managerial tradition at General Motors, Sloan's legacy would also continue in a scholastic format at the nation's business schools, training the next generation of professional managers.

Peter Drucker wrote many years later, "He [Sloan] was not a modest man. He valued his place in American economics and history."[4]

## THE LESSONS OF HIS PLANNING GENIUS

It must be remembered that what Sloan accomplished 85 years ago seems commonplace today—it is almost taken for granted—but the corporate system did not exist in its entirety until he assumed the presidency of General Motors. From the moment he took on the mantle of leadership, the structure of the corporation in the United States, and then the world, would improve dramatically.

Sloan put into practice new ideas and concepts to improve all aspects of company organization. From his earliest days after M.I.T., as a new hire at the Hyatt Roller Bearing Company, his inquisitive mind searched for methods to improve upon outmoded American business practices. These are the key elements in Sloan's revolutionary system:

- Facts and data are the main and only determinants of decision making.

- The company should encourage dissent and differences of opinion.

- Organize via committees a decentralized system with centralized power and control.

- Staff with the most competent people without thought to friendship.

- The president or CEO acts as the absolute ruler though consensus.

Sloan presented the integral part of the reorganization system in the previously mentioned "Organization Study," which he wrote in 1919 and submitted in 1920 to Pierre du Pont, then the chairperson of General Motors. The report is a brilliant example of clarity and subtle persuasion. Sloan despaired of the old system of despotic authority, of management decisions by intuition, and of hiring by cronyism. The work begins: "The object of this study is to suggest an

organization for the General Motors Corporation, which will definitely place the line of authority throughout its extensive operation as
well as coordinate each branch of its service."[5]

Sloan demanded that the new corporate order be guided by two
main principles: granting independent authority to the heads of divisions within the corporation for decision making, but also requiring
them to report to a central authority for financial endorsement and
guidance in the macroeconomic areas of business.

Essentially, the successful American corporate organization that
would dominate the world's business communities began to take
shape when General Motors followed Sloan's innovative ideas. After
him, all public and private institutions would attempt to transform
their organizations into the General Motors style, with a clearly
defined decentralized structure and effective leader or president.


## THE LESSONS OF HIS GENIUS IN PRACTICAL MATTERS

The template for Sloan's reorganization turned General Motors in a
new direction of increased profitability. The proof of the success of
the "Organization Study" was evident in the improved sales of General Motors' automobiles and its worldwide rapid expansion.

In addition to the reorganization, Sloan introduced practical business decisions that are the hallmark of his genius:

- Offer wide customer choices.

- Promote a positive corporate image through institutional advertising and public relations.

- Realize the need for international sales and marketing through
  overseas manufacturing or export.

- Find ancillary businesses beyond the corporation's core product
  or service.

Owing to Sloan's understanding of the benefit of corporate public relations and consumer advertising, the nation awaited the annual
autumn presentation of General Motors new cars with the same ritual
expectation as the seasonal scheduling of baseball's World Series or
the arrival of Christmas. He had made car buying an anticipated

national event, bursting with media hoopla in magazines, news-papers and, later successfully, in radio and television.

It is interesting today to remember generations past when the nation received most of its information from newspapers and weekly magazines like *Life*, *Look*, *Colliers*, and *The Saturday Evening Post*. Immediately after World War II, within the pages of these and other magazines, automobile manufacturers paraded their lineup of new cars. And no parade was as eagerly anticipated as the five popular models from General Motors—each one markedly different but all recognizable in the distinct "Body by Fisher" General Motors styling mold.

## SLOAN'S LEGACY IN PRINT

Today, Alfred P. Sloan, Jr., and General Motors are forever linked, especially after the publication in 1963 of his second autobiography, *My Years with General Motors*. The book's main purpose was to articulate the position of the professional manager as leader and decision maker, in short, an accounting of Sloan's own time and experience at the company. He accomplished this by emphasizing, perhaps for the first time in American business history, that manage-ment is a defined discipline with shape and form and operated by guiding organizational principles.

His autobiography is a must read for any person interested in the historic rise of an American corporate giant. The work serves as an informative business story, a fascinating turn-of-the-century history of the American automobile industry, with brief glimpses into the lives of many of the early pioneers who made it successful. It also provides an insight into the mind of an organizational and manager-ial genius.

The first autobiography, *Adventures of a White-Collar Man*, pub-lished in 1941, is a picturesque narrative of his boyhood, the early time at Hyatt Roller Bearing, and it includes sketches of his General Motors experience up to 1940.

One aspect lacking in both books is any personal information or feelings about victories or defeats. He displays an almost Mr. Spock Vulcan logic–like approach to topics, rendering facts and decisions with little emphasis on how these events affected people or nations or himself. In fact, he waited for everyone mentioned in *My Years with General Motors* to die before he published it, so respectful was he of the lives and privacy of associates.

## SLOAN FOR THE AGES

It is not just that Alfred P. Sloan succeeded so spectacularly at General Motors; it is *how* he achieved the success that is interesting for managers today. Sloan can be considered primarily the architect of the modern corporate structure, the person whose blueprint organizational guide became the bellwether standard to follow for companies and organizations worldwide.

Prophetically but accurately and without boastfulness, he said: "Today it is clear that every man, woman, and child, including generations yet to be born, has a stake in the power of General Motors."[6]

## GUIDE FOR THE BOOK

The different individual names and organizations in this book are akin to passengers on a train trip who get off at one station and return in other guises with other titles later in time. Here is a helpful guide to the most frequently cited names and companies.

### PEOPLE

*Alfred P. Sloan, Jr.* Began working at the Hyatt Roller Bearing Company in 1895 and, later, became its president. After he sold Hyatt to GM in 1916, he was made the president of the United Motors Company, a new unit made up of other GM-owned component companies. His United Motors position also placed him on GM's executive committee. In 1918, he became vice-president in charge of operations at GM and continued in this position through the presidencies of William Durant and Pierre du Pont. In 1921, he became the chief assistant to du Pont. In 1923, he was appointed the new GM president and chairman of the executive committee. He retired in 1956 as chairman of the board.

*William Crapo Durant* In 1904, he joined Buick as general manager and became president. In 1908, he incorporated the name General Motors, issued stock, and purchased Buick's assets. The Olds Company was sold to GM also in 1908. Later, in 1909, he bought the Oakland car company and in that same year Cadillac. (He now had four of the five GM car makes.) He then acquired interest in or outright purchase for GM of 30 automobile accessory companies. By 1910, GM was financially overextended and he was ousted from the presidency. In 1911, he formed the Chevrolet Motor Company. By 1915, using profits from Chevrolet, he repurchased a majority stock share of GM and assumed its presidency again. In 1920, again because of bad financial management, he was forced to resign as president of General Motors.

*Pierre du Pont* From 1915 to 1918, he served as president of the Du Pont Company. (The family name is "du Pont," while the company name is always capitalized "Du Pont.") In 1915, the Du Pont Company purchased a 37 percent share in General Motors. In 1919, he was named GM's chairman of the board, and he assumed the presidency in 1920. In 1921 and 1922, he also served as general manager of the Chevrolet division while retaining the other two GM titles. In 1923, he retired as president of GM.

## COMPANIES

*United Motors Corporation* Created by William Durant in 1916, it included Hyatt Roller Bearing, Dayton Engineering, and other automotive component companies. In 1918, it ceased as a separate company and was folded into General Motors where it was dissolved in 1919.

*General Motors* Organized in 1908 as General Motors Company, it incorporated the Buick Company. Oldsmobile and Oakland Car Company were added in 1908, Cadillac was added in 1909 and also Rapid City Motor Vehicle (the precursor of GMC Truck). It was incorporated in Delaware in 1916 as General Motors Corporation, and it purchased Chevrolet in 1918. GMAC started in 1919. Pontiac, offered by Oakland, was introduced to the public in 1926.

2

# DISSENT, DISAGREEMENT, AND CONFLICT

*S loan's early career at Hyatt Roller Bearing Company...His introduction to the automobile industry and United Motors Company...The dictatorial style of General Motors' CEO William C. Durant...Sloan puts dissent into practice with the memoranda...The GM conflict of the air-cooled engine...Disagreement saves Cadillac...The internal battle over New Coke...Escalating up: the method of disagreement at Marian Laboratories... Circumventing the military chain of command...Soup dissenters at the Heinz Company...The managerial lessons of implementing and controlling dissent within an organization*

❧ ☙

The basic problem of the corporate organization in the pre–Alfred P. Sloan, Jr., era was that no effective or formalized management system existed for hearing differences of opinion among staff. Further, disagreements were not viewed as being helpful to the resolution of problems, and openness was often discouraged in the workplace.

The result was leadership by owner or boss fiat, the "my way or the highway" autocratic control that compelled subordinates to obey or be dismissed for insubordination. In essence, the process was feudal and undemocratic; the top person in the chain of command spoke from on high with an unchallenged and mighty voice to the ordinary workers below. Sloan recognized the inherent problem of one person as absolute ruler: "Dictatorship is the most effective way of administration, provided the dictator knows the complete answers to all the questions. But he never does and never will. That is why dictatorships eventually fail."[1]

At the turn of the twentieth century, in the absence of a cadre of middle managers, total decision making rested in one person's hands, whether that determination concerned purchasing, manufacturing, sales, or marketing. Employees had little or no say in how the enterprise was run; their opinions were either unsolicited or, if rarely given, dismissed.

However, this was to improve substantially under Sloan's guidance. Dissent became an integral part of the management process in the years after he assumed the stewardship at General Motors to the betterment of the corporation and of the workforce.

## SLOAN'S FORMATIVE EXPERIENCE

After graduating from M.I.T. in 1895 with a B.S. degree in electrical engineering, Sloan began working as a draftsman for the Hyatt Roller Bearing Company in Newark, New Jersey. The company manufactured an antifriction bearing that would eventually become a vital component in the automobile industry and that would serve as Sloan's successful entree into General Motors.

At Hyatt, Sloan met an energetic immigrant bookkeeper named Peter Steenstrup. During lunch hours, the men would discuss in detail the business shortcomings of the small company (25 employees), and, especially, its owner, John Wesley Hyatt: "We fell into the habit of talking about the affairs of the Hyatt Roller Bearing Company. As boys will, we spoke our minds freely. We were sure we could run things better."[2]

Sloan and Steenstrup recognized that Mr. Hyatt was not an astute businessman or, at least, not a capable manager with a scope of vision to operate the small plant profitably. (Hyatt was a brilliant inventor who had discovered the celluloid process in response to a $10,000 contest offered by a billiard ball maker that needed a hard substitute for ivory.)

Sloan, as a new Hyatt hire, had no say in the company's operation. He voiced his opinions to Peter Steenstrup but could not talk to the head of the company. He chafed that he could not speak his mind freely. There is no doubt that having received a college degree in engineering, as one of the new breed of university men, he perceived that his viewpoints had merit and should be heard.

These original Sloan-Steenstrup exchanges established a pattern of open, forthright conversations that Sloan would transfer later into the uppermost strata of General Motors' management. He enjoyed the give-and-take with Steenstrup, finding in someone with his own temperament, a good listener and someone not averse to sharing opinions even if they differed from his own.

This first business partnership in 1898—two eager young men in their twenties with the world of opportunities awaiting them—soon developed into the management team at Hyatt Roller Bearing after Sloan's father and an associate purchased the company. Sloan became the general manager and Steenstrup the chief salesman. Freed from the elderly Mr. Hyatt's daily involvement, the two put into practice their long-discussed business ideas. The first order of the day was to halt the monthly cycle of repetitive losses. After six months of reorganization, the firm generated a small profit.

The salient lesson for Sloan was that spirited dialogue produced knowledge, and even friction between employees could benefit the enterprise.

## SLOAN MEETS THE AUTOMOBILE INDUSTRY

In 1899, Hyatt received a request from Elwood Haynes of Kokomo, Indiana, to supply ball bearings for wheel axles. Haynes's company manufactured the newfangled machines powered by gasoline called automobiles.

Fast-forward 18 years, and the Hyatt Roller Bearing Company had become one of the most successful ball-bearing manufacturers to the nation's axle makers that supplied the burgeoning automobile market. In this period, the astute, hard-working Sloan recognized that this emerging auto industry had not yet reached its full production capacity. There was every reason to predict that, as car prices dropped, many more Americans would become first-time auto buyers. This notion became fact when comparing the first year Sloan had operation control of GM in 1921 to the stock market crash in 1929. The number of cars produced had risen from 1.4 million autos in 1921 to 4.5 million in 1929, a 3.1 million-car increase.

The Hyatt Company had one serious sales problem; it sold most of its production to just one axle company, Weston-Mott. In 1906, the then-independent Buick Company lured Weston-Mott from Utica, New York, to build a new plant in Flint, Michigan, next to the Buick factory. For Buick, having an axle maker next door would significantly curtail the delivery time of ball bearings and allow the car company to meet all dealer orders promptly. In 1908, Buick, now formally rolled into the General Motors consortium, purchased 49 percent of Weston-Mott's stock.

Sloan grew apprehensive that either one of Weston-Mott's two largest customers, Ford or GM, would start to manufacture its own line of ball bearings. This would leave the Hyatt Roller Bearing Company with a large plant in Newark and greatly reduced sales because Ford and GM dominated the manufacturing of automobiles.

The Hyatt Roller Bearing Company was typical of a two-person operation; basically, a small company where Sloan performed most of the managerial functions alone and Steenstrup did the selling. In his autobiographies, Sloan does not cite any dissent with his sales manager, the decision making was clearly his own.


## SLOAN AND THE UNITED MOTORS CORPORATION

In 1916, Sloan solved the problem of Hyatt's future by selling the company to General Motors where it became part of a new subsidiary called United Motors Corporation, composed of automobile accessory manufacturers. He had smartly eliminated the economic sword of Damocles that dangled over Hyatt's head should Ford or GM start to make their own ball bearings.

Sloan had not offered the company for sale, rather, the president of GM, William Durant, the automobile pioneer and visionary, tendered an offer to purchase the company's stock. Durant's brilliant plan (revolutionary for its time) was to buy up parts and accessory companies that would sell mainly or exclusively to General Motors. In addition to Hyatt, Durant purchased Dayton Engineering Labs (DELCO), Remy Electronic, Jazon Steel Products, and other component companies.

Durant appointed the 40-year old Sloan as president of the newly formed United Motors, which allowed Sloan the opportunity to run multiple divisions with other managers reporting to him directly. He had a small board of directors for the first time. Working with these other small manufacturing entrepreneurs at United Motors provided Sloan with an appreciation for their fact-driven basis of decision making that was similar to his own.

During this early stewardship, he first experienced opposition to his organizational changes. Critical to the success of the reorganization of many disparate companies into the single, United Motors entity was his ability to channel dissent to his way of thinking.

## SLOAN'S DISAPPROVAL OF WILLIAM DURANT'S MANAGERIAL STYLE

The beginnings of Sloan's radical concept of the modern corporation must have arisen from his disappointment and frustration with the managerial style of GM's president William C. Durant. In essence, Durant, charming, intuitive, speculative, would become the irritating grain that Sloan's inner angst turned over time into a managerial pearl. For all intents and purposes, Sloan consciously decided (whenever the opportunity would arise) to manage and organize as the anti-Durant. Sloan believed that Durant could create but not administer. GM was becoming too big to be ruled without organized administration.

This is not the space to elaborate on the genius or failings of William Durant, who gained and lost stewardship of General Motors twice in his lifetime. He should be regarded as a pioneer in American automotive history as important as Henry Ford. Durant was a salesman by nature and a speculator who routinely made decisions on the fly without consulting others, or without studying fact-driven reports. He is credited with implementing the system of a multi-brand automobile company that offered different lines of cars.

Sloan, who rarely allowed his displeasure to surface in print about any associate or competitor, chose his words cautiously when he wrote about his early association with Durant: "From the time I became president of United Motors, I saw a great deal of Mr. Durant. I was constantly amazed by his daring way of making decisions."[3]

To be fair to Durant, he had made many brilliantly spontaneous decisions with hardly a second's reflection on cost or applicability. He had a knack for finding many different inventors and setting them up with investment money, plant space, and equipment. Once, he was introduced to a stranger who boasted he could make a better spark plug from porcelain. This was the French racing car driver, Albert Champion. With Durant's Buick seed money, Champion soon created a better spark plug for the AC Spark Plug Company that GM acquired totally in 1925.

However, Durant surrounded himself with cronies and yes-men to Sloan's disapproval. Sloan would never tolerate this type of managerial system when he became president; he never wanted to be surrounded by yea sayers.

The classic example of Sloan's shock at Durant's casual style occurred when the GM president decided to look for and then build a new office building in Detroit. The meeting was held at GM headquarters in New York City where the long-held and prevailing consensus was to choose a site in the downtown Detroit area.

Sloan had wandered into the meeting by chance and off-the-cuff offered Durant a different opinion: an out-of-town location would be cheaper and more convenient to the many office personnel that lived in the suburbs. Sloan had studied the problem in depth when he searched for a site to move Hyatt Roller Bearing from New Jersey to Detroit:

> Almost hesitantly, because it was not my responsibility, I volunteered an opinion. "Why pay downtown prices for land? Or downtown taxes?"
>
> Durant replied, "Next time we go to Detroit we will go to the site you recommend and take a look."
>
> We did so. And Durant told me to buy the land. His characteristic approach.

"What about the price?" [Sloan asked]

"Whatever you need to pay. Just draw on the treasurer."[4]

This move—of historic significance since it would eventually be the site of General Motors headquarters—Durant had made as offhandedly as though he had ordered a box of paper clips.

It seems incomprehensible today that a decision as important as a new headquarters site of a Fortune 100 corporation could be made without analyzing the real estate market, taxes, and the multitude of other site location variables. It is inconceivable that a range of diverse opinions would not be heard from the outset and a feasibility report written that outlined the potential location choices. Even before corporations implemented special departments for new factory or office sites, Sloan recognized the need for a specialist in the field to handle these kinds of real estate transactions.

Time and again, Durant's managerial style and his self-governing decisions provoked the taciturn Sloan into paroxysms of dissonance. Durant operated without any input or counsel from subordinates, research, or marketing reports, or, in fact, any coherent committee for managerial decision making.

Sloan tried repeatedly to move the mercurial autocrat on to the path of accountability. It was Sloan who was the first manager to suggest that General Motors should be fully examined by outside, independent auditors, an accounting firm that Sloan had employed while head of Hyatt Roller Bearing. And much to the subordinate's surprise, Durant responded in the same instant reply as he had voiced to the new building location. After Durant consented, Sloan did contact the outside firm, providing GM Corporation with its first audit by Haskins and Snell accountants.

During the many years that Sloan served as United Motors president, he had become convinced that Durant's autocratic, one-man style could not continue to survive as General Motors grew exponentially with new acquisitions and expanded sales: Sloan realized that once Durant made a decision, usually without requesting any other manager's advice, he would hold on to it forever. Sloan wrote, "General Motors had become too big to be a one-man show."[5]

When Sloan moved up the GM ladder—and when Durant had been ousted from the presidency for the second time in 1920—one of Sloan's first objectives was to promote and systematize dissent. He never wanted to create a group of yea-saying "Sloan men." His goal was to democratize General Motors so that all voices were heard. The era of managerial dictatorship passed when William Durant exited General Motors forever.

The new age would soon witness Sloan ushering in his reorganization plan that relied on the free exchange of ideas. Yet there would be one more obstacle for Sloan to overcome before all of his changes could be implemented. It would occur while he was the acting executive vice-president of GM, and the battle royal would pit Sloan against Pierre du Pont, the new president of GM and also against GM's brilliant research inventor Charles Kettering.

One of the most famous disputes in American automobile history would arise over the clash of the air-cooled versus the water-cooled engine. Sloan's active dissent would establish the pattern of forthright disagreement that would later represent the hallmark of his long and successful managerial reign.

But before the battle of the two engines, Sloan had participated in an earlier dissent that would have enormous impact on the future of General Motors: the pending decision in 1920 by Pierre du Pont, the newly installed GM president, to liquidate the poorly performing Chevrolet. It was classic dissent à la Sloan; he scheduled a meeting and brought the facts with him. He wrote: "We urged upon him [du Pont] the fact that many more people always could buy low-priced cars than Cadillacs and even Buicks. That it was an insult that we [GM] could not compete with anyone [Ford]. It was a case of ability and hard work."[6]

Pierre du Pont relented under Sloan's courage of convictions. But soon the practice of dissent, which would become part of corporate structure in the United States, would begin in the pending battle of the two engines. A battle where Pierre du Pont would not be so yielding in his opinion.

## SLOAN PUTS DISSENT INTO PRACTICE

The backdrop to the engine story is this: In 1920, after William Durant's departure, Pierre du Pont, then GM's chairman, decided to assume the hands-on role of president. Sloan reported directly to du Pont who had been impressed by Sloan's clear and concise "Organization Study."

In 1918, Charles Kettering, working at the Dayton Engineering Company, an acquired division of GM, began to experiment with an air-cooled engine (GM used the more lofty marketing term "copper cooled") that could replace the water-cooled engine, then the industry's standard. Water-cooled engines required elaborate plumbing systems and the constant need for water. On paper, air-cooled engines seemed more efficient and less costly. Everyone at GM was enthusiastic about the possible application to its line of cars throughout all the divisions.

Sloan became skeptical months before the air-cooled engine could be tried out on any line of GM automobiles. He reasoned that such a radical and drastic change should be tested first and then slowly introduced into the GM line, beginning with the lowest priced Chevrolet. But the executive committee, of which he was a member, seemed bent on moving ahead with speed. He did not share the enthusiasm for rapid advance and had many reservations about the possibility of the new, untried engine.

Further, this marked the first time into unchartered waters where the research committee (Kettering) interacted directly with one of the managers of a GM division, in this instance, Chevrolet. Whose decision should be ascendant? Research? Or Chevrolet management? Sloan became aware that the executive committee had not resolved the matter. He sensed that a clash was imminent, especially when the executive committee halted production of all water-cooled engines.

For the pragmatic Sloan, rolling the dice with an untried new system that might revolutionize the industry represented more risk than he thought the corporation should take. Of equal importance was that the air-cooled decision represented a departure from the newly realized system of management he had recommended: "From a business and management standpoint, however, we were acting at variances with our doctrine. We were, for example, more committed to a particular engineering design than to the broad aims of the enterprise."[7]

The "enterprise" was the multidivisional GM big picture, and it bothered Sloan that Pierre du Pont did not share his opinion. He knew that widely separated parallel lines of thought could not endure in the long term. And the "doctrine" was his carefully considered "Organization Study." He had labored without a strong dissenting voice for many years under the autocratic dictatorship of William Durant, and he did not ever want to repeat that negative experience.

Sloan's position favoring the continuation of the water-cooled engine was measurably improved when initial in-auto testing produced serious failures with Kettering's air-cooled innovation. Now primed with the results of these first tests, Sloan began the campaign of dissent that he hoped would change the prevailing decision of the executive committee to continue with the air-cooled engine.

The modus operandi of dissension that Sloan employed was the short, fact-filled, and persuasive memorandum. In the annals of corporate dissent, these memos stand out as a clear-cut method to express disagreement in a logical, cohesive, and persuasive manner.

Sloan had used the written page to promote his "Organization Study," and he employed the same hard-copy format to present his counter arguments to du Pont and the executive committee. Often, he utilized bulleted or numbered lists to express an opinion or numbered points to mark down agreements or decisions numerically. In this manner, he kept a record of what he had recommended and what had been agreed. He kept everyone apprised of the decisions that had been made.

The placement of the air-cooled engines in new Chevrolets proved a disaster, and in the summer of 1923, the Chevrolet Division recalled all its cars with air-cooled engines. The executive committee finally pulled the plug on the innovation after being persuaded by Sloan's coherent dissent to discontinue the new type of engine.

Kettering was furious that his air-cooled engine had been shelved. He was convinced that he and his team could make it viable. Outraged that his work had come to nothing, he submitted his resignation to GM and petitioned for permission to take the air-cooled engine technology to another automobile manufacturer.

Sloan held Kettering in the highest regard. In the formative years of the development of the automobile, a few mechanical geniuses and brilliant scientific brains had risen to the forefront of the burgeoning auto industry. And Kettering was the acme of these research men. In 1911, he and Clyde Coleman invented the electrical ignition system, the electric starter motor for cars, which replaced the laborious hand-cranking starter system.

What followed next would also represent Sloan's noteworthy decision on the best method for dealing with a losing side in a significant corporate dissent. He had prevailed in the internecine conflict that pit-ted him and the divisions against Kettering and Pierre du Pont. But the victory was never personal; the debate never rose to mudslinging or generated bad blood between him and the team that favored the air-cooled alternative. He allowed Kettering to tinker with the air-cooled project afterward for a while but eliminated it permanently as a substitute for the water-cooled engines. Sloan knew what his next task was: "My problem was to reconcile Mr. Kettering's natural reactions and enthusiasm for the new idea with the realities in the case."[8]

The "realities" were that in 1923 the automobile market experienced a sales boom and GM had to concentrate on meeting the increased demand with the existing and industry-accepted water-cooled engine. Further, Sloan solved the "problem" by eventually (two years later) inviting Kettering to move the Dayton Engineering Laboratory to Detroit where he (Kettering) would be head of a newly created and expanded General Motors Research Division. He would be given the freedom to do any kind of automobile-related research he wanted. In addition, Sloan (now president of the company) promised to support the research venture with ample capital funding, plant, equipment, and personnel.

Sloan offered Kettering a spanking new and fully funded research facility to do any type of automobile-related research unfettered by any internal General Motors corporate or financial authority. He had flattered Kettering with this carte blanche offer, one that no inventor could refuse and Kettering accepted.

(To induce Kettering to move to Detroit with the research staff, Sloan offered him a raise to $120,000, which was $20,000 more than what General Motors paid Sloan at the time. Also, only Kettering and Walter Chrysler called Sloan "Alfred." To everyone else it was always "Mr. Sloan.")

Kettering accepted Sloan's proposal and brought his team to Detroit, a move that placed him more closely within the GM fold. Sloan was, as always, good for his word. Kettering had the freedom to research whatever he wanted. The result of this decision produced two of the most successful and profitable innovations of the first half of the twentieth century: ethyl gasoline and Freon liquid gas for refrigerators—both discovered and perfected in Kettering's Research Division. And both inventions generated millions of dollars for General Motors.

The partnership of these two men had survived the battle of the engines. Sloan, in keeping with his policy of dissent, allowed all sides of the engine debate to be heard. He had demonstrated the managerial brilliance by identifying in Kettering a scientist who was and would continue to be a valuable player in the company's future. He found a smart way to mollify the frustrated Kettering and his research team.

In 1945, the two men—both made extraordinarily wealthy by their significant salaries and holdings in General Motors' stock— would embark on a groundbreaking medical concept: the founding of the Sloan-Kettering Hospital for cancer research in New York City.

Sloan had prevailed in his first major dissent by relying on facts to sway others to his position. He had also allowed the opposition to air its side in meetings and in reports. Finally, after being the victor in the outcome, he quickly moved to heal the rift with his research genius.

## DISAGREEMENT SAVES CADILLAC

By the 1930s, Sloan's management system was well established and coworkers knew that the General Motors president encouraged dissent. This openness allowed mid-level managers to express differences of opinions, even at the highest level without apprehension of jeopardizing their careers.

The most memorable of these GM dissenter stories concerned the pending decision to discontinue the slow-selling luxury line of Cadillacs during the depression of the 1930s. Cadillac's sales had risen to a record high of 41,000 vehicles in 1928 (including, its new La Salle models) and then began to drop annually for the next four years. By 1932, sales had declined to just 9,153 cars as the nation was in the grips of the great economic downturn.

At the same time, Packard Motors, Cadillac's main competition in the domestic luxury-priced field, had moved down market with its cars, eliminating the highest priced of its automobiles. GM could stop making Cadillac and continue with its newly introduced La Salle brand (1927) to compete with Packard at the low-price end of what remained of the dwindling depression-era, luxury car segment.

In 1932, the GM board of directors met to halt production of the Cadillac, possibly forever, relegating it to U.S. automobile history. A majority of the board did not even want to keep the Cadillac name-plate for a later time.

Owing to Sloan's reception for candidness, a young Cadillac engineer named Nicholas Dreystadt realized that he could ask for a hearing with the board. His topic: how to make Cadillac profitable in 18 months, and he requested 10 minutes of the board's time. At Sloan's GM, the young engineer received a short hearing to present his plan.

Dreystadt argued that Cadillac was the one GM car that was a symbol of status, the car men purchased when they had made it in the business world. But Dreystadt offered other, surprising news to the board; the Cadillac brand was the status symbol for wealthy black men. In practice, General Motors, like all other U.S. car companies, did not market to black people. There were no dealerships in the urban areas or towns where blacks lived. Black men could purchase Cadillacs only by asking white friends to act as surrogate buyers.

Dreystadt recalled the incident of his initial pleading with the GM board, which he recounted years later to Peter Drucker:

> One of the [board] members said, "Mr. Dreystadt, you realize, don't you, sir, that if you fail there won't be a job for you at GM?"
>
> "Of course, I do sir," I [Dreystadt] said.
>
> "But I *don't*," said Mr. Sloan quite sharply. "If you fail, Mr. Dreystadt, there isn't going to a job for you at Cadillac. There won't be Cadillac, but as long as there is a GM, and as long as I run it, there'll always be a job for a man who takes responsibility, who takes initiative, who has courage and imagination. *You* worry about the future of Cadillac. Your future at GM is *my* worry."[9]

Cadillac was a low-sales-volume car with a high profit margin, and thus a small growth in sales could represent the difference between profit and loss. The GM board gave Dreystadt 18 months to achieve his objective by allowing him to pursue more direct sales to blacks. This attempt to sell to blacks marked the first example of niche target marketing in the history of the American motor industry.

The result? By 1934, Cadillac sales had increased to 11,468 cars, and by 1941 sales rose to a record high total of 60,037 under Dreystadt's leadership. By 1962, Sloan could look back with satisfaction at his 1932 decision because in that year Cadillac sold almost 160,000 highly profitable cars and had achieved the preeminent status as America's luxury car.

Cadillac, like Chevrolet in 1920, had been saved by dissent. Saved because Alfred P. Sloan, Jr., insisted upon differences of opinion.

## GM'S ROUND TABLE COMMITTEE OF OPINIONS

Sloan recognized that within GM's divisions, the best way to reach consensus was to schedule committee meetings with all the divergent players present. He contended that it was important for the many disciplines to be in a room together so that everyone learned the thinking and rationale from all viewpoints.

In 1923, he instructed the automobile divisions to meet regularly with engineering, manufacturing, and sales and marketing present. In this format, for example, an engineer who wanted to add an extra feature would learn from production the feasibility of manufacturing the part or improvement and also hear comments from sales and marketing on how the possible extra costs might affect the purchase price. Sloan had learned the painful lesson from the past Kettering engine conflict: "The junctures between staff and line are critical, as we had learned the hard way. The experience with the copper-cooled car showed what a paralyzing effect one of these junctures could have if it were turned into a battlefield."[10]

Sloan never wanted the company to be embroiled in a single conflict that might split apart the smooth working of General Motors. In addition, it must have been a matter of pride that after his "Organization Study" had been accepted, he wanted to ensure that his system worked as well in practice as it had appeared on paper.

Through his tenure at General Motors, Sloan created ad hoc committees where he saw a need for them. In each case, he insisted that these committees had decision-making capabilities, decisions that would assume authority based on the dissenting opinions of its members.

## NEW COKE: DISAGREEMENTS AT COCA-COLA

The tale of New Coke, the magnificent marketing bungle of the mid 1980s, is a classic example of internal corporate dissent that affected a major outcome at a company. Although in the retelling it might seem that company dissenters were steamrolled by the "all systems go" decision to launch the new beverage, the fact is that from its beginning (research and sell-in), middle (reality in the marketplace), and end (scaling back the project), that debate continued with the full airing of disparate viewpoints.

As a result of 20 years of Pepsi's youth-oriented advertising ("The Pepsi Generation"), by 1981 Coca Cola's margin over its main competitor had declined to only 5 percent. This lead was inflated by Coke's fountain and counter-service exclusivity at McDonald's and other fast-food franchises. But in the supermarkets, Pepsi had gained the packaged goods lead over its rival by two share points. The decline was accelerated by Pepsi's boasting to cola drinkers to take "The Pepsi Challenge," a direct, frontal assault on Coca-Cola's taste.

At Coca Cola's headquarters in Atlanta, the situation had reached critical mass. Management believed that Coke had to find some dynamic breakthrough promotional, marketing, or advertising campaign that could halt the erosion of brand share. If no steps were taken, then Pepsi would gradually become the number-one soft drink in the United States at a great financial loss to Coca Cola since each share point was worth millions of dollars in lost sales revenue.

Coca Cola's senior management began to think the unthinkable, to change the existing formula. Initially, this radical idea was viewed as heresy. Coca Cola, perhaps more than any other packaged goods product, served as a symbol, an icon of the United States. In its familiar contoured bottle with its universally recognized script logo set against a bright red backdrop, it was the world's most recognized trademark. The brand was quintessentially American, like Mom, apple pie, and baseball.

(In Venice, Italy, a cafe displays an unusual photograph taken at the break of dawn at the famous St. Mark's Square. The picture—shot from the top of the Camponile, the 325-foot guard tower—reveals thousands of pigeons on the square eating previously placed birdseed; their tangled but arranged mass of bodies spelling out the unmistakable logo script of Coca Cola!)

Who would dare to change the Coke formula? And what would be the consequences of so radical a move? Could the company believe that creating another cola with the words "new and improved" have a positive impact on the future of Coke? Could the company instead try to position the brand to younger consumers and compete with Pepsi head-on for the emerging baby boomer market?

The realities by 1984 were starkly negative; the Coke brand had declined from a 24 percent market share in 1981 to 22 percent in 1984. Armed with this discouraging statistic, the decision fell to top management to look into the possibility of reformulation. The brilliant marketing manager Sergio Zyman (he had launched Diet Coke in 1982) was chosen to head the project. Practical considerations had overridden dissent.

Coke's technical division created a new, sweetened formula. Unconfirmed analyses stated it contained actual sugar and not aspartame, the popular artificial sweetener. This sweeter-tasting version outperformed Pepsi in taste tests.

There was initial dissent to launch the New Coke and to discontinue selling old Coke. The apprehension came from a company traditionalist who believed that withdrawing the 100-year old favorite would create negative publicity. But CEO Goizueta realized that two Cokes would be unacceptable to the bottlers, already burdened with Diet Coke and Cherry Coke line extensions.

In one of the most massive brand relaunchings in history, after only 79 days, Coca-Cola had to restock the nation's shelves with old Coke renaming it Classic Coke. The public had rejected New Coke as though it were the failed Edsel of popular colas. Every prior taste test and piece of qualitative and quantitative research had not revealed the one, true fact: the American public did not want to see the disappearance of its historically favorite drink.

In the end, the country's popular dissent determined the outcome. New Coke continued in some form for a number of years, eventually becoming Coke II. The irony was that Coke's user base became more loyal to the brand after the threat of extinction. As years followed, market share for the old Coke increased significantly. The untouchable aura of Pepsi's youth advertising began to fade, and with it Pepsi's perception of being the better-tasting cola.

The print and broadcast media reaction to New Coke—most of it negative—had provided Coca Cola with hundreds of millions of dollars of free publicity. Every day, each day all the public read about or watched on television was another Coca Cola story. The fitting and unplanned for ironic result was that Coca Cola's market share started to climb.

Again, like Sloan after the air-cooled engine episode, Goizueta fired no one for dissenting or for failing. In fact, the stock price rose in the following years, and he and his team reaped large bonuses. In essence, CEO Goizueta, made a case that had Coca Cola fired all those involved in the dispute, it would have sent an alarming signal to everyone at the company (and at other companies as well), that risk-taking was frowned upon or dissent should not be encouraged.

## ESCALATING UP AT MARION LABORATORIES

Ewing Marion Kauffman, the founder of Marion Laboratories in 1950, held to a number of core business beliefs that allowed him to take a small pharmaceutical company, which he started in his basement, up through a successful merger with Merrill Dow in 1989. Kauffman never referred to workers as "employees"; he always called them "associates."

Few high-ranking executives in American history possessed Kauffman's gift for establishing a warm and cordial relationship between executives and lower-ranking "associates." It is a tribute to his amicable managerial style that people in his organization always called him "Mr. K."

In the approachable atmosphere of Marion Labs, Kauffman encouraged dissent with an interesting and important proviso: associates and executives could only complain upward. His term for this system was "escalating" and not only did it facilitate complaints being heard, it also discouraged the usual, lateral fault-finding among workers of equal status.

Kauffman had heard more than his share of bellyache complaining from others in his early years as a salesperson. But few among his peers wanted to risk losing a job by mouthing off about the boss. The result was that dissent remained rooted on the bottom rungs with little hope for any productive change by speaking to higher-ranking executives. This lead Kauffman rightly to observe that legitimate dissent might lead to a change in direction, and only a decision maker, higher up than the dissenter, could achieve this.

A past example at Marion Labs reveals how this escalating-up system worked to everyone's satisfaction. The chief financial officer had spent months investigating the establishment of a new operation to be based in Puerto Rico that would represent a significant tax abatement. When it came time to green light the project, the president of the company's pharmaceutical division vetoed the Puerto Rican proposal.

The CFO believed that it was vital to the company's financial interests to pursue the tax shelter, and he escalated up by going to see Ewing Kauffman. The CEO listened to the argument—and indeed it held merit—but he explained that the pharmaceutical division was stretched thin as it attempted to launch a new product. The new product's short-term and long-term value to the company represented a greater potential return on investment than the size of possible savings from the tax shelter.

Kauffman's policy was always, "Agree to disagree." He never wanted to make someone wrong, and by allowing voices to go higher, he found a workable system for dissent to be heard. Although their leadership styles could not have been more different, Kauffman and Sloan were of the same opinion when it came to encouraging and then listening to dissent. The positive result was the same for both companies: employees knew they could blow off steam and disagree.

## THE MILITARY CHAIN OF COMMAND

The United States military employs a chain of command from the lowest rank to the highest. This proven method allows orders and decisions to be handed down efficiently. For the airing of dissent or complaints, the military phrase often repeated is "to go up the chain of command." This requires the person with a grievance to first move one step up the command ladder. Once there, he or she might or might not receive permission to go on to the next level. Many times possible injustices or major complaints were stopped at one level up. And if consent was not given to proceed up the chain, the injustice or grievance expired at that level.

In the 1960s, the U.S. Army realized this system might prove inhibiting by forcing new personnel with a legitimate gripe to confront a superior. It decided to initiate a method to allow soldiers to bypass the many-tiered chains of command and permit them a one-time chance to talk directly in secret to the judge advocate general. The process was to open the JAG office one night a month, staffed by a military lawyer. The open-access information was posted in the weekly bulletin in all barracks.

This end run around the chain of command was rarely used. But the knowledge that it existed offered troops an escape valve if they needed it.

Companies that offer escape valves for worker opinion will find that the lid rarely blows if complaints can be heard. One common method is to have organized suggestion systems that encourage employees to consider changes that will benefit the company. Although Sloan's GM pioneered no such formal suggestion idea, its employees knew that the system of openness existed because Alfred Sloan encouraged dissent. Anecdotes and stories at GM about the air-cooled engine or Cadillac's survival became company lore.

## SOUP DISSENT UNHEEDED

During World War II, the U.S. government decided that Heinz Company's soup-making plant would switch from soup to manufacture plastic parts for glider airplanes. This left Campbell as the country's main soup maker during the war years, with the result that after 1945, soup in America was practically all Campbell's. The familiar red and white soup cans (the colors taken from Cornell University's football team, nicknamed the Big Red) dominated the supermarket shelves without many facings left for Heinz.

Over the next 25 years, Heinz tried to recapture some of the soup market share it had lost to Campbell but without success. Campbell's share had risen to between 75 and 80 percent of the soup market, leaving Heinz to divvy up the remaining percentage with regional and specialty soup brands.

Heinz's first innovative attempt to regain market share was Happy Soup, a new kid's version with Disney characters on the can and with fun shapes inside. The thinking was that children would eat their soup and look at the cans. The concept met with pronounced dissent internally at Heinz. There were some clever television commercials but the product failed in the marketplace.

In the late 1960s, Heinz perceived there might be an emerging market for richer-ingredient, higher-priced, and larger-sized soups. The company decided to name the new brand Great American Soup. It was sold in a blue can with a white star and red lettering, the perfect red, white, and blue patriotic label for the U.S. market.

The account was given to the advertising agency Doyle Dane Bernbach, which had achieved success with Heinz ketchup's "slow" advertising. During the next few years, Great American Soup sales never achieved the volume that the Heinz marketing group had predicted. An internal debate followed whether to withdraw the brand or continue selling it nationally. The resulting decision surprised everyone: the comic Stan Freberg was given the brand to advertise to increase its awareness.

Dissent poured in from Doyle Dane's account management, stating that Freberg would prove a disastrous choice for Great American Soup. The comic, whose brilliantly hilarious advertising had worked for Jeno's Pizza and Chun King, demanded total authority over the advertising. He even refused to show storyboards to Heinz or even to discuss his plans for the commercial.

The Great American Soup television commercial, costing a reputed $1 million (an enormous sum in the early 1970s) featured the popular Hollywood dancer Ann Miller. The spot was a spectacular Busby Berkeley type dance number with Miller dancing on top of an eight-foot Great American soup can, surrounded by gushing water fountains, an orchestra, and a line of high-stepping chorus girls. As she taps into the kitchen, her weary husband asks, "Why must you make such a big production out of everything?"

The advertising was memorable but it did nothing for the brand; most people only remembered the celebrated film star and not the soup product advertised. This time the naysayers within the Heinz Company and at Doyle Dane had been proved right. Freberg's ad could not repeat the success of his previous commercials for the pizza and Chinese food products.

Someone should have listened to the dissent from the outset. The expensive commercial marked the death knell for Great American Soup. Heinz began to concentrate on making private-label soups, which is what dissenters had advised for years.

## THE LIMITS OF DISSENTERS

There are occasions within an organization when the dissenter pushes the buttons of disagreement too far. The question is what to do with that hot-tempered person even though he or she may be right.

The answer to the irascible dissenter problem comes from Alfred P. Sloan, Jr. In the years after World War II, GM consciously decided to avoid potential antitrust concerns of the federal government by keeping its market share in and around 50 percent of the U.S. automobile market. The realistic fear was that if the giant corporation started to capture more than half of the market share in the United States, it would be under scrutiny from the federal government for monopolistic practices and be forced to split up into two or more companies.

But a younger member of GM's marketing staff argued forcefully for splitting the company into two entities to permit the auto giant to go after as much of the car market as possible as separate corporations. This radical divide-and-conquer suggestion riled the company's elders as a heretical doctrine that would prove the ruination of General Motors.

The marketing man soon became a despised coworker. Many wanted to give the rebel a bonus and a red slip out of GM. But Sloan dissented, saying, "We don't penalize people for their opinions—we want them to have opinions."[11] Instead, Sloan promoted the dissenting manager and moved him from Detroit to the Electro-Locomotive Division in Chicago that had flourished after Kettering developed a method to make lightweight diesel locomotives: "This way," Sloan said, "he'll make as much money or more through his bonuses as if he had reached a top position at GM. Yet he'll be out of Detroit, where he can't really function with all the enemies he's made, including myself."[12]

Sloan kept a bright person within the company and also did not impair his historic concept for encouraging dissent or for fairness.

## THE LESSONS OF LISTENING TO DISSENT

Companies and organizations should encourage the exchange of opinions, inform employees how these opinions can be voiced, and never penalize those who dissent vigorously. In essence, these three fundamentals comprise a feasible system for hearing divergent opinions.

## FOSTERING OPINIONS
Sloan's GM allowed for and encouraged opinions from all corners. By placing people in different select committees, Sloan's charge to these groups was for spirited argument leading to agreement. His goal was that each committee would enunciate a carefully planned policy.

Newcomers to GM must have learned soon after hiring that this was a company where dissent was permitted and even considered necessary. For Sloan, dissent was the shared path to agreement and to understanding. He realized that agreement lead to consensus.

## VOICING DISSENT
Memoranda represented the modus operandi for continuing dissent beyond the discussions in the committee meeting. GM executives used Sloan's cogent and concise memos as the operating model. His memos were brilliant examples of facts and persuasive arguments.

In effect, the memoranda method facilitated dissent before or after meetings, either to enumerate the topics for the meeting or to make comments afterward.

Many companies utilize a formalized suggestion system as a method for soliciting employee opinions. The BIC Company in Milford, Connecticut, supports an "Ideas That Win" system to generate employee submissions. Each new hire is given a six-page pamphlet that spells out the suggestions system and, importantly, the rewards (beyond recognition) that can be expected. The Dana Corporation of Toledo, Ohio, takes this one step further by requiring each employee to make two new suggestions each month.

When employees can freely express opinions, it fosters a climate of openness.

## ALLOWING DISSENT
As Sloan demonstrated time after time, it was vital to hear dissenters' opinions, no matter how hot-tempered or intransigent they spoke. The first two parts of his dissent system would never have

succeeded had employees been terminated soon after airing a differing opinion.

An example of keeping tempers in check in meetings comes from the CEO of a mid-sized consulting company. He had worked in Spain for two years and attended the occasional bullfight where he noticed that one official decided before the fight if a bull was physically fit to participate in the arena. If the man spotted some deformity of hoof or horn, he rejected the animal and it had to be taken out of the ring. How to remove a massive and possibly enraged bovine safely? The answer: six cows yoked together entered the ring with large cowbells attached to their necks. As they circled the bullring, the bull fell dutifully into line with the females, exiting safely and calmly. The CEO kept a cowbell handy in the conference room and when dissent rose to a level that was personal, or a discussion heated to beyond the boiling point, he would ring the bell loudly to calm the angry (bullish) dissenters.

The last word on dissent: One time a Sloan associate had disagreed with the chairman, and many thought the executive had behaved irresponsibly. General Motors' lawyer asked, "If he annoys you so much, Mr. Sloan, why don't you let him go?" "Let him go?" Sloan queried. "What an absurd idea, he *performs*."[13]

# CHAPTER 3

# OFFERING THE CUSTOMER CHOICES

*istory of American consumerism...Henry Ford, pioneer...
GM models...Sloan assesses GM's model problem...Sloan
has to close GM's luxury car price gap...Sloan introduces
the La Salle...GM's styling department and Harley Earl...Sloan ini-
tiates the annual GM model...Computer industry offers choices...
Clairol and new choices...Marriott, hospitality choices...Hallmark
offers choices...The managerial lessons of offering customers
choices and the pitfalls of too many choices*

ഏൟ ൟൟ

Alfred P. Sloan, Jr.'s marketing genius rested in part on his capacity
to see beyond the consumers' basic utilitarian automobile transportation needs. Whereas Henry Ford turned out the open-aired Model-T
in great numbers at a low price, and always in black, Sloan perceived
that American cars could offer noticeable add-ons in style, color, and
accessories. He was convinced that the nation's great and increasing
national wealth after World War I would encourage consumers to pay
more for car extras.

Sloan gambled that the more models he offered, with more bells and whistles than the competition, the greater the appeal to a larger number of car purchasers. He would produce the widest range of automobiles to please every type of consumer, from the low-income price buyer to the higher-income person who would pay for the maximum in comfort, horsepower, and luxury.

He recognized the four variables that marked the transition of the car market from the old to the new: "…a complex of new elements came into existence to transform the market once again. These new elements…can without significant loss reduce to four: installment selling, the used-car trade-in, the closed body, and the annual model."[1]

## A BRIEF HISTORY OF U.S. CONSUMERISM

The 1920s marked the start of America's consumer society transformation that eventually spread throughout the world and continues to expand globally today. It was during this decade that a considerable variety of commercially made mass-produced goods were newly offered to the public in great quantities and at low costs.

Before this explosion of products and goods, during the decades prior to World War I, a mostly rural America possessed little discretionary income for items other than daily requirements. Mainly people sewed their own clothes and grew their own food. Starting in 1893, Sears Roebuck offered a choice of products by catalog through the mail. Print advertising campaigns in magazines began at the turn of the century. In 1904, Jell-O announced the publication of a recipe book and received 250,000 orders. Americans wanted to buy more types of products and live a better life.

The Roaring Twenties ushered in a time of commercial opportunities sparked by new consumer prosperity despite the off-putting restrictions of Prohibition that most ignored. For the first time, American citizens—but especially those moving to and living in cities—could buy a reasonably priced range of ready-to-wear, form-fitting apparel in department stores. In addition, the consumer could purchase newly manufactured electrical devices and appliances, such as vacuum sweepers, toasters, phonograph players, and radios, at affordable prices.

(Thorstein Veblen, one of the nation's first economists, published *The Theory of the Working Class* in 1898, which addressed the American predisposition to purchase products. It was he who introduced the phrase "conspicuous consumption" that would become a national catchword. The 1920s with its rapid rise in income, mass production of affordable products, and buying on installment credit would witness his theory become reality.)

## HENRY FORD AND AUTOMOBILE CONSUMERISM

In the 1920s, automobiles also advanced on the road to success as sales of cars increased dramatically. In 1919 around 7 million cars traveled on American roads and by 1929 this number had climbed to 27 million, approximately, a car for every U.S. household. Further, in 1920, the country had 369,000 miles of road and 10 years later it had increased to 852,000 miles, a gain of 230 percent.

Henry Ford must be credited with the significant rise of automobile sales not only with his assembly-line production but also with the introduction in 1914 of a five-dollar-a-day minimum wage for his workforce, double the average U.S. worker's salary at that time. His conveyor assembly line reduced the time to manufacture a car from 13 hours in 1912 to an hour and a half in 1914.

The innovative mass production brought about by the assembly line expanded production and proved that volume manufacturing lowered costs. By 1925, a new Ford car cost the consumer $290, or about three months wages for the average American worker. The price would drop to $260 two years later.

## THE NOVELTY OF U.S. INSTALLMENT BUYING

The rise of consumerism in the 1920s was fueled by the growth of buying on credit in the form of loans, and the newly offered layaway plans. Installment purchasing had begun in Paris in the nineteenth century in the department store retail market.

In the United States, Edward Clark, the genius behind selling the Singer sewing machine, introduced installment buying in the 1850s. At a sales price of $125, the timesaving machine was out of the reach of most American households, but Clark began the "hire-purchase plan" with a first payment of $5 down and $3 per month. He is also credited with the trade-in, offering a $50 down payment on any make of sewing machine to consumers eager to purchase a new Singer model. By the 1890s, the cost of a Singer sewing machine had declined to $35. The Singer Company's financing plan was simplified to the famous, "a dollar down, and a dollar a week."

In the mid-1920s, the burgeoning used-car market proved to be the catalyst behind the adaptation and spread of installment buying in the new-car market. Car dealers needed a mechanism to move new models and also to sell old ones. The financing response came from car manufacturers and from some banks that encouraged Americans to attain their automobile dreams by buying on credit. In 1929, more than 60 percent of all cars were sold by a credit purchase, with some of the poorer risk buyers paying as much as 30 percent interest to finance the car.

The age of consumerism had risen on the back of credit purchases, an economic boom that would prove to be one of the major reasons for the nation's severe downfall in the depression. But, once the economy revived in the middle and late 1930s, the return to credit buying would stimulate unprecedented growth in the United States.

## THE GM MODELS TAKE SHAPE

The multicar model array at General Motors in the 1920s, consisting of different makes of cars, had a clear-cut bearing on the company's decision to offer a variety of automobiles for a diversity of consumer tastes. There seemed to be little practical purpose to offering one open-body style, black car in the same horsepower with seven different names.

Historically, William Durant is the pioneer who began the General Motors concept of car consolidation. Between 1908 and 1910 Durant bought 25 auto-related companies, of which 11 manufactured automobiles. Out of the 11, only 5 would survive the Sloan era that began in 1923: Chevrolet, Buick, Oldsmobile, Pontiac (formerly Oakland), and Cadillac.

When Durant was forced to step down the first time from General Motors in 1910, he spotted the talent of Louis Chevrolet and backed him to design a lighter car. Together, the two men started the Chevrolet Motor Company, which showed profits immediately. Durant used the Chevrolet stock in exchange for General Motors shares in an attempt to reacquire a controlling interest in the company.

By 1915, and with assistance of the Du Pont Company, which also held a large GM stock position, William Durant was returned to the presidency of General Motors. More important to the future of the company, was that Chevrolet eventually became part of the multi-car General Motors lineup.

## SLOAN ASSESSES THE PROBLEM

The function and aim of General Motors was clear to Sloan in 1923 when he told stockholders of his strategy of "a car for every purse and purpose."

Sloan, then president of the corporation, was confronted with two clear market problems: the Ford Model-T dominated with greater than a 50 percent share, and General Motors sold different cars in seven separate models at an ascending ladder of prices. The consumer could start with a four-cylinder Chevrolet "490" at the bottom price of $795, continue up the price ladder with a six-cylinder Oakland at $1,395, move higher with an eight-cylinder Olds at $2,100, or top out at a Cadillac for $3,790.

Sloan realized that so many cars, many priced close to another GM offering, created confusion in the mind of consumers. If purchasers could not see the benefits of owning a GM car straightaway, Sloan perceived that these buyers would be awash in too many choices and decisions. Moreover, 1921 was a time when automobile advertising was still in its infancy so it was difficult to distinguish one model from another except by visiting a dealership.

Sloan sorted out the price segmentation by eliminating two poorly performing makes (Scripps-Booth and Sheridan) and diminishing the price points from seven to six. At ascending price points, a consumer could buy the highest priced Chevrolet for $x$ dollars or buy a better-made Oakland without many add-ons also for $x$. Continuing up, a consumer could buy a more deluxe Oakland for a few hundred dollars more at the $y$ price or choose an entry-level basic Oldsmobile also at the $y$ price. Often the difference in price was in the number of cylinders, starting at four and increasing to eight cylinders.

The innovations in choice of model and enhancements within a specific model, now first offered to the consumer in 1921, would become the keystone to the next six decades of General Motors' success. Sloan was specific in this GM quality image: "General Motors should place its cars at the top of each price range and make them of such quality that they would attract sales from below that price, selling to those customers who might be willing to pay a little more for the additional quality."[2]

## SLOAN CHANGES CHEVROLET

In 1900, the U.S. census listed a national population total of 76 million with 30 million urban dwellers (39 percent) and 46 million in rural areas (61 percent). Thirty years later in 1930, the nation's population increased to 123 million, but the largest growth had occurred in the cities. The urban population had increased to 69 million (56 percent), while the rural population rose to 54 million, which declined to 44 percent of the national total.

Sloan was confident that the American consumer would opt for a better-looking car and pay a slightly higher premium for added interior benefits. Moreover, another consumer theory came into play; Henry Ford had purposely turned out a simple, low-priced car (Model-T) for the rural and farm segment of the population while Sloan (an Eastern-bred and educated cosmopolitan) perceived the car as a potential status symbol for the suburban and urban population. He summed up General Motors' most serious problem: "From the inside the picture was not so good. Not only were we not competitive with Ford in the low-price field—where the big volume and substantial future growth lay—but in the middle, where we were concentrated with duplication."[3]

Sloan saw an opportunity where others saw stagnation or defeat. He categorized the challenge to meet Ford head-on as being fortuitous when he wrote: "I say luckily for us [GM] because as a challenger to the then established position of Ford, we were favored by change…for us, change meant opportunity."[4]

In 1925, General Motors' engineers presented a newly designed Chevrolet, which the company named the K model. Under Sloan's leadership, the K had been designed with new, consumer-appealing features: a longer chassis, more leg room, a finish of Duco (a better paint finish created by Charles Kettering), Klaxon horn, overhead light, and improved clutch and rear axle. The revitalized, improved model led Sloan to say: "Chevrolet's internal statement of policy at this time was that it was our objective to get a public reputation for giving more for the dollar than Ford."[5]

"Giving more for the dollar" represented a shift in consumer marketing thinking within the automobile industry. This particular innovative strategy had a dual objective: a better-quality Chevrolet with more benefits and a specific competitive target, Ford's Model-T. In 1925, General Motors still ranked second in share, but in 1924 (when all car sales increased on the nation's economic buying boom), Ford Motor Company's one entry, Model-T had dropped from 54 percent to 45 percent of the market.

With the introduction of Chevrolet's K model, Sloan had correctly anticipated that Henry Ford would not read the tea leaves of change nor ponder the statistics of a declining market share. There are few instances in American business where one genius (Sloan) deduced flawlessly the actions (or lack of them) that another genius (Henry Ford) would take in regard to the dynamics of the market. Sloan's plan was uncomplicated: to decrease the price differential between the Chevrolet K model and the Ford Model-T: "It was our intention to continue adding improvements and over a period of time to move down in price on the Model-T and our position justified it."[6]

## SLOAN CLOSES THE LUXURY CAR CONSUMER GAP

Sloan's second phase of targeting the consumer was to fill the price and style variances between the five GM models. The first step was to close the wide price gap of $2,000 between the Buick "6" and the lowest-price Cadillac. The former was perceived of as a commendable mid-range car on the high end, and the latter, the highest standard of luxury automobile in the United States. In 1921, for example, the lowest-price Buick cost the consumer $1,795, and an entry level Cadillac started at $3,790.

General Motors had an important reason to compete in the $2,000 and above price range; it was a luxury market that was being dominated by the stylish, powerful, and competitive Packard, which was taking share from Cadillac on the high end. In addition, Buick owners were trading up to the more expensive Packard line but were not willing to spend more money for the highest-priced Cadillac.

Historically in 1904, the Packard Company had built a four-cylinder aluminum race car called the Grey Wolf, a speedster with an aluminum body. The racing aspect was new to American automobile buyers, and the sleek car caught the attention of a public intrigued by the new machine and also by the daring men who drove at great speeds. By 1919, a Packard racer had captured the world's land speed record of 149 miles per hour at Daytona Beach. The race car's success brought Packard widespread fame. The company concentrated on making high-end, luxury automobiles with elegantly square bodies in eight-cylinder models that were the epitome of style and elegance.

Sloan and his staff studied the Packard price gap problem and two main lines of thought emerged: one, to make a better Buick to sell above its $2,000 range and, two, to make a less expensive Cadillac to offer under $3,000. As Sloan considered the choices, he was cognizant that upgrading Buick or downsizing Cadillac were options that might have a potentially adverse effect on the consumer. The public did not consider Buick a high-end model, and there existed a justifiable possibility that Cadillac's luxury status would be diluted with an entry of a lower-priced car.

In 1927, Sloan proposed a solution to the price gap that surprised the automotive industry: he ordered a study for the creation of a *new* General Motors car. The automobile would not come from purchasing another car company: it would represent a newly designed, manufactured, and named automobile. The result was the La Salle, which would become the mid-luxury car that would fill the Buick-Cadillac price gap. Cadillac dealers would sell the La Salle. (Coincidentally, both models were named after French explorers in America.)

General Motors launched the La Salle in 1927 with an eight-cylinder engine in a closed four-door sedan at a price of $2,685, $100 more than the Packard fifth series model. Sloan had found the perfect answer to the price gap conundrum.

## THE LA SALLE BEGINS GM'S STYLING PROGRAM

During the 1920s the American automobile underwent a significant modification, it changed from an open-air car for transportation to a closed-body car for transport and leisure. In 1924, the closed-body models represented 43 percent of U.S. industry sales, and by 1927 it had risen dramatically to 85 percent. Sloan summed up the change as moving from *mass* to *mass-class*.

The rapid growth of the closed-body car demanded greater attention to the styling of the exterior and interior, especially at General Motors where Sloan was quick to see the appeal of style on the consumer. Soon most of the U.S. auto companies switched to closed-body cars, and the public preference for this change accounted for the abrupt and sharp downfall of Ford's Model-T, and with it, the substantial decreases in revenues of the Ford Motor Company. Sloan stated the case matter-of-factly: "The rise of the closed-body made it impossible for Mr. Ford to maintain his leading position in the low-price field, for he had frozen his policy in the Model-T...preeminently an open car design."[7]

In 1919, General Motors had acquired the Fisher Body Company, which had been organized in 1908 when it made 150 closed-bodies for that year's Cadillac. The seven Fisher brothers were known for their quality workmanship in fabricating chassis, and two of them, Fred and Lawrence Fisher, would later be appointed members of GM's executive committee.

Fisher Body was another of GM's brilliant vertical integration acquisitions whereby the company obtained the skills of experts in a certain automotive field. It was to Lawrence Fisher that Sloan entrusted the task of designing the new La Salle. Sloan wanted nothing less than a stylishly elegant car to match Packard's speed and sophistication.

Fisher's attention turned to southern California where a young, Stanford-educated engineer named Harley J. Earl had shown exceptional design skill in a custom body shop, making coach-built bodies for special order Cadillacs. Earl had advanced the art of automobile model design by using clay, an advancement over plastic and wood and easier to mold into different shapes.

Earl was brought to Detroit in 1926 to try out ideas for the new La Salle. The automotive stylist was free to experiment without restrictions of a specific GM look or design. He found the one luxury car model to emulate, the classic European-built Hispano-Suiza. The fabled "His So" was a masterpiece of automobile styling, the most expensive car in the world and the favorite of Hollywood stars, millionaires, European royalty, and maharajahs. In its time, it was considered the premium car in the world, even superior to the handsomely stylish Rolls Royce.

Sloan was delighted with Earl's La Salle model because it provided General Motors with a more modern look and a car styled and priced to meet Packard head on in the mid-$2,000 price range. A more important La Salle historic yardstick: the car represented the first U.S. mass-production automobile to be styled by design. Many considered it the best-looking luxury automobile in America. Earl had given the outer body added pizzazz with a two-tone finish, an exciting innovation in 1927.

More than the successful first appearance, the car started the wheels of change moving in Sloan's mind: to increase consumer demand, all of General Motors other five makes also needed styling. He recognized that "The market made it clear that appearance was selling cars."[8]

## CREATION OF GM'S STYLING DEPARTMENT

Sloan had been thinking about style as a vital component of automobile sales from his early days at Hyatt Roller Bearing. As far back as the turn of the twentieth century, he had been curious why more emphasis was not placed on this aspect. He wrote later: "In my dreams of what might be done I visualized an organized effort to promote the maximum in eye appeal—a styling approach separate from the usual engineering approach."[9]

Sloan's dreams met styling reality in the personage of Harley J. Earl. For all intents and purposes, Earl is the father of American car styling, the first car designer to be called a "stylist." Originally asked to come from California for the La Salle project, his talent and car design induced Sloan to realize an earlier aspiration: the creation of a separate styling department devoted solely to the appearance of General Motors' cars. Sloan asserted: "I was so impressed with Mr.

Earl's work that I decided to obtain the advantages of his talent for other General Motors car divisions."[10]

In 1927, Sloan presented to the executive committee an immediate plan for the creation of a special department that would deal exclusively with styling. He promoted Earl to head this new division to be called the Art and Color Section. Word circulated at GM that Earl was looking for other talented people interested in design within the corporation. Soon he had 50 people working in the section; the first car department fashioned to deal with the elements of automotive style.

Sloan sent Earl to Europe in 1927 to bring back any styling ideas that he found. Over time, per Sloan's suggestion, Earl invited noted European car designers to Detroit. But Sloan and Earl always remained cognizant that the American consumer preferred big cars with big trunk space and big horsepower to the smaller, European models.

Sloan listened to the dissent from the divisions that resented one person (Earl) having the power to change the look of the entire GM line. The executives within GM were apprehensive that Earl would have total control over all models and that soon all GM cars would look alike.

The GM auto men griped that the new Arts and Color Section was becoming a "beauty parlor." Much criticism was directed at Earl who was handsome, arrogant, and flamboyant. He dressed in cowboy boots and casual attire and installed mauve curtains in the office. No wonder Sloan heard loud dissent from the staid GM staff. He gathered in the differences of opinion and then responded to the emotional but unfounded complaints against his genius stylist: "Mr. Earl...recognized that it will be impossible for him to revise eight or nine lines of cars every year."[11]

Ironically, the first GM car of the line that Earl designed, the 1929 Buick, failed to appeal to the consumer. Too round for the market with a noticeable circular bulge, it was referred to as the "pregnant Buick." Sloan perceived that the change was too radical and thought that the public preferred small changes as opposed to drastic alterations in the cars.

Sloan moved the Arts and Color Section into the General Motors Annex purposely to provide easy access to other GM executives from all the divisions. He wanted everyone's voice to be heard by the stylists.

He viewed the development of new cars as a community effort and relied on Harley Earl to decide on the finished model. In the1930s, Sloan changed the name of the department to the Styling Section to encompass its total function.

Earl contributed perceptibly to General Motors' automobile styling dominance in the U.S. market with his styling creations. His career numbered many milestones, including, the first person in the automobile design profession, inventor of the concept or "dream" car, the use of modeling clay, and the designer of the Corvette. The models went from the Styling Section blackboard, to clay models, and, finally, to the consumer

Sloan's biographer summarized the importance of Harley Earl: "Sloan saw a high potential for increased sales in Earl's work. His basis for this judgment was strategic: eye appeal would transform the car market. Consumers would purchase cars not just for utilitarian transportation but for personal pleasure and self-expression."[12]

Of historic note, the Styling Section provided women with their first opportunity to work at General Motors. This represented the first hiring of females in significant numbers within the male-dominated U.S. automobile industry.

The Styling Section and the clear price definitions of the six General Motors cars led Sloan to fit in the final piece in General Motors' consumer targeting: the annual model. This one event would dominate America economically and ceremonially as no other commercial event had in the nation's past or would ever do in its future.

## THE ANNUAL MODEL CHANGE

For more than 50 years, from the 1930s onward, the annual Detroit ritual of the automobile model change dominated the American consciousness. The "Rites of Autumn"—as the event was called—captured the nation's attention in consumer-driven commercial hype and hoopla of advertising and promotion. Alfred P. Sloan, Jr., was the driving force behind this influential experience that revolutionized the concept of America's way of doing business.

Sloan always used the term *dynamic obsolescence* (later known pejoratively as *planned obsolescence*) to describe the modus operandi of the American consumer purchasing a new car and trading in the old one about every two years on average.

The system seemed elementary in concept: U.S. automobile companies would unveil new models annually, offering the public visible improvements in style and interior. He wrote: "Each year we must produce a line of cars which embodies advanced engineering and styling features, and which will be competitive in price and meet the demands of the retail customer."[13]

General Motors promoted the idea that annual change was positive to the consumer and to the economy. The GM company redefined car ownership as being about prestige, status, and self and not just about transportation. Sloan put forward a revolutionary concept about car ownership into the nation's psyche without ever shouting it directly: "You are what you drive."

Naturally, Henry Ford voiced displeasure at the idea of changing models, having advocated simplicity and design and proving the economies of scale to mass-produce one car. Begrudgingly though, he stopped production in 1927 of the Model-T and closed all Ford plants for seven months. When the new closed-body Model-A was launched, it caused a nationwide sensation that allowed the Ford Motor Car Company to regain the automobile market lead temporarily in 1929 and 1930.

Sloan started to champion the annual model change as corporate strategy, but it would take until the early 1930s for this to become policy. He had finally put in place the variables that he needed to embark on the annual strategy. General Motors sold six distinct car models priced in differing segments from the low-priced Chevrolet to the high-priced Cadillac. Sloan had hired Harley Earl and started the Styling Section to concentrate on designing cars in a conscious attempt to appeal visually to the consumer. Sloan recognized the options open to the buyer: "A customer can, over a wide range, really have his car in any color he desires and trimmed with material he fancies. In mass production there has been developed such an amazing flexibility that it well may be said that every car in certain particulars could be a custom job."[14]

The last piece was to formalize how and when these model changes would be offered to the public. Sloan considered all the production and marketing variables: the lead time for a model change, the engineering required, the raw materials needed, and, increasingly more important, how to advertise the new cars to the public.

GM would begin each new model with body and engineering changes so that the public could give a thumbs up or down to the new shape. If the styling appealed to the consumer, the following years would witness minor, cosmetic changes to the chassis and, often, greater alterations inside the car.

Sloan knew that to spur sales he needed advertising campaigns, starting as early as the late summer to talk to or excite the consumer about the upcoming new models presented in the fall. At first, during the 1930s the ads appeared in magazines; then radio was added in that decade, and finally, television in the 1950s. Some of the TV jingles still resonate today. For example, people still recognize Dinah Shore's singing of the popular "See the USA in your Chevrolet."

General Motors was also an innovator in linking its annual model change to a vision of progress for the nation. At the 1939 New York World's Fair, a promotional coup was the company's classic Futurama exhibit, the number-one visitor-attended hit at the fair. People waited two hours to take a seated ride into the future of 1960 for views of the cities and cars of tomorrow. (The futuristic automobiles resembled spaceships in the 1936 Flash Gordon movie serial.) But the message to the nation was clear: GM had demonstrated that automobiles would be at the center of American life in the world of tomorrow 20 years away. And the one American car company to supply that vision of the exciting future would be General Motors.

At the end of World War II, Sloan started another consumer-oriented vehicle for displaying the annual models: the GM Motorama show. Running from 1949 to 1961, the Motorama captured the public's interest and also generated excellent press. The 1949 premier drew almost 600,000 people in New York and Boston. And the 1953 Motorama is best remembered for Harley Earl's introduction of the Corvette, a fiberglass dream car of the future. The zenith of promotion was the 1955 Motorama show aired on CBS television, hosted by Bob Hope and seen by millions of viewers.

There was a time when the five model GM cars were recognizable to every motorist in America. Even at a distance, the distinguishing GM grillwork from the Body by Fisher designers and a product of the Styling Section would clearly identify the GM model whether it was the stripes on Pontiac or the fins on the Cadillac.

Sloan had changed the concept of automobile merchandising by varying the GM style annually throughout its five-car lineup. He realized that offering consumers many exterior and internal choices would spur sales: "Today the appearance of a motorcar is a most important factor in the selling end of the business—perhaps the most important factor—because every one knows the car will run."[15]

## COMPUTER INDUSTRY OFFERS THE CONSUMER CHOICES

The world's personal computer industry parallels the history of the rise of automobile manufacturing by also offering consumers many choices in models and styles at different price points. Correspondingly, the constant upgrading among all the many hardware component variables (video card, chip speed, memory, modem connection, etc.) follows Sloan's concept of dynamic obsolescence and continual model change.

In 1905, imagine the delight and surprise of a person driving an open-air, hand-cranked car at 20 miles an hour for the first time. The feeling of wonder would be the same as a person's excitement and astonishment utilizing a 1980s model CP/M computer with a single large floppy disc slot, spell checking automatically, and then printing out the work with a slow and noisy dot matrix, daisy wheel printer.

The public viewed the first marketed personal computer with the same uneasiness and nervousness as the earliest automobiles. And similarly, no one in 1980 could foresee that waiting around corner in the decades to follow was the Internet, AOL, e-mail, and Google in the same way no one in 1911 could predict the massive interstate highway system of the 1950s, the two-car garage, or other improvements like air-conditioning, in-auto VCR systems, or opening and locking car doors with the click of a special device.

The spectacular and swift improvement in computer technology arose from rapidly increasing consumer demand for easier-to-use office and industrial equipment. In 1962, the Massachusetts Institute of Technology and the Digital Equipment Corporation built the first personal computer at a cost of $43,000. The first personal computer, the MITS Altair 8080, was released in kit form in 1975, and a few thousand units were sold to hobbyists. By 1983, consumers could purchase a Radio Shack laptop Tandy model with its Microsoft DOS operating system at below $2,000.

There exist other analogous consumer parallels to the automobile and computer industries: both were started by tinkerers with a passion for new technology, often turning out ungainly models with superb functionality and little aesthetic style. Eventually, in both industries, the models would become lighter, faster, and lower in cost.

Some of these precursors of the "modern" (read MS-DOS operating systems) models were the CP/M machines like the Osborne, Commodore, Eagle, and the Kay-Pro (named after Andy Kay) that first surfaced in great number in the early 1980s. The Kay-Pro was introduced in 1982 with one serial port, 2 full-height floppies, and a 2.5 MHz Z-80 processor. For all intents and purposes, these early models traveled figuratively at the same slow speeds of those early automobiles. But these new machines worked, and their operation (slow and clunky by today's efficient standards) was a significant improvement over electric typewriters and word processors.

In 1986, a year after Microsoft developed Windows for IBM, U.S. households using a computer numbered a scant 8.2 percent. By 2004, consumer usership had risen to 75 percent. The growth of the Internet has witnessed a more spectacular increase in a shorter time. In 1998, 18.6 percent of U.S. households had a connection, skyrocketing to 67.6 percent in 2004, representing more than 190 million connected U.S. households

In every newspaper in the United States or online, consumers can view an array of computer choices and systems from low-priced towers to high-priced laptops. The purchase decision corresponds to the selections in the automobile industry, options for entry-level utilitarianism or costly technical works of art. In addition, the ancillary offerings of monitors, keyboards, mouse clickers, etc. are similar to the automobiles industry's many interior style offerings.

The U.S. computer industry, similar to the Big Three American automakers, has been winnowed down to a small group of manufacturers from hundreds. The leaders in 2004 were Dell (32.8 percent) and Hewlett Packard (20.5 percent), which generate more than 53 percent of the PC industry sales in the United States. Gateway is third with 5.2 percent; and Apple has a 3.3 percent share and also has a distinct and a loyal user base.

Consumers can keep a computer for years or trade up annually as new models appear. These new models are constantly being marketed in a push for the new and improved, which harks back to Sloan's annual model change. But the computer industry surpassed the automobile industry for planned obsolescence by eliminating the trade-in allowance. And there is no used computer market.

The two main computer manufacturers, Dell and Hewlett Packard, adhere to many of Sloan's policies for discovering what consumers want. Both companies do extensive research; both qualitatively by conducting focus groups and one-on-one interviews in the field, and also doing quantitative surveys with user and nonuser groups.

The entire computer industry also follows a Sloan tenet of offering postsales service (online and often free of charge). This customer service remains one of the most important variables that influence a purchase decision and Dell and HP have established excellent reputations for assisting purchasers of their product. These companies may not have established a GM-type Mr. Goodwrench advertised repair service but, down the road, this kind of repair may become an important consumer choice.

In the old days, an American would say, "I buy a new car every two years." Today, the computer is the machine of constant change, providing new improvements and options. In the future, expect to see more different kinds of computer choices offered to the consumer in terms of size, color, and price. It may well be that Sloan's automotive slogan will change to "a computer for every price and purpose."

## CLAIROL EXCELS AT OFFERING CHOICES

Sloan's insistence on providing consumers with many choices to reach niche markets was not limited to the automobile industry (nor to the computer industry that followed years later). The key to his concept was the term "for every purpose" meaning that manufacturers had to concentrate on many varied and distinct aspects of the marketplace.

An example of a new industry that followed Sloan's examples was the hair-coloring market. In this business one company originally dominated the market in the same way that GM dominated the automobile field after Sloan took over as president. That hair-coloring company was Clairol.

This company's successfully historic introduction of home hair coloring for American women demonstrated the importance of knowing and developing a customer market that was comprised of many demographic and psychographic segments. Clairol's success was predicated on the ability to identify that many niches existed within a particular consumer base and that to succeed the company had to create discrete, and differently named and advertised, products for each user segment (like GM's five-car lineup).

The history of Clairol (basically also, the history of hair coloring in the United States) began in 1931 when Lawrence Gelb, a New York chemist, traveled to Europe to look for new cosmetic ideas not then made or sold in the United States. One product by the Mury Company of Paris intrigued Gelb; a hair-coloring treatment called Clairol, the French phrase for "light color." Gelb purchased the patented formula for $25,000 from the owner, a German chemist.

In the 1930s, hair coloring in the United States remained exclusive to hair salons. But most women would rarely dare to be seen having this treatment. Instead, they had to use rear entrances at the salons and enter in secret. Inside, the coloring procedure was performed in booths hidden behind curtains. A significant problem for the hair salons of that era also was the dull or brassy color finish that came from the low-grade quality of hair dyes.

Gelb set about to convince the hair salons that the Clairol formula was more efficacious and that the end result would look more natural because the coloring process penetrated the hair shaft. To encourage inquiries from salons, his wife used the invented name of Joan Clair, an expert who answered all questions about the new coloring treatment. Finally in 1950, Gelb established a laboratory in the United States to develop new hair-care products with the renowned Austrian biochemist Dr. Bernard Lustig to legitimize the company's product as being scientifically formulated.

Clairol might never have continued further than a hair salon treatment had it not been for the Toni home permanent wave product introduced to women in the late 1940s. The first ad for this radical idea—that American women could style their hair at home almost as easily as shampooing it—showed two beautiful twins with gorgeously styled coiffures and challenged the reader to guess which sister had been to the beauty parlor and asking, "Which twin has the Toni?"

The success of the Toni home permanent system convinced Gelb that American women might be willing also to try hair home coloring if it were simple and effective. The sales potential for selling hundred of thousands of consumer products over the counter was substantially greater than selling a finite and bounded number of coloring treatments in hair salons.

Gelb realized that the name of the product currently sold to hair salons, Miss Clairol Hair Color Bath, would not achieve the objective of convincing women of the ease and benefit of the one-step, 20-minute hair-coloring process. After considering many names that would appeal to the consumer, finally, Clairol came up with Nice 'n Easy. The product description said it was hair coloring made simple. The name proved to be genius as it accomplished the dual goals of ease of preparation and beneficial end result.

The next step was to advertise Nice 'n Easy to women that had scant knowledge of hair coloring outside of hair salons. The creative problem was to introduce the new product to generate interest, and to convince women they could color easily at home. The result in 1957 was one of the most memorable advertising campaigns in history: the photograph showed an attractive woman with lovely hair and the headline asked provocatively, "Does she or doesn't she? Only her hairdresser knows for sure." (This ad was judged the ninth best U.S. advertising campaign of the twentieth century by *Advertising Age* magazine.)

The advertisement, created by the Foote, Cone and Belding agency and penned by copywriter Shirley Polykoff, caught the attention of American women immediately with its challenging and sexually subliminal question. Nice 'n Easy sales skyrocketed as more and more women decided to try to color hair at home rather than pay money for a hair salon treatment. In addition, many millions of women who had never considered going to a hair salon, purchased the product to see if it delivered salon-quality results.

With the spectacular success of Nice 'n Easy, Clairol executives looked to expand sales by appealing to two different markets that had not been stimulated to buy Nice 'n Easy in great numbers. One market was younger women with blonde hair or women who wanted blonde highlights. For this segment Clairol created the Born Blonde product. Again, the advertising provided the motivation for coloring hair; it said, "If you have only one life to live, live it as a blonde."

The other market segment that Clairol needed to reach were older women with gray streaks who wanted to touch up the gray with a choice of how much hair to color. The new product for this segment was Loving Care, and it, too, was advertised with the brilliant campaign: "You're not getting older. You're getting better."

By the mid-1970s, Clairol (now part of Bristol-Myers via a 1959 acquisition) owned a 60 to 70 percent share of the domestic hair-coloring market. The company operated a hair-coloring school in its Manhattan offices, and all new hires had to attend for a week to learn the process. Clairol relied heavily on hair and hair-coloring research, periodically measuring the domestic market in depth.

In the early 1970s, data indicated there were a growing number of younger American women with long hair. This lead to Clairol's successful launch of Long and Silky conditioner followed by a shampoo with the same name. At the same time in the 1970s, Clairol came out with its Herbal Essence fragrance shampoos. This product also came from examining consumer trends and deciding to offer a variety of naturally scented shampoos to ride the wave of the "go natural and organic" trend in the country. Health food shops had started to proliferate, offering all-natural, nonchemical shampoos in different formulas like rosemary, chamomile, and citrus.

The Clairol shampoos marked Bristol-Myers' attempt to challenge Procter & Gamble, Lever Brothers, and Colgate in the large shampoo market. Users had no problem accepting that Clairol, a name synonymous with quality hair coloring, could also make a quality shampoo. The shampoo represented a carryover of a quality name in the same manner that General Motors could manufacture quality refrigerators.

## THE MARRIOTT HOSPITALITY CHOICES

The 2004 hospitality industry in the United States was an $86 billion business with the revenue leader Marriott generating $9.2 billion. No hotel company has been as successful as the Marriott organization offering the consumer a range of low-end and high-end lodging both in the United States and overseas. Its 21 percent share of the regular hotel business (not including revenues from economy hotels) leads the other two large hotel chains—Hilton at 16 percent and Starwood at 11 percent.

Important also to the worldwide chain has been the corporation's successful branding of the Marriott name onto the many economy-level lodging chains like Fairfield Inn and Residence Inn without any dilution to the flagship JW Marriott Hotels and Resorts. The sole exception to Marriott branding is the high-end, luxury chain of Ritz-Carlton hotels, a 1995 acquisition, which is not advertised as being operated by the Marriott. (There is precedence for keeping the mid-priced name off of the luxury acquisition, as in the case of Ford not putting its name on its line of Jaguar cars.)

The Marriott organization has been reinventing itself since its founder J. Willard Marriott opened a nine-stool A&W root beer stand in 1927 in Washington, D.C., and named it the Hot Shoppe. In 1937, the company branched out into the airline food service field with its 1937 In Flite Catering business for American Airlines and the now defunct Eastern and Capital airlines.

For the next 30 years after its founding, the corporation remained exclusively in the food service business, operating under the Hot Shoppes name a series of successful and ubiquitous cafeterias in Washington, D.C., and Baltimore, Maryland. During World War II, the moderately priced, good-quality meals served the workforce of the burgeoning defense industry and the thousands of military personnel that passed through the nation's capital.

In 1957, it opened its first lodging site, a 365-room motel in Arlington, Virginia, called the Marriott Twin Bridges Motor Hotel. This marked the first time that the Marriott name was ever used as a consumer brand name. Seven years later the company changed its name to Marriott-Hot Shoppes.

From that point onward in the company's history, it moved slowly into the hospitality industry; building or acquiring hotels. The modus operandi has been to build company-owned properties or to construct hotels by franchise agreements. It may come as a surprise to travelers, but more than 40 percent of all Marriott properties are run by franchise owners. In the latter case, Marriott assists with the building plan, design, and furnishing and also trains staff. The company receives franchise and incentive fees and is unburdened by real estate problems, which are left to the franchise owners.

(The hospitality industry uses the exclusive term REVPAR [revenue per available room] as the industry measurement to gauge the productivity both of individual hotels and also cumulatively for chains. The REVPAR is calculated by combining the occupancy rate and the average price of a room.)

Building new locations or buying out other chains, today, Marriott and its affiliates offer franchises for seven hotel brands in the United States and five hotel brands internationally. The domestic operations include Marriott Hotels, Resorts, and Suites; Courtyard; Residence Inns; Fairfield Inn Hotels; TownePlace Suites; SpringHill Suites; and Renaissance Hotels.

To examine Marriott's offerings from the low-end budget sites to the high-end Ritz-Carlton is to see a replication of Sloan's five-car General Motors lineup and to follow his dictum with the revised slogan "a hotel room for every price and purpose." This Marriott multi-tiered price and quality strategy permits the servicing of all types of consumers.

The expectation at Marriott, as at General Motors, was that as consumers' incomes rose, they would upgrade their lodging from the bare-bones basic hotels to the deluxe Ritz-Carlton with its "appointed" rooms and first-class, or Cadillac, service.

## HALLMARK OFFERS CHOICES

Hallmark cards represents another successful example of a company that offered many choices and also dominated its industry in the same way that GM achieved a dominant market share under Sloan's leadership.

Founded in Kansas City by the Hall brothers in 1910, the greeting card company realized that to attract the greatest number of potential consumers, it had to produce and market cards for every sentiment and, eventually, for every occasion or holiday. One of the first cards offered a pick-me-up to people down on their luck. The card read, "When you get to the end of your rope, tie a knot in it, and hang on."

A key marketing decision was that the company understood that to succeed it had to sell a broad and varied "line" of cards. This, effectively, set the tone and direction for designing and printing cards for more than birthdays, graduations, and Valentine's Day. The first Mother's Day cards appeared for sale within the company's in-house store. They were so popular among the workers that soon these warmly sentimental cards were offered to the public with great success.

(Hallmark does not name official holidays; this can be done only by a Congressional resolution. Christmas generates the greatest number of cards within the greeting card industry, totaling almost three billion annually. Valentine's Day generates about one billion cards. The lowest end for a celebratory occasion is Nurse's Day with barely half a million cards sent out.)

Similar to GM, Hallmark created a memorable and successful institutional advertising campaign in 1944 with its slogan "When you care enough to send the very best." (This ranked 68 in the top 100 advertising campaigns of the twentieth century). In addition, its signature and crown logo that appeared in 1949 remains one of the America's most recognizable and most respected corporate designs, as similar in substance as General Electric's script initials or the Coca Cola logo.

The company has always been up-to-date on evolving national consumer trends and has reacted to the social changes in the nation's lifestyles with different lines of greeting cards. Hallmark launched its humorous Shoebox Greeting line in 1986. Recently, it has added religious cards via acquisition of other card companies. In 1999, it started to offer a complete line of cards in Spanish.

Realizing the importance of the low-priced market like Sloan with the Chevrolet, the company started its Warm Wishes line of 99-cent cards. And consumers can now create their own cards with the Personalize It! in-store computer system.

Taking a page from Sloan's willingness to find ancillary businesses, Hallmark acquired Binney and Smith whose product line included Crayola, Magic Markers, and Silly Putty. It also bought Revell-Monogram, the world's largest manufacturer of model kits. And most of the ribbons, wrapping paper, and bows on the market are also made by Hallmark.

Whatever the sentiment (except perhaps risqué ones), Hallmark has created cards for each and every consumer need and wish. Its continuing success as a $4 billion company depends upon maximizing its choices to consumers. Founder J. C. Hall said, "I'd rather make eight million good impressions than 28 million bad ones. Good taste is good business."

## THE LESSONS OF OFFERING CUSTOMERS CHOICES

In examining Sloan's "a car for every price and purpose" strategy, it is key to realize that it succeeded because it offered customers the right choices. Taking the multicar offerings from William Durant's earlier acquisitions, Sloan was one of the first and smartest executives to understand that Americans took pleasure in the freedom of consumer choices offered. The self-determination was, in effect, an extension of the democracy of voting.

Sloan sensed that in a nation where citizens prided themselves on their individuality, offering many choices contributed to self-expression, especially, in purchasing an automobile. As Sloan stated, since everyone knew the car would run, the variables that comprised the purchase decision revolved around price and style and freedom of choice.

### TOO MANY CHOICES

Too many possible choices are off-putting to consumers and cause dissonance. Currently, an average supermarket stocks over 40,000 different items, and many are line or size extensions of popular brands. The result is what psychologists call *choice overload,* which results in Americans questioning their purchase decisions and setting themselves up for failure when products do not meet high expectations.

A prime example of a popular and growing business that is indifferent to choice overload is the cell phone industry, which offers a spate of often confusing options. Newspaper advertisements and online promotions offer a sea of multiple cell phone proposals and mind-boggling calling plan alternatives.

The proliferation of cell phone offers, many free to the consumer, and an increasing number with money back, are the enticements to lure new customers into long-term phone plans. There is a correlation between the superiority and higher price of a phone and the price of a calling plan; the more expensive the phone, the more costly the customer's monthly fee. The industry is unsure of whether customers are doing the math, comparing the outright purchase of a cell phone (neither free nor cash back) and then negotiating for a lower, monthly plan price.

Finally, phone calling distributors like Lets Talk, Smart Price, Get Connected are type 2 provider communication companies that contract to buy phone time in bulk from the type 1 providers, which are the larger phone company suppliers like AT&T, Verizon, and Sprint. Type 2 companies resell phone service to customers at a discount, frequently, with cell phone prices significantly lower than the major players. This kind of discounted service adds on another choice to the already perplexed cell phone consumer. What type 2 consumers do not realize when they opt for cheaper services is that if a circuit designated for them goes down, the type 2 provider can do nothing but wait for the main carrier to correct the problem. The customer has no recourse but to wait also.

Consumers make choices using an empirical mental model that analyzes awareness of benefits, costs, and risks. However, the most recent research studies indicate that when potential customers are faced with too many choices, their minds begin to shut down. They cannot compute all the combinations and permutations of multibenefit offers. The negative outcome is that when these choices, like cell phone or cell phone plans, become overwhelming, customers do not purchase at all.

Consumer research indicates also that many shoppers do not enjoy choosing from a wide range of options because they tend to second-guess themselves and worry about making a bad selection. Retailers have started to curtail the number of offerings, trimming back the total number of items, and surprisingly, generating higher sales.

## WHEN GOOD CHOICES GO FROM BAD TO WORSE

Two different customer-based choices—both from General Motors—indicate how often good choices at the beginning can turn out to be bad choices years later. The lessons in these case studies are how to cut losses early or not to offer a radically new idea at all.

In December 2000, General Motors announced the unthinkable, that in 2004 the company would discontinue manufacturing the Oldsmobile, the oldest continuing American car model. It was started in 1897 by Ransom Olds and marked the second automobile to be incorporated in 1908 into what would become the General Motors Corporation.

Oldsmobile at one time was GM's most innovative model. It offered the first automatic transmission in 1938 and was the first GM car to offer a high compression overhead valve V-8 engine in 1949 in the legendary Rocket 88. Sales peaked at 1.2 million in 1985 when its Cutlass model was the most popular car in the United States. (In 1987, Oldsmobile sold 400,000 fewer cars than in 1986!) But by the year 2000, total sales had dropped precipitously to below 300,000, the lowest total since the 224,684 cars sold in 1952.

Why did GM discontinue Oldsmobile? The simple answer was that it had misplaced the car's identity; gone was the historic essence of being an Oldsmobile with a clear-cut model concept, recognizable shape and grill, and superpowered names like Rocket 88, Cutlass, or Tornado.

In the decade of the 1980s, when the entire GM line lost its distinct styling appearance, all of its models started to resemble one another. Or, put another way, the cars started to look like the successful Japanese competition. (The term at GM for the sameness in look was *badge engineering,* which referred to the five car divisions sharing as many parts as possible to lower the production costs. The unfortunate result was that a Chevy looked too similar to a Buick.)

The decision GM management made, the ill-fated choice that would open the door to future retirement of the Oldsmobile brand, was to reposition the restyled, look-like-every-other-car Olds as an alternative to Honda. In twenty-twenty hindsight it proved a predestined mistake to pursue the high brand loyalty, quality-made Honda and Acura lines. The Olds had built a deserved reputation as car known for power and sleek styling. How could GM anticipate that existing Honda (or comparable Toyota, Nissan, or VW) buyers would switch to Olds, which had never generated the quality performance ratings and high resale value?

The Oldsmobile cancellation decision harks back to Sloan's discontinuation of the Scripps-Booth and Sheridan cars in the early

1920s, which were the sixth and seventh automobiles (and superfluous) in his five-car reorganization lineup.

Sloan was not involved in the termination of another GM car, the Corvair, a small, rear-engine car that appeared in 1957 to meet the new challenge of smaller European models. Ironically, although the novelty car was small and economically fuel efficient, its Monza model with bucket seats deluxe trim, etc. captured the consumers' fancy, building up the price and diminishing the most important reason for purchasing a small, inexpensive car with good gas mileage.

In a similar vein, GM's decision to manufacture the Saturn car as a GM-manufactured but anti-GM automobile (a quality *Japanese-type* car made in the United States by Americans) represented a brilliant and necessary marketing choice. But today Saturn has proved to be a multibillion-dollar misstep with no prospects of the anticipated success as GM's "car of the future." (One investment banker called it "GM's new division of the present.") Ironically, it enjoys the same high customer loyalty and performance ratings as Japanese makes, but it has never generated the high volume sales totals as its Japanese competition.

The Saturn, a quality car with its own no-hassle, set-price dealerships, suffers from a paradox that has judgmentally inhibited greater sales: why would U.S. customers who prefer a Japanese car purchase an American car manufactured in the Japanese style? In some automotive circles, introducing Saturn at such a considerable start-up cost was similar to GM's initial 1920s insistence that the air-cooled engine would become an enormous success and the wave of the company's future.

Saturn car sales in 2004 totaled about 221,000 cars, down 58,000 from 279,000 in 1996. Historically, the car never generated the 500,000 target goal needed to be profitable since the first car rolled off the assembly line at the newly built, state-of-the-art Tennessee plant in 1990. More bad news occurred for GM when research indicated that more than 40 percent of Saturn buyers had already owned another GM vehicle.

What can managers learn from these two examples? In the Oldsmobile case, it was clear in the mid- to late-1980s that the car had, altering Sloan's phrase, "no purpose." It had failed to continue its long-established and distinctive niche as an Oldsmobile in the mind of the consumer. It had lost its link back to the turn-of-century Old Scout model that in 1905 had blazed a record-breaking trail across the continent, and it had also lost any association with its historically named power models.

Further, with the green light given in 1983 to manufacture Saturn, where was the room in the GM five-car lineup for a model like Oldsmobile with no perceptive identity? Some 20 years later with rapidly declining sales and an unhappy dealer network, GM finally pulled the plug on the Olds model in the same way that Chrysler had discontinued the once popular Plymouth. These two discontinued makes would join the Willys, Nashes, Studebakers, Packards, La Salles, and step-down Hudsons in the graveyard of the American automobile industry.

The lessons about choice in these instances are twofold: Olds should have been discontinued in the mid-1980s when it was obvious that the American market had changed significantly, with U.S. customers preferring better-quality cars with higher resale value and less need for postsales service. The choice to let the Olds brand continue in a repositioned challenge to Honda doomed its existence since it could never deliver the benefits of its competition. The Oldsmobile could never enter some cocoon of change and emerge as a new and beautiful Japanese model.

The Saturn choice is similar to a professional baseball club that looks good on paper but never performs up to expectations in the field. In retrospect, would it have been hypothetically more profitable for GM to have acquired an existing Japanese automobile manufacturer (if that were ever possible) in order to offer choices in the favorable niche that all Japanese models own with consumers worldwide.

The GM strategy of purchasing a foreign car company did not seem to work in Europe with the recent GM-Fiat Auto of Italy acquisition, which GM backed out of in 2005, agreeing to pay $2 billion to Fiat *not* to complete the transaction.

(Auto nomenclature trivia: The name of the famous Italian car company Fiat is actually an abbreviation and should be spelled F.I.A.T. The letters in Italian represent the words *Fabbrica Italiana di Automobili Torino,* or the Italian automobile factory at Turin. Similarly, the A.L.F.A in Alfa-Romeo in Italian stands for *Anonima Lom-*

*barda Fabbrica Automobili* or the Lombardy car-making factory. Nicola Romeo added his name in 1916.)

## SLOAN AND CHOICES

Sloan had put into the works a product policy that emphasized smart choices, realizing at all times that General Motors sold to the consumer. The overriding strategy was to make automobiles at least equal in design to GM's competition but not risk creating vehicles with radical designs or radical ideas (e.g., Saturn).

As for the basics of customers choosing one car over another, Sloan always enjoyed quoting William Knudsen, general manager of Chevrolet, on why the automobile in all brands achieved such instant popularity. Knudsen said, "Everyone wants to go from A to B sitting down."[16]

# FACTS DETERMINE DECISIONS

*S*loan insists upon the facts...The old GM no-facts system...The first fact-based Sloan plan at GM...Facts for purchasing decisions...The global teen market: new facts...Facts about baseball ownership...Analyzing content...Chrysler relies on facts for supply-side purchasing...Facts determine change of course in Navarre, Spain...Quick facts at a test product's end...The managerial lessons of relying on facts and the dangers of using only facts

It is common practice in modern corporations and organizations of today to seek projections and numbers that will determine the status of many variables, including sales and profitability. The vital statistics in the form of reports serve as a yardstick for how the company or organization performs. In addition, a well-run organization asks its chief personnel in staff positions throughout the divisions to provide interim numbers for short-term and long-term planning. These facts and statistical estimates have a direct bearing on the corporation's expectation of future success.

There was a time in American business when facts did not play the important part that they do today. It was a time when—particularly in the emerging automobile industry—business was conducted without reliance on data or planning. It was a time of one-man rule with little or no accountability and, rarely, the request for data beyond sales figures and production-run totals.

At General Motors, Alfred P. Sloan, Jr., changed this outmoded and dangerous practice of doing business without adherence to facts. He would insist upon numbers from the various committees that governed the central operation of General Motors and also from the many divisions that reported to the CEO. He had no interest in any person's intuition and frowned upon casual, spur-of-the-moment or hunch decisions: "The great difference in managerial technique between the industry of today as compared with that of yesterday is what might be referred to as the necessity of scientific approach, the elimination of operation by hunches; this affects men, tools, and method."[1]

He would emphasize the "scientific approach" through fact-finding in every aspect of General Motors, through innovative quantitative research, and also by consumer surveys. To this end, he was one of the pioneers of generating feedback from the General Motors dealer network and from automobile customers. Always, the goal was to study the data available: "My business experience has convinced me facts are precious things, to be eagerly sought and treated with respect."[2]

## THE GENERAL MOTORS SYSTEM SLOAN INHERITED

When Sloan became vice-president in charge of operations at GM, the company had been operated in a haphazard and disorganized system by William C. Durant for many years. Durant had surrounded himself with cronies to whom he had given plum jobs, heading up the various car divisions. He conducted few meetings with these division heads and did not require reports or projections of long-term sales or inventory planning. To his many associates, Durant seemed more interested in his position in the stock market and conversing with investment counselors on the many phones in his office.

For Durant, the key to success was to make as many cars as General Motors could produce, sell the output, generate revenue, and then realize a profit. Since he also was heavily invested in the stock market, a rise in General Motors stock, on announcement of short-term sales, would also drive up the share price and make his large holdings worth considerably more.

Pierre du Pont sensed that the company in which he had invested so much of the du Pont family fortune was being poorly run under Durant's aegis. In 1919, he sent over John Pratt, a savvy Du Pont executive, to poke his nose around the General Motors operation. Pratt was astounded at what he learned: "No one knew just how money had been appropriated, and there was no control of how much money was being spent."[3]

Pratt also discovered that the process of pitting divisions against each other to vie for available money and resources encouraged vote swapping; you scratch my project's back, I'll scratch yours. Sloan's biographer described these events as the time-honored tradition of political horse-trading: "General Motors, ironically, was being run in accord of the oldest legislative political traditions—'logrolling'—in which votes are traded without concern for the common good in order to secure 'pork.'"[4]

In sum, as early as 1918, Pierre du Pont, chairman of the Du Pont Company's board of directors, began to experience firsthand Durant's loose stewardship. Since the Du Pont Company was heavily invested in General Motors stock ($50 million), it was able to attempt some reorganization by sending over its own staff of executives to provide Durant with a more capable managerial staff.

But in 1919 Durant with his substantial share of GM stock remained president, and Pierre du Pont and the other investors could do nothing to change GM effectively. It was during this year that Alfred P. Sloan, Jr., submitted his "Organization Study" to Pierre du Pont, who read the work with considerable interest. Here, at last, was an organizational plan to run GM in an efficient managerial system, a system based solely upon facts.

## SLOAN IMPLEMENTS HIS FIRST FACT-BASED PLAN

By 1920, Durant's tenure as head of GM came to an abrupt end because of overexpansion and declining sales. Pierre du Pont assumed, reluctantly, the role of president. But when he looked around the company for someone who shared his objective for tighter manufacturing and financial controls, the one name that came to the forefront was the author of the "Organization Study." Du Pont appointed Sloan as his personal assistant and also as vice-president in charge of operations.

For Sloan at age 45, the role of being the architect to change the entire structure of General Motors represented the opportunity of a lifetime. Later, he would write of this chance to influence the future outcome of the company: "The immediate problem was to weld an unwieldy and incoherent mass into a correlated and coordinated whole, by elimination and addition, through an organization based upon fundamental managerial policy of first determining the facts."[5]

Determining the facts became the primary task of the new du Pont–Sloan team, and the first area they examined was the sales and profitability of the automobile divisions. It is relevant to know that the General Motors sales and marketing strategy was to offer many cars in seven different models at price ranges that started with the lowest offering, a four-cylinder Chevrolet at $795, and topping off at the highest, at an eight-cylinder Cadillac at $5,690 with all the extras.

GM's 1920 sales totaled 393,000 cars, or only 37 percent of Ford's production that year of 1,074,000 vehicles. These numbers translated to Ford Motor Company holding a 47 percent share of the U.S. automobile market of 2,300,000 manufactured cars and General Motors having a mere 16 percent as the second largest car manufacturer share in the country. In 1921, GM dropped to 12 percent and Ford increased to 60 percent.

But Sloan's insightful mind looked at all these sales numbers with a different perspective from William Durant's sales-anywhere-at-any-costs strategy. Sloan observed that Chevrolet was not competitive with Ford in the lower-priced, higher-volume segment, which offered significant growth as each year more Americans entered the market as first-time car buyers at the lowest price point.

In addition, Sloan's gathering of the facts revealed another GM problem, the middle-priced cars, Oakland (later changed to Pontiac) Olds, Scripps-Booth, Sheridan (the latter two cars were Durant acquisitions and soon discontinued), and Buick competed with each other and, in effect, cannibalized each other's sales. Sloan realized that price reform was needed: "Some kind of rational policy was called for. That is, it was necessary to know what one was *trying* to do."[6]

Further, by 1921 General Motors was losing money, and this included the popular Chevrolet division. It seemed that GM was on its way to being overwhelmed by Henry Ford and his Model-T. These ominous facts necessitated Sloan to write: "...and we needed a research-and-development policy, a sales policy, and the like, to support what ever we did."[7]

What Sloan did, based upon the careful examination of all the variables, was to form an advisory committee, composed of people with automotive experience. The task given was to reexamine thoroughly the company's product line. The committee's findings were handed to the executive committee for review and action.

It was at this point that Sloan articulated one of the most revolutionary axioms in American business. Sloan wrote: "The primary object of the corporation (i.e., General Motors) therefore, we declared was to make money, not just to make motor cars."[8]

The first decision was to regenerate the Chevrolet line so that it did not compete with Ford on price. Instead, GM would offer a higher-priced car that would be superior to the Model-T. The new Chevy would cost a little more, but it would be within the uppermost (but affordable) price range of a consumer looking for a quality, low-priced automobile.

In 1923, Pierre du Pont resigned and Sloan replaced him as the president of General Motors. Sloan also became chairman of the executive committee, which increased substantially his power to effect additional changes. It was the notable beginning of a long reign of unprecedented success. There was no crowing over the appointment, only work to do: "I became president under the auspicious policy of the corporation. The period of development lay ahead."[9]

## SLOAN APPLIES FACTS TO PURCHASING

The reorganization of the committees that had begun at Sloan's recommendation under Pierre du Pont's time in power would soon experience more changes.

In 1922, Sloan created a general purchasing committee to concentrate on the efficiencies of large-scale volume in acquiring raw materials, parts, and other vital items necessary to making General Motors more profitable. In fact, Sloan's estimate was that efficient purchasing could save the company between $5 million and $10 million a year.

The acknowledgment that a centralized purchasing department would have difficulty incorporating the needs of the many divisions was key. Here Sloan ran into the reality that the diverse technical requirements of the divisions could not be realized by personnel with just purchasing expertise. His solution was to staff the purchasing committee with experienced and savvy automobile men from the divisions. The net result was the standardization of items across the departments, which led to buying in volume and a lowering of inventory. The new way to look at purchasing data allowed GM to become a more lean and efficient company.

## TURNING OUT FINANCIAL FACTS

Once Sloan set in place his decentralized system, granting much autonomy to the divisions, he put into practice financial controls with the assistance of experienced Du Pont executives. In 1921, one of the most prominent was Donaldson Brown who had previously hired economists and statisticians at the Du Pont Company, an uncommon occurrence in American business in the first years of the twentieth century. Sloan insisted that Brown be GM's vice-president in charge of finance: "He and I shared similar views on the value of detailed, disciplined controls in the operation of a business."[10]

While at the Du Pont Company, Brown submitted a report to its executive committee that presented a novel method for analyzing return on investment. His ROI formula revolutionized the practice of corporate accounting. Eventually, after it was adopted at GM, it allowed the company to calculate overall profitability across the diverse company, a vital process based upon facts that had been missing under William Durant's no-facts and no-accountability presidency.

Sloan welcomed Brown who shared his affinity for facts as decision makers. In addition, Sloan was pleased to have a financial expert at hand, since he possessed a good but rudimentary knowledge of accounting. Most of all, Sloan was delighted to put in place workable financial controls that fit in with his decentralized system: "When Donaldson Brown came to General Motors he brought with him a financial yardstick. It was a method of crystallizing facts bearing on the efficiency of management."[11]

Brown was another of the new university men who had been trained in science and math. He had graduated from Virginia Polytechnic University in 1902, and later he did graduate work in engineering at Cornell University. His main contribution was recognizing that the American corporation needed more rigorous cost accountability. He can be regarded historically as the one of the nation's first real "numbers" men.

Sloan was also impressed with an innovative technique Brown used at meetings, using charts for presentations. The chart system would become commonplace at GM as a useful tool for submitting and analyzing the facts.

Soon, under Brown's accounting tutelage and Sloan's overall direction, GM's financial operation established effective controls for capital spending, cash control, inventory assessment, management, and production control. Once these were set in place, the huge company hummed with the constant process of fact gathering.

One of the groundbreaking statistical concepts was Sloan's request for annual estimates from the division managers to control production: "I requested them to predict for the coming year what their sales, earnings, and capital requirements would be on the basis of expectations that were pessimistic, conservative, and optimistic."[12]

Sloan discovered, however, that there was an inherent difference in the predictions between those operating by numerical controls (finance, accounting, and manufacturing) versus the sales and marketing staffs that were more optimistic and tended to overstate expectations.

Throughout the many years of his stewardship, Sloan always listened to the confident predictions from his sales and marketing staff. He always wanted everyone's opinion heard. But he knew from years of experience at Hyatt, United Motors, and GM that business was cyclical and reality had to be determined by cold, hard facts and not by the Pollyanna expectations of the sales force.

It is a leap of many years to travel from Sloan's time at General Motors to the fast-paced world of the new marketing paradigm on the Internet. However, whether selling cars on dealers' lots or on e-Bay, the only important variables are the facts of the transaction. This is true whether in the United States for adult car buyers or as in the next example, worldwide for teenagers. Every marketer everywhere needs to rely on facts.

## DIVERSE FACTS OF THE EMERGING GLOBAL TEEN MARKET

Amid the postwar economic boom in the United States in the 1950s, teenagers became a prominent spending segment of the economy for the first time. Marketers recognized that in the expanding suburban society, teens possessed large amounts of discretionary income to spend on music, clothing, and food. This emergence of teens paralleled the growth in the 1920s of the new breed of middle-class American consumers.

The consuming power of the 13- to 19-year-olds increased exponentially as more teens entered the marketplace with more cash to spend. But over the years one question remained unanswered: Was the U.S. economy the only marketplace where teens spent considerable sums on themselves? How could companies market to teens in other countries, many with vastly different populations and cultures from their neighbors? Of special interest was the proliferation of teenagers in the newly developing Third World markets of China, India, and Brazil. How many were there? And what did they spend?

To answer this global teen puzzle, The Brain Waves Group, a research and consulting company, proposed a massive study in the 1990s to gather facts that no corporation or institution had amassed before. The company had done projects for Coca Cola, Procter & Gamble, Philips, and Burger King, and one of the questions that surfaced from these international marketers was the unknown fact about teens worldwide.

The questioning about this global market went beyond the basic demographic facts of the total teen population per country. The number of teens could be easily gleaned from United Nation's or country statistics from their U.S. embassies. Marketers wanted to know psychographic information: What did these teens think? How different were they from the prototypical U.S. teenager? And, most important, how could global companies sell and market to teens on an area-by-area or individual-country basis?

The Brain Waves Group began a multiyear research project sponsored by the giant advertising agency D'Arcy Masius Benton and Bowles. It was called The New World Teen Study, and it set out to generate facts that would be constructive to marketers, providing an in-depth picture of teens in 44 countries around the globe. The Brain Waves' president acknowledged that the key to the study was to develop groupings by type and then to segregate the types by their similarities and differences.

In effect, what The Brain Waves Group did was comparable to Sloan's going in the field to visit the dealer networks. The research company went into the international field, carrying out quantitative research via local telephone surveys and also doing qualitative research via focus groups and one-on-one interviews. The goal was to gather facts and then dispel hunches and false notions about teens worldwide.

The initial findings generated numerous surprises: U.S. teens did not rank as the highest in the world in weekly spending (they were sixth) nor in credit card usage (they were twelfth). Previously held suppositions had to be thrown out and replaced by new, fact-based information.

In a second-wave study of brand identification among global teens, the report produced no surprises: The highest of the 75 recognizable rated brands were Coca Cola, SONY, Adidas, Nike, and Pepsi, all internationally marketed products. But what caught everyone's attention was the tenth-ranked logo: the Chicago Bulls of the National Basketball Association. How had the Bulls ranked so high? The answer had four distinctive parts: the growth and accessibility of the Internet, the universal popularity of Michael Jordan, the broadcasting of NBA games on local television, and the NBA's highlights, which were also aired nightly on cable channel CNN in English throughout the globe.

When The Brain Waves Group parsed the data on brand identification, it discovered that the cross-cultural media world of teens also shared a common variable that marketers could immediately activate: 85 percent of teens watched MTV. Further research indicated that

MTV programmed U.S. and British bands and rock stars but also customized the musical broadcasts to include local singing stars, varying the format country-by-country.

The Brain Waves fact-finding survey aided global marketers to identify the enormous (575 million) teen market. It helped these marketers by laying out, for the first time, the real facts. As Sloan has indicated, "facts are precious things," and the new data served as an eye-opener to global manufacturers. No more would hunches about teens influence decisions.

Worth noting is that Alfred Sloan had taken numerous railroad trips across the country to speak to dealers about their observations and opinions. By doing this kind of work in the field through research, he discovered firsthand the facts from the dealerships. Also important to advertisers and marketers were The Brain Waves' worldwide subjective findings about personal and societal attitudes relating to economic, marital, and political variables, including, importantly, knowledge of and need for technology.

## THE FACTS ABOUT BASEBALL OWNERSHIP

A curious myth existed about owing a major league baseball franchise: That no matter what the purchase price, an owner would not only reap significant profits during ownership but also receive a great capital windfall upon the sale of the club. From coast to coast, every new male American multimillionaire entrepreneur with spare cash and a large ego decided that a good investment was to buy a baseball team.

The true facts were radically different. The reality was that owing to tax code and other economic variables, baseball ownership was a losing proposition.

In 1981, the facts of the economics of baseball ownership were revealed to the public in an iconoclastic speech delivered to Mid-Continent Perspectives (a prestigious lecture series) by Michael E. Herman, president of the Kansas City Royals. He also served as a member of the Major League Baseball Player Relations Committee.

Herman's financial analysis indicated that the economics of baseball are not positive and this situation was different from the earlier, profitable days of owning a franchise. The facts revealed that as franchise costs rose annually, especially players' salaries, the breakeven attendance figure rapidly increased. Revenues were capped by the saturation of media markets.

Further analysis revealed that in the decade of the 1970s, while broadcast and gate revenues increased at about 7.5 percent and ticket prices by 4.3 percent, ballpark attendance only grew by 4.4 percent, which was attributed to fan resistance to higher ticket prices. Worse for the owners, inflation continued at 7 percent, substantially higher than the increase in ticket prices.

But the analysis delved deeper into the economics, going beyond potential profit and loss on the ledger sheet. The IRS tax code presented a negative incentive to baseball ownership when it came to depreciating an asset because the franchise did not have a determinable life like a factory, office building, or railroad car.

Players' contracts could be depreciated on the theory that, over time a player, like any other object in constant use, would function at a lesser capacity at the end of five or seven years. But when purchasing a team, the IRS was specific that only 50 percent of the player's salary could be allocated and for only five years. After that, there were no more tax breaks to be awarded.

The five-year period of tax depreciation meant that in the sixth year, owner losses became negative cash flow with more money going out than coming in. And in that sixth year, there was no longer the use of depreciation.

If all of this depreciation bad news stacked against an owner's generating a profit was not enough, there was the existence of free agency, which allowed players to seek new contracts with any teams after a certain number of years in the league. Herman's startling study indicated the marginal revenue of a player's worth grew faster than his marginal productivity: The older a player became, the more money he was paid but at a decrease in his productivity.

The statistical analysis of selling a team provided the biggest shock. Over the period in which Herman examined the facts, a baseball owner made between 3 and 6 percent pretax return on the investment. This sum compared negatively to the average profit of other investments: farm real estate at 9.5 percent, new home ownership at 7.5 percent, and even triple-A bonds, which returned a firm and constant 6 percent. Baseball was a high-risk, low-return investment—and not a liquid one at all.

Herman also correctly predicted the future and widening disparity in big-salary versus small-salary clubs and the corresponding big-city versus small-city gap. Over time, those teams that paid the largest salaries and purchased the more costly free agents would show a higher winning percentage than the lower revenue generating clubs.

In 1996, a reexamination of baseball facts comparing the financial statements of the 27 major league teams, using 1990 and 1996 data, revealed that owning a baseball team—on average—was a losing proposition. The key determining factor, worth of franchise value, indicated that in 1990 the average franchise was worth $136 million, and this declined $2 million by 1996 to $134 million. The wealthy, top revenue drawing New York Yankees had only increased its franchise worth by 6 percent over the seven-year period. The New York Mets, which had a seven-year bad patch of mediocre teams, witnessed its franchise value decline from $200 million in 1990 to $144 million by 1996, a $56 million paper loss, or a 28 percent loss.

The study is an example of facts not having much influence on the purchase decision; new owners with big egos are never going to be that interested in the bottom line, especially when they are making emotional decisions. The fact is that baseball owners experience the pleasure of proprietorship and seem less worried that over time, owning a team is a poor investment. Alfred P. Sloan would never have understood this irrational decision.

## ANALYSIS OF THE FACTS

During Sloan's 40-year tenure at General Motors, the nation experienced a radical change in the methods of deriving commercial data. The Roper organization was one of the first professional public opinion research firms, and its contribution would forever alter how U.S. companies derived facts from the American public.

Over time, the burgeoning research industry has spawned a cottage industry of small and mid-sized firms that deal with questioning consumers on products and politics. Sophisticated telephone surveys track public opinion on a daily basis. Focus group facilities with two-way mirrors can be found in almost every major urban and suburban area.

Everyone wants the facts that Sloan indicated were vitally important. Each year, companies develop new innovative systems for research, attempting to delve one or two steps deeper into the nation's psyche with the goal of solving business problems with found facts.

One of the newest methods is to examine customer feedback from telephone calls or e-mail. In essence, companies or organizations—large or small—accumulate a treasure trove of valuable information from customer comments or consumer feedback. If these are analyzed at all, the reports usually provide only top-line data, indicating, for example, the number of complaints, and then listing these by frequency.

Although these quickly gathered facts are helpful, they may be only directional, and they do not reveal the reasons for customer discontent. The electronic recording of these data in text form opened up the possibility for greater analysis. Initially, software companies developed minimal programs to parse through the text data and provide a nominal look at what was recorded. These reports told "the what" but not "the why."

The challenging problem was to improve upon the basic counting of facts and come up with a program that could find hidden meaning among the myriad of textual statements. The solution came from a new, start-up company called Intelligenxia that began in a Jacksonville, Florida, new-business incubator.

Intelligenxia developed a sophisticated software product called Virtual Analyst that scans and analyzes text found in all forms of electronic documents. The software takes disregarded or unanalyzed information and converts it into a productive factual asset. It finds hidden relationships by quickly extracting key meanings from a multitude of documents in a variety of formats and platforms.

This type of sophisticated content analysis becomes useful if there exists a large collection of records. Or it is helpful if a company has an ongoing and steady stream of unanalyzed textual data. The old saw that knowledge is power holds for mining accumulated text records. Currently, the company is assisting the Department of Defense to mine field intelligence.

Intelligenxia brings up the kinds of facts that spur decision making, which is the key to Sloan's insistence that facts and only facts determine outcomes.

## AUTOMOBILE SUPPLY-SIDE FACTS

One of the best kept secrets of American business in the 1930s was that the Chrysler Corporation, maker of Dodge, Plymouth, and Chrysler vehicles, manufactured only the engines; the rest of the parts and components were purchased from outside vendors. In essence, everything else was contracted out to suppliers. As Peter Drucker writes: "Production was a pure assembly job, and while requiring great technical skill assembly requires few business decisions. . . . Assembly is done by hand with the wrench being the most complicated tool."[13]

This cost-effective manufacturing method ended for Chrysler after World War II when it expanded to become the second largest automobile company in the world, employing more than 100,000 workers. However, for many years after, the company retained a historic legacy back to the low-capital and small-plant 1930s when it earned the highest rate of return of the Big Three U.S. automobile companies.

Fast-forward to the 1980s, when Chrysler's sales had slipped significantly and the company had to reconsider how it did business with its vast supply chain. The truth was that in past times, Chrysler's engineering department would decide on necessary new components, and then the company's purchasing department would seek the lowest bids for the parts from a host of suppliers. The constant squeezing of profit margin from among these component manufacturers engendered an adversarial relationship between the auto manufacturer and its suppliers.

Chrysler management realized it needed a restructuring of its purchasing policy and examined other existing supply-side methods. Time and time again, after studying the supply-chain facts, one international model emerged for Chrysler to follow, the Japanese business philosophy called *keiretsu*. In the manufacturing area (as opposed to the financial), *keiretsu* denoted a vertical relationship, incorporating a pyramid of suppliers and parts manufacturers in one structure. This could be termed a partnership arrangement with manufacturer and supplier acting in conjunction with each other rather than as opponents forever haggling over the lowest price.

Once the decision was made to embark on an American form of *keiretsu*, Chrysler reduced its supplier base from 2,500 companies to a manageable 1,100. Along with the reduction of suppliers, the company eliminated unrealistic supplier specs with difficult-to-achieve delivery due dates.

The new partnership system was characterized by inviting the supplier into the decision-making process. From these harmonious meetings—where both parties cooperated for their mutual benefit—new benefits arose with a shorter production development cycle, lower production costs, and, most significantly, lower procurement expenses. Chrysler profit per vehicle increased from $250 in the 1980s to $2,000 in 1994.

Additionally, Chrysler improved upon the supplier collaboration by instituting a cost-saving program called SCORE (supplier cost reduction effort) that encouraged supplier-partners to reduce their component costs. The auto company assigned each supplier an annual 5 percent reduction target. A bonus to suppliers who participated in the savings plan was that Chrysler remitted 50 percent of the savings.

The SCORE program had an added hook for a supplier; it could keep the 50 percent savings or return its share back to Chrysler. The returned (or untaken) dollars increased the supplier's SCORE rating. The higher the rating, the more business Chrysler agreed to purchase from the supplier in the future.

Magna International, a diverse original equipment manufacturer (OEM) of automotive systems, assemblies, modules, and components, returned half of its $38 million savings back to Chrysler, significantly raising its supplier SCORE rating. The auto giant rewarded Magna by doubling its sales to $1.5 billion.

By closely examining the facts of its supply chain, Chrysler (before its merger with Daimler-Benz) generated almost $4 billion in supplier savings.

## FACTS AFFECT ECONOMIC DEVELOPMENT

The region of Spain with the highest economic indices is Navarre, the northern province where Pamplona is the capital city. After a total reorganization plan 25 years ago, the autonomously run province changed dramatically from an agricultural region to a highly industrial one.

As proof of the plan's success, the largest Volkswagen plant outside of Germany was built in 1983 in Navarre. It became the centerpiece of the region's large automotive component manufacturing, attracting companies like Bosch, Siemens, Delphi Packard, TRW, and other well-known European, Japanese, and American companies.

The long-term key to this successful economic conversion was the establishment of a quasi-public economic development agency called SODENA (Society for the Economic Development of Navarre) created to induce foreign companies to come into the region. The two main investors were the Navarre Savings Bank and the provincial government. SODENA is unique in economic development because it is the world's only publicly traded stock corporation with profit-making objectives.

During the mid 1990s, Jésus Zabalo was appointed director of SODENA. Trained as an industrial engineer, he had been the former president in Spain of Lucas Varity, a leading manufacturer of brakes, and other car components. He had learned that the only way to make a business decision was to study the facts.

In Pamplona, with a population of about 250,000 (the size of Louisville, Kentucky, or Birmingham, Alabama), Zabalo started to meet with other regional executives to learn their thoughts on future development for Navarre. Many perceived the best direction was to continue searching for other auto component companies to build upon the region's excellent reputation in this field.

During these discussions—often among acquaintances he had known all his life—Zabalo listened to plans and ideas. But when executives shared social chitchat about family and children, he also became aware of an interesting fact: The college-educated daughters of Navarre families could not find work in their home province.

From this anecdotal evidence of daughters having to relocate to Madrid or Barcelona, Zabalo commissioned a research study of employment and unemployment data in Navarre. The report confirmed that although overall unemployment was low (at around 7 percent), when examined by gender, the numbers confirmed that the total unemployed females were more than double the regional average. Further examination revealed that many of these unemployed females had university training and college degrees.

Clearly, in 25 years SODENA had done an outstanding job of bringing new business into Navarre, but the new companies had created primarily, blue-collar factory jobs that were exclusively performed by males. The relevant fact from the research pointed to a lack of available positions for university-educated females in the region's heavy-labor manufacturing environment.

Armed with the facts, SODENA shifted the focus of its search from heavy machinery to medical and biotechnology. The main reason was that medical, biomedical, and biotech companies relied upon people with technical training; positions that women could fill. For two years, and mainly in the United States, SODENA presented its Navarre economic story to more than 75 U.S. medical and biomedical firms as a possible new European base for medical companies.

The anecdotal information that Zabalo gleaned from associates about their daughters generated a factual study, which allowed SODENA to alter the target of its global industry search.

## FACTS END A NEW-PRODUCT TEST

On occasion, some facts quickly gathered can provide direction to smaller or less important projects. Often, these data can be obtained at little or no cost.

An example occurred in the mid-1970s, when the Colgate Company decided to end forever any further sales or advertising of Alpen, an imported natural-health cereal made by the Weetabix Company in the United Kingdom. Although all importation of the cereal had ceased, and sales had declined dramatically in two test markets, the company wanted to know if the brand had generated awareness or, perhaps, a positive attitude among consumers who had seen months of Alpen television commercials and some local print advertising in the two test markets.

The advertising agency account supervisor on the brand suggested a one-day supermarket research project called a "mall intercept," where 100 people would be stopped to answer a short, two-minute questionnaire about the cereal. The key question to be asked was, "What does the name Alpen mean to you?"

The Colgate product manager of Alpen and the ad agency's account executive went to the two test markets (Washington, D.C., and Boston) at night, and the next day questioned 100 people at random in front of two supermarkets where the cereal was still on the shelf. The two-city combined data was tabulated back in Manhattan the next day, providing 200 responses to the questionnaire.

At a mid-morning meeting that day, the facts of the day's research were presented to Colgate management. Eighty-five percent of the respondents answered that Alpen meant "Alps, Swiss, or Switzerland," obvious answers to the main question. Only 7 percent answered "Cereal, health cereal, or good-tasting cereal," a poor result.

Alpen had been the first health-food cereal to be marketed in the United States. But its muesli formula—a blend of whole grain oats and dried fruits—proved less appealing to consumers than the American-made and sweeter granola health-food cereals, which entered the market nationally a few months after Alpen's test marketing introduction.

For Colgate, Alpen's new-product launch had been disappointing in the company's first attempt to market a food product. The quickly gathered facts had indicated no encouraging awareness or positive attitude toward the cereal. The project ended officially after the presentation of the research facts.

## THE LESSONS OF EXAMINING FACTS

Facts are essential to decision making in all aspects of an organization or a corporation. These can be in the form of primary or secondary facts but, regardless, the main use of data is to design programs that will better the organization, allowing it to perform and to prosper.

The prominent reason for using facts is to have access to the real world opposed to relying on hunches, which may not be the reality. Alfred P. Sloan, Jr., used the term "scientific approach" to categorize his changing over from the guesstimates of business projection and into a fact-based world of reality.

### THE DANGER OF RELIANCE ON FACTS ONLY

How often has a manager heard "statistics lie" or "the facts can prove any opinion"? Many times decision makers want to rely solely on the facts or they feel comfortable only with the facts. But there are many occasions when facts do not reveal the true story.

A New York City bank executive was promoted to the position of director of commercial banking in charge of all the retail business banking in the city's five boroughs. He sent out memos to the vice-presidents in charge of the local branches who had direct contact with the commercial accounts in their areas.

The director was captivated by facts, creating sophisticated formulas and constantly looking at complex statistical variables. He scheduled visits to meet these subordinates and install a sense of central, factual thinking and precise bookkeeping on the disparate locations.

Eventually, he met with the retail banking loan officer whose branch was located in the heart of the clothing manufacturing area bordering Seventh Avenue. The director asked this officer what he thought was the most important fact in determining that branch's profitability for the next fiscal year?

The branch manager replied without hesitation, "Oh, for certain, it will be tennis wear."

The bank director expressed surprise at the response, thinking that interest rates or ease of loan applications or other financial variables would be the main facts that affected the branch's revenue estimates. He asked for more clarification on the odd "tennis wear" response.

The branch officer replied that most of the bank's clothing manufacturing accounts had chanced their next season's business success on women buying more tennis wear. If this style gamble proved successful, the local manufacturing accounts would pay back the bank's loans on time. If tennis wear proved to be a short-lived fad, the clothing manufacturers would be stuck with unsold merchandise. This, in turn, would lead them to default on the loans and, consequently, the bank's profitability would decline. The branch manager smiled and said, "And those, sir, are the *facts* for my branch."

The story illustrates the occasional inconsistency between data and the real world. Intermittently, anecdotal evidence can provide more direction than the balance sheet or the quantitative survey. In some instances, facts do not reveal the "why" of an important question (i.e., purchase decisions, political candidate preference, etc.), and for these answers, more in-depth qualitative research is usually needed.

## THE COST OF FACTS

A large and extensive market exists for companies, large and small, supplying data for countries, industries, segments of industries, and the like. The problem for managers is whether the cost of the facts merits their purchase.

The key considerations for a company stem from Sloan's questions: What data do we need? Why do we need these facts? and How much will it cost to acquire the data? Many times, self-generating data from customer or client surveys can provide useful information at little or no cost.

One special commercial example of how finding facts can potentially save considerable money comes from the New York City–based consulting firm of Morgan Anderson. The well-known company specializes in assessing client and advertising agency relationships. Over 20 years, it has developed sophisticated and accurate metrics that can analyze and redefine compensation agreements and also demonstrate whether an advertising campaign or a media buy has been successful. These are facts that companies cannot assess by themselves since they do not possess the formulas or know-how of either how to generate facts or to understand them.

There are countless other examples of outside fact-finding consultants, agencies, and data banks that can either present data electronically or analyze the facts on a project basis.

In all fact-finding cases, the data will provide a more accurate picture than well-intentioned hunches. As Peter Drucker states: "Procedures (i.e., facts) can work only where judgment is no longer required.... But the most common misuse of reports and procedures is as an instrument of control from above."[14]

C H A P T E R

# THE NEED FOR INTERNATIONAL BUSINESS

*T*he first U.S. manufacturing ventures overseas...Car companies going international...Sloan pursues Citroën in 1919...GM's British acquisition...GM examines other European possibilities...Mr. Paarboom, the deal maker, introduces Sloan to Opel in Germany...Sloan and GM choose Opel for acquisition...GM's last stop: Australia...Poor U.S. nomenclature and ad decisions internationally...Looking at Europe with American eyes...Establishing a presence by outright purchase of overseas plants...Business International, how to succeed internationally...Pepsi's modern overseas options...The cola wars in Venezuela...Establishing a new market abroad: Häagen Dazs...American entrepreneurs pursue ice cream in Ireland...The managerial lessons of doing business internationally

ও৩ ৩৬

American companies have eyed international markets, especially Europe, with interest for more than a hundred years. Exporting from the United States represented the easiest method for selling products into Europe without incurring significant real estate and labor costs necessitated by establishing an overseas base of operations. There have always been marked advantages to exporting by accepting international orders or, in more sophisticated operations, hiring an overseas agent to represent the company.

## EARLY U.S. SUCCESSES MANUFACTURING ABROAD

H. J. Heinz, founder of the Pittsburgh-based company that bears his name, made an initial foray abroad when he brought seven U.S.-made products to England in 1886. They were accepted by the prestigious Fortnum and Mason food shop in London. The Heinz Company continued exporting until 1919 when it built its first factory in the United Kingdom. (Many British citizens, lovers of the locally made baked beans and the creamy salad dressing in the bottle, were surprised to discover that Heinz was not originally a British company).

Similarly, the Colgate Company began manufacturing in the United Kingdom in 1929 after it acquired the Palmolive-Peet Company in 1928. The merger provided Colgate a toehold, on which it capitalized by expanding onto the Continent, where it has dominated the oral care, soap, and detergent markets since. Today, approximately, 70 percent of Colgate's revenues come from long-established worldwide operations in Europe, China, and South America.

## CAR COMPANIES GO ABROAD

The Ford Motor Company exported its first car to the United Kingdom in 1903. In 1905, Ford opened a showroom in London, selling 400 automobiles. As local automobile demand in the United Kingdom increased, Ford established its first manufacturing facility outside North America, building a factory at Trafford Park near Manchester in 1911. The company began its well-known assembly-line production—the United Kingdom's and Europe's first—in 1913.

The European road system in the 1920s was no different from America's: a few paved roads in and around the larger cities and dirt roads elsewhere. Historically, the Italians designed the world's first car-only road in 1924. The German autobahn, the first multilane high-way system began in 1935 and traveled from Frankfurt to Darmstadt at a distance of 22 kilometers (12 miles). The first major British roadway, the famous M1, was started in the 1950s, connecting London with points north. It was finished in the 1970s, and today is 200 miles long.

The Ford Motor Company's success in the United Kingdom caught the attention of Alfred P. Sloan, Jr., when he was vice-president of operations. The question for Sloan and his General Motors' executives was how to compete successfully with Ford and the other European car manufacturers in the international markets? Sloan stated clearly the classic concern for American companies: "We had to determine whether we wanted to be exporters or overseas producers."[1]

In a nutshell, he identified the major U.S. dilemma of doing business abroad, a dual problem that still exists for U.S. managers today: to export, keeping costs low, or locate abroad, incurring large capital outlays in expectation of significantly higher sales and revenues.

## SLOAN FIRST COURTS THE FRENCH

In the fall of 1919, Sloan and a group of General Motors executives visited Europe with the idea of purchasing 50 percent of the Citroën Company of France, named after its founder, André Citroën. It would mark General Motors first serious attempt at international expansion by acquisition.

André Citroën was a graduate of the École Polytechnique, France's most prestigious engineering college. A prominent biographical fact was that while serving in World War I as an artillery officer, he noticed that the French Army had an insufficient supply of munitions, particularly shells. He had visited Henry Ford's Michigan factory in 1912, and he convinced the French government that an assembly-line system (similar to Ford's automobile line) could manufacture 10,000 artillery shells a day. Located eventually at Javel, France, it was probably one of the first modern mass munitions manufacturing factories in the world.

André Citroën turned his attention back to motorcars after World War I and, like Henry Ford, decided to produce a single model, the Type A, which he launched in 1919. The French engineer understood the advances and improvements made by U.S. car manufacturers and perceived that selling 50 percent of his company to GM would pro-vide both capital and American automobile know-how. But obstacles to the deal rose immediately as Sloan wrote: "For one thing, the French government did not like the idea of American interests taking over an enterprise that had contributed importantly to the war effort."[2]

The horrors of World War I—and the appalling death rate among all combatants—still permeated in France where most of the trench fighting on the Western Front had occurred. The French nation's resistance to an American takeover was a problem of nationalism, a recurring circumstance that U.S. manufacturers would face through-out the globe for the rest of the twentieth century and into the next.

In addition, the consensus of the talented General Motors staff (Sloan, Chrysler, Kettering, Mott, and Champion) was that Citroën management did not meet the high U.S. corporate standards. The acquisition fell through when both Walter Chrysler and Sloan declined to move to France and head up Citroën.

(André Citroën prospered without GM's financial assistance. In the 1920s, he established an assembly-line system in France and was known as the "Henry Ford of Europe." His innovative advertising and marketing efforts targeted women. By the 1930s Citroën was the fourth largest car company in the world after America's Big Three automobile companies.)

This initial General Motors foray into European expansion by merger or acquisition whetted Sloan's interest in looking into further acquisition possibilities. But he had learned some constructive lessons from the Citroën experience: the most important one being that foreign countries did not want to see their native industries swal-lowed up by giant American corporations.

In 1923 GM opened a small assembly plant in Denmark for the Scandinavian market, but it was not considered a base for larger, European expansion.

## AN ENGLISH ACQUISITION

In the 1920s, after the unsuccessful acquisition of Citroën, General Motors turned to Great Britain, where American automobile manu-facturers experienced serious import tax protection. These were known as McKenna Duties, named after Reginald McKenna, British Prime Minister Hebert Asquith's Home Secretary and Chancellor of the Exchequer. His task was to fund the mounting World War I cost, and he accomplished this by raising the income tax and also leveling import duties. Sloan wrote: "The so-called McKenna Duties raised a formidable barrier to all foreign vehicles."[3]

These duties were originally stopgap measures beginning in World War I but they were so successful in raising money and in protecting British manufacturing that they were kept on the books until 1956.

American car companies also endured an additional costly British regulation that assessed car license fees based upon units of horsepower. This statute favored the small-bore, long-stroke British engine and punished the larger American types. Sloan calculated that a Chevrolet owner paid slightly less than double the annual fee of a British-made car. Clearly, exporting was detrimental to the U.S. car manufacturer with the twofold difficulty of expensive import McKenna Duties and the higher horsepower license fees.

In 1924, Sloan sent a GM team to England to investigate the purchase of the Austin Company that produced 12,000 cars annually. Negotiations broke down over a disagreement on the asset valuation of the English company. Sloan said: "I was actually relieved to hear the news. For it seemed to me that Austin had largely the same disadvantages that bothered me about Citroën six years earlier; its physical plant then was in poor condition, and its management was weak."[4]

General Motors' attempt at foreign automobile acquisition experienced nationalism for the second time when British journalists referred to GM as the well-heeled American suitor come to court the eager and coy maiden (the Austin Company). Further, the U.K.'s jingoistic press questioned whether British industries should remain in the hands and ownership of British subjects and not be sold to foreign concerns, especially, the rich American cousins across the Atlantic.

Sloan was undeterred by the negative comments in the British press and assented to the purchase of the British-made Vauxhall Motors, Ltd., which had made a five-horsepower car as early as 1903. General Motors perceived that the acquisition would be viewed as an experiment in overseas manufacturing. However, Sloan remained doubtful: "I took the line that in the next few years that we should move slowly and cautiously until we had worked out a clear policy for overseas expansion."[5]

In 1928 the next question was what size car Vauxhall would manufacture in England, with Sloan favoring a small-bore engine to avoid the British high license fee tax. But the more he studied the prospect of a small Chevrolet-type of car for Europe, the more he started leaning toward its manufacture in Germany and not in England with the Vauxhall purchase.

The prospect of such a major, international undertaking was fraught with other risks beyond profit and loss. Sloan was an Eastern-born, college-educated, and cosmopolitan person who recognized that a potential General Motors' operation in Europe might have other consequences: "The advent of General Motors abroad is bound to stir up a great deal of discussion, both within industrial circles as well as with Government circles."[6]

## GENERAL MOTORS EXAMINES THE POSSIBILITIES

During the 1920s, it had taken Sloan seven years to establish his system of multidivisional success at General Motors, increasing sales and taking significant domestic market share from the Ford Motor Company. As he and his staff examined past statistics in the U.S. automobile market, he realized that car sales were cyclical with dramatic upswings and downturns in the marketplace. These changes were not based on poorly accepted model designs or on serious production problems. The swings went hand in hand with the fluctuations of the economy.

By 1929, General Motors and its competitors started to experience a serious downtick in auto sales. In that year, many of the smaller, less successful automobile companies failed and disappeared from the marketplace. The Big Three U.S. car companies represented more than 75 percent of total U.S. sales.

Sloan had no forewarning that the year 1929 would be the start of the Great Depression, fatefully commencing on Black Tuesday in October of that year. But he did acknowledge that expanding General Motors' market to Europe could provide a future buffer to those down years when U.S. car sales lagged. Since 1929 was beginning to shape up as poor sales year, it was time for Sloan to return to Europe for another look at the European market. In fact, GM exports declined from a high of 290,000 vehicles in 1929 to only 42,000 by 1932.

Exporting would not prove to be the successful model for General Motors. Sloan recognized the problem: "Many years ago I recognized that it was impossible to assume that the most important manufacturing countries would continue to permit the exploitation of their markets from without, especially for such a vital need as motor transportation."[7]

## MR. PAARBOOM INTRODUCES OPEL TO SLOAN

As Sloan studied the European market, he was drawn to the Adam Opel A.G. Company in Germany. The story of how Opel came to his attention must be told by narrating the tale of the brilliant but eccentric Willem Paarboom, a Dutchman who had learned the intricacies of finances in colonial Batavia in the Dutch East Indies.

History knows Paarboom through the pages of Peter Drucker's autobiography *Adventures of a Bystander* published in 1978. The noted economist first met the Dutch investment advisor when he accompanied him during a house-buying trip in England in the mid-1930s. The 6 foot 5 Paarboom was always dressed in black from head to toe.

Paarboom is one of the twentieth century's first corporate merger consultants, a proven balance sheet genius. He specialized in bringing together companies for their mutual good, and his most important historic coup was to recommend the merger between the English soap maker Lever Brothers and the Dutch-based company, Margarine Unie.

Paarboom realized that both companies had similar business models and were engaged in comparable marketing of consumer household products throughout Europe. The result of his initiative was the formation of Unilever in 1930, which was then large enough as a single unit to compete in Europe with the soap giants Colgate-Palmolive and Procter & Gamble. The key to the merger was establishing a two-country corporate British and Dutch organization. Paarboom is also credited as the mastermind who advocated a single Unilever board of directors for the two firms.

In the late 1920s, Paarboom intuited that the five aging Opel Brothers had become weary of operating the Adam Opel A.G. automobile company begun in 1899 in Rüsselheim, Germany. He knew that the German government, for reasons of nationalism, would not permit the company's purchase by another European car manufacturer.

The answer, which only he envisioned, was to find an American automobile purchaser, and General Motors was the one company that caught his attention. He traveled to Michigan to meet with Sloan after having worked out the transaction financials in detail. When GM demonstrated an interest, he returned to Germany and convinced the Opel brothers to take the American deal. The German government voiced no objection.


## SLOAN OPTS FOR OPEL

Sloan knew that the Adam Opel Company was one of the first European car manufacturers to utilize production assembly lines similar to the American system. It had become the largest automobile company in Germany as local demand for cars increased significantly in the mid-1920s after the country started to recover from the runaway inflation that characterized the period after World War I. In 1928, Opel's total output of 43,000 vehicles was small when compared to the total production of America's Big Three car companies.

In characteristic Sloan fashion—gathering the facts, seeking committee consensus, and encouraging divergent opinions—he formed an official GM overseas study group to examine the Opel factory and to analyze the German and Continental markets. He was cognizant of the importance of such an overseas manufacturing move to the financial picture of General Motors: "As a matter of fact, this is one of the most important steps from the standpoint of capital investment and expansion that the Corporation has made since the present management has been connected with its administrative side."[8]

After reviewing the relevant facts about Opel, its dealership network, and its manufacturing plant, General Motors agreed to purchase 80 percent of the company at a total price of $26 million with an option for the remaining 20 percent at $7.4 million. By 1931, General Motors owned 100 percent. The German government approved the takeover plan without reservations: "In acquiring Opel and building up Vauxhall, General Motors underwent an important change. It was transformed from a domestic to an international manufacturer, prepared to seek markets for its products wherever they existed."[9]

General Motors immediately invested capital in new Opel plant facilities and refurbished outdated buildings. Sloan moved I. J. Reuter, general manager of Oldsmobile, to head up the Opel acquisition. Reuter came from German stock and spoke the language. By 1936, Opel made 100,000 vehicles, which rose to 140,000 by 1936. Under the ownership of General Motors, Opel production had increased in eight years more than threefold from 1928's preacquisition 42,000-production level.

(By 1962, the last year Sloan used statistics in his second auto-biography, Opel recorded 378,878 sales, a remarkable increase from the 26,312 in 1930 when it was acquired by GM. Of note is that the German government took possession of the Opel factory from 1940 to 1948 when it was returned to General Motors' ownership.)

For General Motors, the 1929 Opel purchase was fortuitous since it allowed the company to establish a European base *before* the onset of the Great Depression. Not only did U.S. automotive sales plummet domestically in the early 1930s but export sales declined precipitously as well. By 1937, after the worldwide economic recovery, GM manufactured more vehicles in Germany and England (188,000) than it exported from the United States and Canada (180,000)—the first year in the company's history when manufacturing abroad was greater than total global export.

In 2003, Opel produced 630,000 vehicles and ranked as the largest automobile company in Germany. An unexpected outcome of the merger was the fact that, over the decades, few Germans knew (or cared) that the American automotive giant owned Opel. By keeping the Adam Opel name (he manufactured quality sewing machines in 1862, and later made bicycles with his five sons, starting in 1886), General Motors had improved on a German brand with great success.

## AUSTRALIA

Sloan's final major expansion was to purchase the Holden Motor Body Builders, Ltd., in Adelaide, Australia, in 1931 to comanufacture components and automobile chassis. The Australian government requested proposals for domestic manufacturing and approved General Motors' entry into the country in 1945. By 1948, the first Australian-made GM cars rolled off the line under the GM-Holden name.

An interesting sidelight of GM's Australian expansion after World War II was Sloan's aversion to doing business in a socialist country. In those days, the Australian government owned the railroad system and the telephone company much as corporations were operated in Great Britain under socialist government ownership

Sloan, a typical American capitalist, believed in laissez-faire, free-trade economics and was resistant to dealing with those countries where the central government exerted control over any industry that was unregulated in the United States. He was always leery of government power, whether by the U.S. Congress or by foreign governments.

## ASSESSMENT OF GM'S INTERNATIONAL EXPANSION

Sloan's foresight and careful planning—along with some trial and error with the failed Citroën and Austin acquisitions—helped establish General Motors profitably as a manufacturer overseas. In 1959, GM opened a small plant in Brazil. In 1999, General Motors acquired Saab, the Swedish car manufacturer (at the same time that Ford purchased Volvo). Globalization would also see GM plants built around the world in Argentina, Chile, and Venezuela.

Sloan had gone abroad cautiously and wisely, learning that each country had a different culture and that GM had to tailor its way of doing business accordingly.

## GOING ABROAD AND MAKING OVERSEAS MISTAKES

One of the main objectives for companies entering foreign markets is to develop an understanding of local customs and cultures. There have been many instances of businesses or products that have failed in their overseas development by not accommodating the products or services to different foreign commercial traditions or translations.

When President John Kennedy visited Berlin, he said, "*Ich bin ein Berliner,* meaning to say, "I am a Berlin citizen." The problem was that *"ein Berliner"* meant a sweet roll in German. Correctly in German, he should have said, *"Ich bin Berliner"* without the *"ein"* to convey his solidarity citizenship with the isolated city.

If the Harvard-educated President of the United States made such an innocent language gaffe, it is not surprising that companies, both American and foreign, have also failed to do their language homework when naming or advertising products sold or promoted in other countries. In fact, the instances of such faux pas are legion:

- The Chevrolet Nova was to be sold in Central and South American under its U.S. brand name until the company realized that *no va* in Spanish means "It doesn't go." It was soon changed to the Caribe.

- The German hardware chain Götzen opened a store in Istanbul under the name Got, which means "rear end" in Turkish.

- American Motors attempt to sell its Matador in Puerto Rico met with local scorn since the word means "killer" and bullfighting had been outlawed on the island hundreds of years ago.

- Advertising in China, Pepsi tried to translate its U.S. slogan, "Pepsi Brings You Back to Life," but, unfortunately, the Chinese characters stated "Pepsi Brings You Back from the Grave."

- To find a pronunciation in China that would sound like "Coca Cola," the soft drink company achieved that similar sound but the characters meant "Bite the wax tadpole." The Chinese characters were changed to mean "Happiness in the mouth."

- The reason why the U.S. baby food giant Gerber never expanded into France under its original name is that the verb *gerber* in French means "to throw up." (At least *this* company did its overseas homework.)

## VIEWING EUROPE WITH AMERICAN EYES

In the 1960s, a leading American manufacturer of cashmere cloth for women's overcoats realized that the market in the United States had started to trend downward. The textile company manufactured cloth in volume to achieve a low sales price, and it carried large inventories of fabric. It faced the gloomy prospect of a declining and over-saturated domestic market.

The company imported its cashmere yarn from Belgium and spun the cloth in the United States. A European Common Market's exporting incentive declared that if locally made raw material (yarn) was imported back into any of the seven member states (Belgium, France, the German Federal Republic, Italy, Luxembourg, Netherlands, and the United Kingdom) as finished goods (cloth), there would be no duty charged on the imported merchandise.

The American company decided to open up a European operation by sending over a marketing and sales person. The objective was to sell cashmere cloth in the 15 colors that the company hoped to sell to European women's coat manufacturers to reduce the large U.S. domestic inventories. The company's export sale price per bolt of cloth would be considerably lower than other European-made cashmere because of the volume production in the United States and also because of the Common Market's no-import-duty incentive.

The representative's first step was to visit the buyers of women's overcoats at the leading European department stores Au Printemps and Galleries Lafayette in France, De Bijenkorf in the Netherlands, Rinascente in Italy, and Kaufhuas and Kaufstadt in Germany. These department store coat buyers concurred that at the low import cost the expensive cashmere cloth could be made into ready-to-wear coats and sold at a reasonable retail price throughout the department stores in the Common Market countries.

The search began, country-by-country, for coat manufacturers, with some initial sales of a few bolts of cloth. Coat manufacturers agreed that only two colors (fawn and camel) would be acceptable for the European women's coat market, which considered cashmere a luxury item and acceptable only in two traditional shades.

The coat manufacturers rejected the bolts of green, orange, yellow, blue, red, pink, etc., the rainbow assortment that had sold in department stores throughout the United States. These Europeans could not comprehend American women's strange taste for these multicolored, nontraditional colors in a luxurious cashmere coat.

The U.S. sales representative found that the largest European women's coat manufacturer was located in West Berlin. In an effort to keep the island city populated and commercially solvent, the West German government significantly reduced the nation's sales tax on products made in the enclave, then surrounded by East Germany.

The West Berlin coat manufacturer studied the low import price of the American-made cloth and also analyzed the German market potential. After months of market studies, it offered to buy the cloth in large quantities if it received an exclusivity for the Common Market, an order that would total $1 million, shipping and duties included. This seemed like the perfect deal to introduce ready-to-wear women's cashmere coats inexpensively into European department stores through the German coat company's existing distribution network.

However, the German coat manufacturer would make up its large order in only the fawn and camel colors. The American company rejected the two-color only deal. The West Berlin coat manufacturer would have to take the order in all 15 colors!

The U.S. textile company had received countless reports from its representative that a cloth as expensive as cashmere could only be sold in Europe in the two, time-honored tan colors. But it chose to view the European market mistakenly with the same American business worldview, and naively (or stubbornly) insisted that European women would purchase coats in the 15 multicolor rainbow selection. The rationale was that if American women bought pink and yellow cashmere coats, European women should do the same.

No rational argument could persuade the American textile executives to change their minds. This once-in-a-lifetime deal to enter the European market fell through. This was a clear example of not bending to meet the cultural and commercial requirements of the local market. The result was a sales opportunity lost forever.

## EXPANDING OVERSEAS BY PURCHASING PLANT AND PEOPLE

Once a company has exported effectively, it may seek to establish a base of operations overseas, usually in manufacturing. The options are to buy land and build a new factory or to convert existing premises to the specific needs of the enterprise.

The Genzyme Corporation of Cambridge, Massachusetts, has utilized a third method successfully to expand into the European market. The giant drug delivery corporation purchases an existing European drug or pharmaceutical company and retains the entire workforce.

In essence, Genzyme looks for a factory in Europe that meets its rigorous standards for pristine drug production (laboratory space, clean rooms, adequate electric power, etc.) and in a short time frame changes the product line to its own. In this way, it does not have to embark upon expensive feasibility studies, land acquisition, architectural plans, construction costs, and costly delays to bring Genzyme drugs to market. Further, the company incurs no added personnel costs (hiring or interviewing) to find and train an experienced workforce; it already exists when it acquires a scientific company.

Naturally, there is a short delay while the changeover occurs. However, since the company makes drugs and drug delivery products, there is no substantial change in the internal plant equipment as would occur, for example, in making a differently manufactured automobile or another piece of machinery.

The company's first acquisition was the Whitman Biochemical Company in Kent, England, in 1981, which established Genzyme in the European Union for the first time. Later, this facility was enlarged as demand for the company's products grew.

In 1994, Genzyme purchased the Sygena Company in Switzerland. The new operation made a different Genzyme product line (peptides and lipids). Additional expansion followed the same way by purchasing companies in Waterford, Ireland, and then in Geel, Belgium, the latter for production of protein molecules.

This method of overseas expansion has three benefits:

1.  It is a cost-effective approach that requires lower capital investment for plant and equipment.

2.  There is a reduction of time for senior staff to be involved in any new site selection process.

3.  A trained workforce is converted to perform similar manufacturing tasks without incurring the costs and time of hiring a new staff.

Genzyme is constantly being solicited by international economic development agencies seeking to attract the drug company overseas. But Genzyme is not interested in land deals or even empty factories, it seeks only to purchase other drug production facilities and incorporate plant and people into the Genzyme system. This takeover concept emulated Sloan's insistence that all the European car company acquisitions follow the methods of quality manufacturing in the successful General Motors way.

## SUCCESSFUL STAGES OF INTERNATIONAL EXPANSION

Often, a U.S. company will succeed in its international business plan by being the first one in the marketplace and offering a unique product or service that no one else provides. When Sloan brought American auto manufacturing know-how to Europe, along with his renewed emphasis on style and choices, GM changed the way the consumers reacted to the automobile industry.

An interesting case is Business International a publishing firm that early on recognized the value of providing data and information on a weekly basis to American companies interested in overseas markets. It altered the way American companies considered the need for and the use of international data.

BI, as it was called, was founded in the late 1950s by publisher Eldridge Haynes to meet the growing, post–World War II demands of U.S. companies impatient for information about global rules, regulations, political events, and economic conditions. Well-written and up-to-date reporting was not available in depth in local or national newspapers or economic magazines.

The key to BI's early success was to recognize the void in international business reporting and fill it with a weekly, eight-page newsletter (also called *Business International*) sold by subscription. BI was able to form a global correspondents' network that provided on-site reportage, unavailable from any other U.S. publication.

The reporting was broad-based, providing a macroeconomic picture of economic and political happenings around the globe. But often there would be an article on a specific business opportunity in a country, a promising lead that a U.S. company learned about for the first time in the weekly newsletter.

Gradually, BI added other revenue-generating products as offshoots of the main newsletter. For example, it scheduled and ran roundtable meetings overseas, offered consulting services for a particular industrial segment or country, and published white-paper-type booklets on international topical subjects, many of which were expanded summaries of the roundtable meetings. In addition, the company began to print a series of instructive "how to" books about doing business in different countries.

BI remained the preeminent supplier of international news and information throughout the 1960s. As American companies expanded overseas, especially in Europe, BI opened its first international office in Geneva. It started *Business Europe*, a second publication, also sold by weekly subscription. The new newsletter enlarged the correspondents' network on the Continent and provided more in-depth coverage on European market conditions.

BI had done frequent and informal customer surveys to ascertain what additional services or information its clients requested. Many U.S. firms were interested in the emerging Central and South American markets, particularly, the development of the Latin America Free Trade Association (LAFTA) created in 1960 to establish a common market by reducing tariffs for its member nations: Argentina, Bolivia, Brazil, Chile, Colombia, Ecuador, Mexico, Paraguay, Peru, Uruguay, and Venezuela.

In 1965, an experienced, American-educated, Spanish-speaking BI staffer was sent to Montevideo, Uruguay, headquarters of LAFTA, to report on the developments of the organization. Two years later in 1967, BI began *Business Latin America*, a third BI newsletter sold also by weekly subscription. This new entity copied the successful *Business Europe* format, establishing a wider correspondents' network and arranging roundtable discussions and seminars for clients.

The final piece to the company's globalization expansion was the publication of *Business Asia* in Hong Kong in 1970. Much of the first reporting on business conditions in China came from interviews conducted by the *Business Asia* publisher with governmental officers.

By the mid 1970s, BI's clients could choose from a menu of weekly and regional publications. In 1981, *The Economist*, the British magazine, acquired Business International to add on consulting and roundtable services.

For almost 30 years, Business International provided vital information on worldwide conditions to American and foreign companies. The newsletters and the booklets served as models for the information that U.S. companies would require as the ensuing years saw the rise in globalization. What BI had done with data collection was similar to how GM had transformed the European car industry by introducing many innovative sales and marketing methods.

## ACCESSING NEW MARKETS AND OLD MARKETS

The example of Pepsi and its attempts to expand internationally in the cola market is an interesting study of where tomorrow's foreign markets are and where they are not. It is also a history of maximizing opportunity.

The international story begins when Coca Cola opened some bottling plants in Europe in the 1920s. Then in World War II, Coke followed the GIs to Europe with the U.S. government's approval; Coca Cola technicians dressed in army fatigues mixed Coke for the soldiers in mini–bottling plants. After the war, Coca Cola retained its standing as the only American cola on the European continent.

It is important to remember that the two soft drink giants' core business is actually selling syrup, mainly to franchised bottlers in the United States and also abroad. Although both companies may own or invest in some bottling business, the syrup sales by themselves generate a high rate of return since capital and labor costs are low. Pepsi and Coca Cola invest heavily in advertising and promotion, but it is the independent bottler who must incur the large capital outlay for plant, bottling machinery, production personnel, and distribution costs, including trucks and delivery staff.

Where was Pepsi during World War II? In 1941, Pepsi was a fledgling national brand purchased regionally in the south. To support the war effort it changed the colors of its bottle crowns to the patriotic red, white, and blue. But other than a few registered trademarks in some overseas countries (e.g., Argentina and the Soviet Union), Pepsi had little international business in the 1930s and did not start to look for bottlers until the late 1940s. It then faced Coca Cola's insurmountable and well-established franchise not only in Europe but also elsewhere around the globe. In the mature European market, no matter how well-planned Pepsi's advertising and marketing plans, the day after the promotion began, "the big red trucks rolled on the highways," said a former Pepsi company official.

In the mid 1990s, Pepsi realized that to grow internationally, it had to battle Coke in the newly emerging markets of India, China, and Brazil. Population projections reveal the wisdom of this move; by the year 2025 China will increase from 1.2 billion people to 1.4 billion, India from 1 billion to 1.4 billion, and Brazil from 176 million to 216 million. Even if Pepsi cannot be the market leader in any of these three countries, there exists a large enough market for profitability.

The difficulty in China is that foreign companies cannot select their local partners as in other countries but must accept the central government's regional choices. Often, the local bottling partner in China may have no prior soda experience and, in some cases, has been specifically designated to increase employment in an area where many are out of work.

Additionally in China, Pepsi and other foreign companies seeking joint ventures or partnership agreements do not have the latitude of deal negotiations that they enjoy in Europe and South America. The Chinese government is always the "silent" partner in the deal.

Pepsi has little choice but to continue spending heavily in China, India, and Brazil where it can battle Coca Cola. Economies of scale dictate that sufficient market share can exist in these heavily populated, and growing, Third World countries.

The future of international expansion is ripe with possibilities as the standard of living improves throughout the Third World. But domestic managers have to learn to crawl internationally before they walk; the pitfalls are many and profits elusive.

## THE VENEZUELAN COLA WARS

In Venezuela in 1955, Pepsi locked in the exclusivity of bottler Oswaldo J. Cisneros, a local businessperson. For 47 years, the well-connected and business savvy Cisneros family created a successful Pepsi franchise. Venezuela was the only country in the world where Pepsi's share (42 percent) was greater than Coke's (12 percent). For all those many and frustrating years, Coca Cola wasted many millions of advertising and promotional dollars in the Venezuelan economy to try to cut into Pepsi's market share. But, thanks to the Cisneros, the country's cola remained Pepsi blue.

How did Coke stop feeling "blue" about the Venezuela market? In 1996, it offered the Cisneros family $1.4 billion to switch manufacturing, bottling, and distribution to Coca Cola! Overnight, every blue Pepsi vending machine, supermarket cooler, restaurant napkin dispenser changed to the red of Coca Cola. In the stroke of a pen, almost five decades of Pepsi supremacy in Venezuela vanished without a trace.

Pepsi's response was to sue Coca Cola and win a judgment in an international court. It also signed quickly with another Venezuelan bottler. Both soft drink giants have begun a mammoth spending battle for market share with Coca Cola now at a 70 percent share and Pepsi at 24 percent.

## HÄAGEN DAZS INTRODUCES ICE CREAM TO EUROPE

There are occasions when a product or service from the United States may not find a sales or marketing opportunity overseas because of cultural differences or the lack of a certain technology. One example is American-style ice cream, a late arrival in the European and Asian markets.

When the Pillsbury Company acquired Häagen Dazs ice cream in 1983, the first decision was to expand the operation by increasing supermarket distribution. The large retail market provided the best opportunity to boost sales, especially among adults who would be willing to pay more money for the higher-quality, rich-in-butter-fat premium brand.

Less promising for future domestic growth were the thousands of Häagen Dazs retail shops, operated by individual or group franchise agreements. These stores had opened after the ice cream appeared in specialty stores and supermarket freezers. When Pillsbury management assessed the franchise operations, it realized that the nationwide quality of the product and the look of each store were dependent on the franchise owners. And to management's dismay, some of these retail shops were inefficiently run and not up to quality standards.

In 1992, Pillsbury, which had also purchased Burger King in 1980 and then the Green Giant Company in 1986, was itself acquired by Grand Metropolitan Corporation, the British hotel conglomerate. The British GrandMet management was more worldly and savvy than Pillsbury about Europe, and it envisioned greater Continental opportunity for expansion for all the Pillsbury-acquired companies.

When GrandMet studied the Häagen Dazs prospects for European growth, it realized that, historically, ice cream on the Continent was a novelty food consumed mainly by children. Throughout the United Kingdom and Ireland, ice cream was a summer seasonal item sold by a small fleet of independently owned vans. In Europe, ice cream—actually sorbet, gelato, or ices—was also sold in street stands and small street wagons. Most noticeable to American tourists all over the Continent was the omnipresent Cornetto from Unilever, a vanilla ice cream in a soft cone topped with a chocolate and nuts. A definite kids' treat item.

(In the United Kingdom, currently experiencing a significant increase in ice cream sales that top $1 billion annually, the semantics for specialty items like the Cornetto cone is referred to euphemistically as the "wrapped impulse market." By contrast, the U.S. ice cream market is estimated to exceed $9 billion in 2004. Some 93 percent of Americans consumers keep some form of ice cream product in their freezers year-round. Ice cream represents approximately 9 percent of total U.S. milk production.)

In the late 1980s, no European ice cream was made or mass marketed, and no locally made ice cream approximated the rich, butter fat creamy taste of high-priced American premium brands. It was difficult to assess the market potential because of three variables: the long-standing adult rejection of ice cream, the uncertainty that bulk-packed pints could be sold in the supermarket chains, and the absence of an ice cream making plant in the European Union to supply product on a volume basis.

GrandMet decided that an inexpensive and quick way to test Häagen Dazs in Europe was to open one or two inner-city retail stores. The green light was given to launch downtown flagship stores in London (Leicester Square) and Paris (Place Victor Hugo) with imported ice cream from the United States. The locations were chosen because of their high pedestrian traffic that would also include many U.S. tourists. These retail outlets would approximate the best-looking franchised outlets in the United States, with the one difference that GrandMet owned and operated the business itself.

The stores opened with great fanfare and excellent public relations, particularly in the food sections of the local newspapers. On the first day, long lines began to form in both cities, and customers started to come in at all hours for a taste. Word of mouth spread quickly through the expatriate American communities that "real" premium ice cream was finally available. Soon, curious Europeans began to sample the rich flavors, and they, too, gave a thumbs-up to the Häagen Dazs establishments.

(A similar Häagen Dazs retail system was started in Tokyo, Japan, with GrandMet coproducing with the local Sunatory company. In Japan, the most popular ice cream flavor is green tea.)

Häagen Dazs opened a manufacturing facility in Arras, France, to supply the rapidly increasing demand of its European business. But more important for future expansion than the retail shop revenues has been the acceptance of premium ice cream as a take-home item in European homes and the ice cream's subsequent appearance in the freezer sections of European supermarkets.

Häagen Dazs was the first company to introduce American ice cream and their flavor varieties to Europeans. By 2004, the brand was sold in 700 cafes in 54 countries, including new operations in South America. In 2000, the company renovated the Leicester Square, London, location and placed comfortable burgundy sofas inside. This stylish seating addition differs radically from the historic U.S. ice cream shop eating experience.

The market potential is untapped for Häagen Dazs as worldwide demand increases for its ice cream, sorbets, and frozen yogurt products. By starting small with downtown cafes, the opposite of the traditional American in-store ice cream distribution system, the brand found the right approach to launch its international business.

Success at home for General Motors with a new styling concept might eventually find its way into the European car market. But there was as much resistance to America's big cars and ungainly fins as there was to consuming American-style ice cream.

It takes time for innovations to cross national boundaries. Sloan never was adamant that the American big-car style replace the smaller European cars. He recognized that incomes (actually, the amount of weeks an average worker needed to work to make a car down payment) were lower in Europe and also that Europe did not possess the elaborate U.S. coast-to-coast highway system.

## SUPERPREMIUM ICE CREAM COMES TO IRELAND

On the heels of Häagen Dazs' success in Europe, other American companies like Ben and Jerry's looked to see whether there was room for two ice cream producers on the Continent. At the same time, in Ireland, the European country with the third highest per capita ice cream consumption and an emerging market for super-premium products, two American entrepreneurs were planning to go toe-to-toe with Häagen Dazs for ice cream supremacy.

The story of the Murphy Brothers is a David confronting Goliath tale but, so far, without the slaying of the giant. In case study terms it reveals the smart moves a small start-up company can take to become profitable by taking a slice of market share from the established brand leader in a niche segment. It is also an example of how to enter an international market as a new brand after the first one has paved the way.

Kieran and Sean Murphy come from Rockland County, New York, and hold dual Irish-American citizenship because their father Finnbar was born in Ireland. For 40 years, their parents owned and operated the American branch of the worldwide Weleda Natural Care and Weleda medical products. Both sons spent their teenage years and postcollege years working in the family business in production, marketing, and sales. They were versed in operating a small company with a specialized product line.

Three years before their parents decided to retire from business, the family chose the small, picturesque town of Dingle (population 2,000) on the west coast of Ireland (where the motion picture *Ryan's Daughter* was filmed). Here they purchased a large cottage, hoping to establish a natural therapy center with massage and aroma therapy. Kieran managed the operation.

After a few years of mixed results at the center, Kieran looked for another business to start. In the back of his mind was to find an

American idea—a service or product—that might succeed in the new economic boom that was occurring in Ireland. While vacationing in Europe and England in 1999, he noticed that he was able to buy Häagen Dazs in the major cities, eventually, finding a thriving ice cream cafe in Dublin.

Could Dingle—with its steady stream of summer tourists, many from the United States—support a small American-styled ice cream shop?

In 2000, the Murphy brothers decided to open an ice cream shop as a launch pad for a new national Irish brand. Sean attended an ice-cream-making school at Penn State University. New ice-cream-making equipment was shipped via London, costing extra money and time.

The Murphy's set up the ice-cream-making equipment in April, 2000, in a small, refurbished shop in downtown Dingle. The hope was to work out the purchasing and production kinks before the arrival of the summer tourist trade. With great anticipation, they made their first batch of chocolate ice cream—the promise of a potentially profitable business career—and to their shock discovered that the local super-rich Irish cream had produced chocolate butter! The local milk was pasteurized but not homogenized, a necessary requirement to make ice cream. Fortunately, there was one supplier of homogenized milk in Ireland.

The first summer witnessed good business. Gradually, even local skeptics were convinced that American ice cream was tasty and refreshing and worth the extra price. But at the end of the season, the town returned to its small, native population, and the store closed. The brothers worked out a business plan to expand by opening up a second retail shop the following year in another Irish resort area populated by American tourists in the summertime.

But when the Murphys checked rental prices in other western Ireland tourist areas, they were shocked at the steep price for rental space. A second retail store could not become profitable, selling ice cream only four or five months a year. And no off-season food concept—chili, burgers, fish and chips—seemed sensible when towns reverted to their local and small populations in the off-tourist season.

The Murphys shifted their focus to production of prepackaged pints and to challenge Häagen Dazs in the supermarket business. But clearly, how could an undercapitalized and unknown small company take on a multibillion-dollar superpower in the same market segment?

The capitalization came from a combination of private money and economic assistance from a national Irish development organization. With new funds, the company rented factory space outside of Dingle to mass produce and package the ice cream for store and supermarket sales. The differentiation came by developing an exclusive product specifically for Irish tastes and made with local ingredients while the American brand competition made its ice cream in France.

To embellish the all-Irish, native-son manufacturing, the Murphys' Web site emphasizes the made-at-home in small batches concept and prints the names of the flavors in English *and* Irish (i.e., *risini* = rum raisin, *fanaile* = French Vanilla, and *seacláid* = pure chocolate).

Today, Murphy's ice cream is an award-winning item that can be purchased throughout upscale supermarkets in Ireland's largest cities. As consumption of superpremium ice cream increases exponentially, the Murphy Brothers are in the position to meet the new national taste for premium ice cream. And, it may even be possible for Murphy's Ice Cream from Ireland to be exported to other European Union countries and compete with Häagen Dazs.

## THE LESSONS OF INTERNATIONAL BUSINESS

Companies that seek additional revenues can look internationally to foreign markets. In the brave new world of globalization, emerging market countries like China are on the brink of a great consumer expansion. The question is the same one posed by Alfred P. Sloan, Jr., in the 1920s: What is the best way to pursue international business?

## EXPORTING

Exporting is the easiest, most economical method with the least amount of financial risk and, strikingly, the business method that has caused historic anxiety among U.S. companies. Whereas, for example, a Boston-based company will ship across the country to Seattle without a moment's worry, the same firm may experience disquiet if a similar order comes from Liverpool, England.

Exporting should be the first step every U.S. company takes to establish a market for a product or service abroad, especially, in the countries of the European Union, which have comparable sales channels and similar financial procedures. Exporting will serve as a market test that will indicate whether some new business can be launched overseas. A successful export program can lead to other international possibilities, such as joint ventures, licensing, and, potentially the most lucrative, establishing a sales office or manufacturing base in a foreign country or region.

Before committing to exporting, a company should ask:

- Does the product or service sell well in the United States? If yes, do similar conditions exist in certain countries for possible export sales?

- Is the product or service difficult to reproduce abroad? Does the company have some proprietary or exclusive product or system that would be in high demand in overseas markets?

- Will the company devote the personnel and the time to pursue the potential opportunities for export? Will it take a long-term view to achieve profitability?

Too often, a U.S. company will decide to implement an export program and then give it short shrift by not committing staff or resources to the project. Another lack that guarantees failure is not to write specific export objectives coupled with a strategy on how to achieve those goals. And, finally, without any empirical basis, often the initial export sales projections are set too high and are therefore impossible to attain.

American companies that decide to export frequently make the misjudgment that they have to find markets in all parts of the world. The best objective is to seek out that foreign market that most closely resembles the domestic one. Focusing on one country or one region is the smart way to begin.

There are two excellent organizations that excel in assisting U.S. companies find export markets and export partners: the United States Department of Commerce and the World Trade Centers Association; offices of the latter are found in some major U.S. cities. The U.S. Department of Commerce provides a wealth of information online at www.export.gov or in pamphlet form. In addition, the

USDC trade service division conducts seminars, sponsors traveling U.S. trade shows, and also arranges trade missions to all foreign countries.

The World Trade Centers Association was established in 1970 to foster and promote international business relationships. Its Web site (www.wtca.org) lists the cities in the United States and abroad that currently have a WTC certified office and which cities are under consideration for future membership. For American companies, these WTC offices are a local phone call away and are usually situated in the city's business district. Many informational services are free, with nominal charges for specialized projects like appointment making, seminars, or collaborating.

Contacting the USDC or a WTC office is tantamount to two-stop shopping for information related to the duties on products for all foreign countries, the names of exclusive sales representatives abroad, and face-to-face advice on the mechanics of exporting, including using letters of credit for payment and also finding the right export management company for the product.

Most preliminary steps establishing an export business can be handled simply and easily without the need to hire extra staff.

### FINDING LOCATIONS OVERSEAS
For many U.S companies a location abroad is the next step after exporting has proved successful. This move can be either a sales office or site manufacturing. The decision entails a long-term commitment to the enterprise and a significant outlay of capital.

Before a company decides to look overseas for a new location, it should investigate what incentives will be offered by the country, city, or province in the areas that seem best for future international operations. The first place to look is online by country. On all these Web sites, the word to look for is *development,* which has become the universal term for economic expansion within countries. Whether it is French *développment,* Spanish *desarrollo,* or German *Wirtchafts-förderung,* links will be found that go to that country's main economic agency for dealing with inquiries about internal development.

Europeans have formed their own organization called EURADA (European Association of Development Agencies), which has 150 regular and associate members in 25 countries. Founded in 1991 and headquartered in Brussels, this association coordinates activities for European Union (E.U.) regions. The site can be accessed and perused at www.eurada.org.

The tax and other fiscal incentives that a European region can offer to a foreign company are determined by the E.U.'s assessment of a range of economic variables. For example, in the Portugal region of Alentejo, located east of Lisbon, which is primarily an agricultural area with a low wage rate and some industrial development, the incentives can be the maximum. The E.U. wants to encourage investment in those regions with lower economic indices to balance growth within the member states, and it allows these developing regions (like Alentejo) to submit proposals with supplementary incentives.

By comparison, the German region of North Rhine Westphalia, a highly successful industrial and scientific area with 23 of Germany's 50 largest companies, cannot offer the same high tax and fiscal package as the E.U.'s poorer developed regions. But GfW, the economic agency for the region headquartered in Dusseldorf, can put together more sophisticated development packages. For example, it has attracted the QVC shopping network that needed a centralized and large distribution space on the Continent. GfW also specializes in offering a low-cost, full-office facility with many secretarial and consultant services to allow foreign companies to test start-up European activities for a low cost.

Countries in the Pacific Rim, Near East, South and Central America, and Africa all have their own Web sites with economic development information.

## CULTURAL DIFFERENCES

Foreign countries have different cultures and ways of doing business. Many times the initial strategy has to be modified to suit the particular business model of the foreign corporation.

A story that illustrates this point concerns the famous Bata Shoe Company of Czechoslovakia, the first modern shoe manufacturer. After World War I, Thomas Bata made a trip to the Far East to open up sales offices. In India, he noticed that the footwear of that country consisted mainly of sandals made from strips of leather. His mind flashed to all the unusable leather strips left daily on the floor of the shoe factory in Zlin, which produced more than two million pairs per year. If the company could export the leather strips to India and make sandals under the Bata name, it could reap a double profit from using the discarded leather and from the new, foreign operation sales.

Thomas Bata contacted the Indian embassy in Prague, informed it of the company's objective to manufacture sandals in India, and requested that native sandal makers be sent to Czechoslovakia for instruction in the Bata shoe-making system. The embassy reported that India was composed of 12 distinct ethnic and language areas and brought over 24 sandal makers, two from each region.

Thomas Bata's next part of the plan was to hire local Czech managers who would return to India and oversee production, one administrator for each of the 12 regions. His instructions to the managers were explicit, "For the next months, live with your sandal makers, learn their native dialect; this is what you will speak to sandal maker workers in India when you return."

After six months in Czechoslovakia, the Indian sandal makers and the Czech managers returned to India to begin making sandals. Now, thousands of pounds of scrap strips of leather were collected and shipped from Zlin to the main Bata office in Calcutta, where they were then redistributed to 12 Bata branches in the Indian hinterland.

After a year, Thomas Bata returned to India to assess the operation, visiting each of the 12 regions before heading for a final stop at the main office in Calcutta. Sales within the country had been excellent, and the company's head manager expected a very pleased boss whose brilliant sandal making plan had proved to be highly profitable.

The manager, upon first welcoming Thomas Bata, said, "Sir, I am sure you are very pleased with the success of the new Bata sandal operation in India."

Bata scowled, "No, I am not happy; the entire jungle is speaking *Czech*!"

Take a good lesson from Pepsi International, which employs a universal "gold standard" for its Lay's potato chips to ensure uniformity across the line in every country *but* allows flexibility for regional tastes and native seasonings. The U.S. manager must realize from day one that no matter how similar the international market or the consumer looks to the domestic market, culturally and sociologically it is a different market.

The moral from these cases is that U.S. firms must adapt to the culture and customs of the local country. Most foreign businesspeople will speak English to some degree, but it is always a mark of interest for overseas companies to learn the language of the native operation. Sloan always insisted that the European car divisions be staffed with native executives and that they be allowed the authority to deal with local situation without having to ask constantly for Detroit's approval.

## SLOAN'S VIEW

Alfred P. Sloan, Jr., was one of the first U.S. corporate executives to mount and carry out a foreign policy of expansion. He envisioned that overseas markets could accept General Motors' products with some modifications of style and price, which explains why the company manufactured mostly smaller cars (e.g., Opel) for the European market.

Sloan never tried to convince Europeans that the supersized American cars with their greater horsepower and larger trunk space should become the cars of the Continent. In his chapter on international business in his second autobiography, "The Company Overseas," Sloan asserts that the American corporation has a function and a mission to do international business but do it differently. He wrote, "For the overseas market is no more an extension of the United States market."[10] Even though Sloan instituted established American business principles, he understood that foreign markets took on a different character and required a different automobile.

# BUILDING A PROFESSIONAL STAFF

*T*  *he difference in organization between GM and Ford...Sloan decides on how to pick the right people...Sloan uses the organizational chart...GM's staffing goals and objectives...Walter Chrysler, the automotive genius...Sloan inherits the Du Pont Company's staff ...Sloan's men: John Raskob, visionary; Donaldson Brown, financial expert; William Knudsen, hands-on manager; Charles Wilson, the modern GM executive...William Bernbach, ad agency staffing genius...Staffing the modern Ford...The managerial lessons from correct staffing*

It can be said with some hyperbole that Alfred P. Sloan, Jr.'s career at General Motors and the talented men who staffed the various divisions could be considered a constellation of stars in the firmament, so brightly did this assemblage glow with each of its components shining luminously.

A claim can be made that before Alfred P. Sloan, Jr., brought together at GM the group of brilliant and enterprising staff, the nation's only prior successful organizational staffing had been during the Civil War under the generals Robert E. Lee and Ulysses S. Grant. For a trip further back and to another county, another victorious military model would be the highly talented staff of marshals who served with Napoleon in nineteenth-century France.

There exists a corollary between the structure of an efficient corporation and a regimented, well-run military organization. In fact, praise and criticism of GM under Sloan and afterward, found parallels between the layered military configuration of battalions and the many corporate arrangements by divisions.

When Sloan became president of General Motors in 1923, he presided over one of the largest assemblages of workers in the world. What differentiated GM from other large companies of the day was the well-defined divisional aspect comprising five automobile companies, truck manufacturing, locomotive production, and a collection of component and accessories companies. As GM expanded, Sloan established separate staffing sections for styling, engineering, finance, marketing and, finally, personnel.

Sloan valued the decision on hiring as the CEO's uppermost priority:

> This corporation pays me a pretty good salary for making important decisions, and for making them right. You tell me what more important decision there is than that about the management of people who do the job.[1]

Under Sloan's decentralization system, these divisions required autonomy and strong, independent leadership. Part of Sloan's genius was the ability to choose the highest caliber of executives to run the many sections and divisions. Historically, Sloan's GM is one of the first examples of corporate staffing on a distinct divisional basis.

The General Motors practice of hiring the best managers would serve as an example for all later organizations—business and otherwise—for years after. That achievement would be highlighted by Sloan's insistence on professionals to manage the various GM divisions. He was circumspect when he stated the hiring question:

> The decision about people is the only crucial one. You think and everybody thinks that a company can have 'better people;' that's horses apples. All it can do is place people right—and then it'll have performance.[2]

## THE ORGANIZATIONAL CHART

Sloan drew detailed organizational charts for the corporation and also for its various divisions. In the landmark chart for the 1937 General Motors Corporation, Sloan placed the stockholders in the top slot, a reminder that a corporation exists primarily for increasing the equity of its shareholders. Below stockholders, Sloan positioned the board of directors and under this slot are two subsections, policy committee and administration committee. Both of these flow through the next level—policy groups—into the CEO and the board of directors.

Spread out in both directions from the CEO are lines connecting to the specific policy groups: distribution, engineering, manufacturing, public relations, labor relationships, overseas operations, executive personnel, and financial relationships. For Sloan it was clear that policy decisions rested above the operating levels of divisions and subsidiaries. It was also clear that in his decentralization system, the policy groups would report to the CEO.

The organizational chart of Ford Motors during the 1920s would have looked much different: the top slot occupied solely by Henry Ford. There was no method for managers in Ford's company to express an opinion, and certainly not one that differed from Henry Ford's. When the only product was a Model-T, the organization worked like an efficient army pursuing one objective successfully.

While there were other U.S. business organizational charts drawn before Sloan's, his 1937 chart is the most spread-out because of the many slots to accommodate the eight main operating divisional groupings (e.g., overseas, accessory, car, truck and body, etc.) and the more than 75 different divisional slots within the eight main groups, consisting of specific operational functions (e.g., General Motors Acceptance Company, Frigidaire, Buick, Bendix Aviation, General Motors South America, etc.). And all of these many slots had to be staffed with managers.

## SELECTING THE RIGHT PEOPLE

Alfred P. Sloan, Jr., enjoys a distinction shared by few people in any field: He wrote two business autobiographies. The first was published in 1940 and its title, *Adventures of a White-Collar Man,* provides insight into how Sloan perceived himself as a professional manager, working in an office with a staff of people. In his later work, *My Years with General Motors,* Sloan makes many references to the dictatorial managerial practices of Henry Ford and GM's own William Durant. Sloan saw clearly that a larger and diverse corporation like General Motors had to be staffed with professional managers with identifiable skills.

Sloan succeeded in ending the era of American business dominated by the "owner" with unlimited, unchecked powers. He effected the transition to era of the "manager" and with this changeover created the opportunity for mid-level and high-level managers to participate in the great wealth of a corporate career. Sloan had a knack of finding, keeping, and rewarding the right people to fill the many divisional slots that he and General Motors' expansion had created. There is no pat Sloan formula for selecting the best staff, no pithy words (often clichéd) about ambition, autonomy, or experience. Sloan did offer these words on hiring:

> You think I should be a good judge of people. Believe me there's no such person. There are only people who make people decisions right, and that means slowly, and people who make people decisions wrong, and repent at leisure.[3]

Sloan was a strong proponent of the 30-day rule, which stated in effect, that if GM had made the right managerial choice, the corporation would have the first 30 days of that new hire's employment to train a person in the GM system sufficiently so that this manager would perform capably for General Motors the rest of his career.

It surprised Peter Drucker, when he sat in at meetings for two years at General Motors to produce his book *Concept of the Corporation,* that an inordinate amount of time was spent discussing "people rather than decisions on policy."[4] It astounded him further when he realized that CEO Sloan was involved as an active participant in these many hirings. He questioned Sloan on the time a committee had taken to select a position of master mechanic in an accessory division:

> Drucker asked, "Mr. Sloan, how can you afford to spend four hours on a minor job like this?"

Sloan replied, "If we don't spend four hours on placing a man and placing him right, we'd spend four hundred hours on cleaning up after our mistake—and *that* time I wouldn't have."[5]

Drucker describes how these hiring discussions at General Motors often became animated and impassioned. The members of the committee knew they could voice their opinions freely in front of Sloan. Sometimes Sloan would listen to the committee debate the pros or cons of a candidate but decide differently, especially if he felt a person was getting short shrift.

One Sloan dialogue about a manager went as follows: "All right he's not brilliant, and not so fast, and looks drab. But hasn't he always performed!"[6] And this candidate, Drucker reported, turned out to be one of the most successful managers of a big GM division, his job saved by Sloan's intervention.

It is important to examine the executives with whom Sloan worked or hired at General Motors to learn firsthand the abilities in these coworkers that influenced his later staffing decisions. Sloan inherited some of these men from the Durant and du Pont regimes, but he was savvy enough to realize that all possessed outstanding traits.

In truth, there would not have been a cogent "Sloan system" of management had he not met and worked along side the likes of Walter Chrysler, John Raskob, and Donaldson Brown.

## WALTER P. CHRYSLER

Walter P. Chrysler served as the one person who most influenced Alfred P. Sloan, Jr., on the efficient method to run and staff an automobile company. Sloan, whose background was not automobile manufacture, realized that he had to find men that possessed Walter Chrysler's temperament, automotive knowledge (self-trained), and engineering genius. The time that Sloan and Chrysler spent together at General Motors was brief—only a few years—but their close, personal friendship lasted until Chrysler's death in 1940.

Walter Chrysler had begun his career in 1911 at GM when William Durant appointed him the Buick Company's works manager. By 1916, Buick had become the most successful car manufactured in the world, rising from a production of 40 cars a day to 500 under Chrysler's energetic and perceptive leadership.

When Packard Motors offered Walter Chrysler the presidency, Durant raised his Buick salary from $50,000 to $500,000. And of course Chrysler stayed at GM. Of note is that under Chrysler's leadership, Buick generated a $50 million annual profit and proved the wisdom of Durant's megasalary offer.

Ironically, as Chrysler moved up the hierarchy to executive vice-president of General Motors, he experienced firsthand the slapdash Durant management style. A conflict of territory arose between the dynamic Durant and Chrysler, the brilliant automotive genius, mainly over Durant's cronyism that collided with Chrysler's objectives for production efficiency.

In addition, Chrysler could not tolerate Durant's constant habit of taking phone calls during meetings or keeping his top staff (Chrysler, Sloan, etc.) waiting for hours in GM's New York building's hallways while he chatted to Wall Street.

Finally, Walter Chrysler threw up his hands in disgust and quit General Motors in 1920. He had the foresight to see that Durant's overexpansion would soon result in a financial squeeze, and he was proved right when GM's budgetary and inventory crisis began in 1920. By the time the Du Pont Company's chief executives, Pierre du Pont and John Raskob, had stepped into the GM picture to rescue the company, Walter Chrysler had already received a lucrative offer to become the CEO of the financially distraught Willys-Overland Company. At the end of his two-year Willys contract, Chrysler had reduced the struggling Willys company's debt from $48 million to $18 million, an extraordinary cost-saving feat in any industry.

During the period when General Motors had overtaken Ford Motors as the leading car manufacturer in the mid 1920s, Sloan sensed that if the trend continued GM could be under increased monopoly scrutiny from the federal government. It was not in the corporation's best interest to dominate the car and truck industry by more than a 50 percent market share. Sloan had a brilliant solution to the problem: "Sloan persuaded him (Walter Chrysler) to strike out on his own. Chrysler started the automobile company that bears his name in large part because Sloan clearly saw that with Ford rapidly going downhill, GM, in its own interest, needed a strong competitor."[7]

Sloan had found an early friend in Walter Chrysler at GM, and also the prototype of a successful manager of an automobile company who knew the mechanical ins and outs of a vehicle. Chrysler was one of the first to complain about William Durant's slipshod leadership style in conversations with Sloan. Then, when Walter Chrysler bolted GM, it created the fortuitous opening for Alfred Sloan to move to the top company spot. And with Sloan in power as GM's president, he could suggest to Walter Chrysler to begin his own car company.

In 1928, Walter Chrysler, by now a successful car company owner and a fabled millionaire, was named *Time* magazine's Man of the Year. He bought land in Manhattan between East 42nd and East 43rd Streets and built the magnificent art deco Chrysler Building with designer William Van Alen. For a while, its 77 stories marked it the tallest building in the world until the construction of the Empire State Building. In his own skyscraper, Walter Chrysler could always see out the office window the smaller and less attractive General Motors building on West 57th Street.

## SLOAN INHERITS THE DU PONT COMPANY'S STAFF

During the beginning of the twentieth century, the Du Pont Company changed over from a manufacturer of powdered explosives to a chemical company. The three du Pont cousins, Thomas, Alfred, and Pierre, who oversaw the company's modernization, had all attended the Massachusetts Institute of Technology. They were convinced that the new century would usher in a new form of industrialization.

For the Du Pont group, the GM stock purchase was a necessary risk; the Du Pont Company's once exclusive and profitable military business had ended with the conclusion of World War I. It had no equivalent possibility of generating dividends from any of its new chemical divisions. It had to diversify into other industries, and the budding automobile industry looked promising. In addition, it could find a captive market in General Motors car production for its Fabrikoid and Pyralin paint and varnish business.

The Du Pont Company owned at first 24 percent of General Motors, which increased to 50 percent when GM faced bankruptcy in 1920. Pierre du Pont (B.S. in Chemical Engineering at M.I.T., Class of 1890) had already overseen a management restructuring at the Du Pont Company with other executives.

When Pierre du Pont assumed the position of president of General Motors in 1920 (at Sloan's urging in their first meeting), he brought with him some of the Du Pont Company's trained financial managers. One was John J. Raskob, who had originally recommended the sizable Du Pont Company purchase of General Motors' stock and who was an early believer in the automobile industry, General Motors, and a profitable future of both. The second person was Donaldson Brown.

## JOHN J. RASKOB

John J. Raskob began his career as a private secretary at the Du Pont Company, doing typing and stenography. But he caught Pierre du Pont's attention, primarily because Raskob was a whiz at finance. Eventually, he was promoted to treasurer of the Du Pont Corporation, later serving on its board of directors and also the executive committee. (Sloan cited Raskob's "Alger-boy career," referencing back to the Horatio Alger poor boy makes good penny-novel tales.)

Pierre du Pont needed Raskob's financial skills at General Motors and appointed him vice-president and chairperson of the finance committee. Raskob was a good speaker, a bon vivant, chummy with the Wall Street crowd, and, for a while, served as the public spokesperson for General Motors. He also stayed on at the Du Pont Company as vice-president in charge of finance.

In this 1920 and 1921 period under Pierre du Pont's leadership, Alfred Sloan stood second in rank of importance after Raskob at General Motors, although he was a member of the executive committee and Pierre du Pont's main assistant. After du Pont resigned and appointed Sloan his successor, relations between Sloan and Raskob amicably both professionally and socially.

Sloan called Raskob "brilliant and imaginative" a complementary personality to the more sedate Pierre du Pont whom Sloan called "steady and conservative." Sloan was quick to praise Raskob's talent: "His faults, if they should be called that, were those that go with an aggressive, impatient, intelligence—the very thing that made him good. Not many men foresaw the future of the automobile industry as well as he did."[8]

The Sloan-Raskob partnership flourished over the next seven years, paralleling the sharp rise in revenues and profit at General Motors. Raskob could assume a role of semi-independence since he still retained his Du Pont Company position and had become wealthy from salary and stock investments in both companies.

Raskob's management achievements at GM included changing the system of financial accountability, the start of the General Motors Acceptance Corporation (GMAC), and importantly, the beginning of an employees' savings and investment plan. However, his most significant contribution was a new cash system, which reduced cash balances in the company's many banks and also expanded the amount of readily available credit that General Motors could borrow. The new method permitted GM to invest excess cash in short-term securities, increasing the company's amount of short-term earned income.

In 1928, Raskob embarked on a new career, becoming the chief fund-raiser for Democratic presidential candidate Al Smith, and later, the head of Smith's presidential campaign. Raskob's new political interest collided with Sloan's model for the responsibilities of the professional manager, whom Sloan believed should remain politically neutral in public.

As the 1928 presidential campaign continued, Sloan grew dismayed that GM was now permanently linked in the media to one political candidate because it created the impression that General Motors had taken sides versus the Republican candidate, Herbert Hoover. Sloan believed that taking sides was bad for GM, a perilous mix of politics and business. Raskob exacerbated the situation by convincing Pierre du Pont (chairman of the GM board) to support Al Smith with money and publicity.

The conflict ensued at GM whether Raskob should resign (Sloan's choice) or take a leave of absence until after the election (Raskob's choice). Sloan prevailed with GM's board, and Raskob was forced to submit his resignation. As Sloan's biographer wrote: "Sloan was helping to invent a new role for the American businessman: corporate manager. Blatant public partisan political maneuvering was not appropriate behavior in a corporate officer."[9]

Soon after, Pierre du Pont was also caught up in this political imbroglio, and he had to take a leave of absence from his duties as chairman of the board.

The final action in this matter forced Sloan to come out publicly for Republican candidate Herbert Hoover in an attempt to balance the Raskob-du Pont Al Smith preference. The announcement neutralized negative sentiment—much of it from GM's conservative

Midwestern auto dealers—that the corporation tilted to the Democratic candidate of Al Smith, a New York Irish Catholic who favored the repeal of Prohibition.

The Raskob incident demonstrated two of Sloan's foremost principles: that the corporation was paramount and impartial and that General Motors' executives should take no action that would potentially harm the image of the company. Raskob and du Pont had argued forcefully that American executives had a right and an obligation to try to effect social and economic change through the political process. Sloan agreed in principle but only if no harm came to General Motors.

Not surprisingly, Sloan did not even hint of this awkward and disheartening political incident in either of his two autobiographies. Perhaps, he believed that the retelling might also do harm to the image of General Motors.

The political arena would continue to bother Sloan throughout his career, particularly, FDR's New Deal. He would never want either himself or General Motors drawn into national battles of policy or politics. These political forays always distracted from the smooth operation of the company. Later, with other GM executives, he was as unsympathetic to their political beliefs as he was to Raskob's, even to those men who left General Motors to serve in high positions in the federal government.

The ultimate praise of the financial acumen that began at the Du Pont Company in the early years of the twentieth century came in *Time* magazine's 1928 Man of the Year issue about Walter P. Chrysler. It compared the differing managerial styles of GM and the Chrysler Corporation, saying: "General Motors uses the financial wizards of the Raskob-Du Pont (company) type."

## DONALDSON BROWN

Donaldson Brown was the second Du Pont Company executive that Sloan inherited in 1921. He would serve as GM's vice-president of finance and then be appointed to the executive committee in 1924. His mathematical and ordered mind fit in perfectly with Sloan's "Organization Study" for revamping the corporation.

His biography in brief: At 13 he attended the Virginia Polytechnic Institute and graduated at 17 with a degree in electric engineering. At 24, he joined the Du Pont Company, rising to the position of treasurer. While at Du Pont he was one of the first financial executives to see the importance of economists and statisticians to assist with long-range planning for the company.

Under Pierre du Pont's stewardship, Brown was instructed to implement a tighter fix on controlling the cost accounting variables that contributed to the Du Pont Company's operation. His innovative answers were to introduce the principle of return on investment (ROI), return on equity, capital turnover, and the precise forecasting of sales and costs based upon facts. He transported all of these financial and accounting systems when he moved to General Motors in 1920 to aid Pierre du Pont and Raskob.

Sloan realized the importance of these financial controls and assessments when he wrote: "Financial method is so refined today (1964) that it may seem routine; yet this method—the financial model, as some call it…is one if the chief bases for strategic business decisions."[10]

After the Durant-inspired GM crisis of 1920, Brown developed a long-range policy of inventory control. Sloan could boast that Brown's written reorganization plans "to control inventories to accord with finance committee policies or good business practices"[11] was the first and essential action in the new financial control system for General Motors.

In Donaldson Brown, Sloan had found a like-minded executive (another college-educated engineer) who believed in the importance of facts and internal controls. Once Sloan had experienced Brown's expertise in the financial area, he assigned Brown to study the tricky business of estimating production. The result was a four-month forecasting system that included plant investment, working capital, sales, and inventory commitments.

Brown was also primarily responsible for the policy on how the company should expand overseas. He studied the best method for the company's groundbreaking bonus and compensation plans, the latter, one of the first statistical models in corporate America. Finally, he suggested a procedure for choosing and then promoting the highest caliber of managers.

Brown also worked out a specific return on investment to measure the success of each of GM's divisional operations. These intricate systems allowed Sloan to examine how the amount of inventory and working capital affected the turnover of capital. In essence, it gave Sloan and his executive committee a precise tool for establishing standards of performance, division by division.

Brown's contribution to General Motors in the 1920s and onward was substantial. He was one of the few GM managers who impressed Peter Drucker with his ability and also with his slight eccentricities. Drucker said that senior management referred to Brown as "the brains of GM, but doesn't speak any known language."[12] Here is how Drucker described the deep-thinking financial genius: "But first he would recite, like the very worst of Germanic professors, all the footnotes, qualifications, and exceptions in a language that was half mathematical equations and half social science jargon, without any indication where he was headed."[13]

In fact, Brown could speak this arcane language because Sloan could translate the mathematical nuances to the other General Motors' executives. It was a measure of Sloan's confidence in Brown's loyalty that he was appointed the company's spokesperson after the historical United Auto Workers union GM strike in Flint, Michigan, in 1936 and 1937.

Donaldson Brown stayed with General Motors until 1946 when Sloan officially retired the presidency. He remained on both the GM and the Du Pont Company boards until the Supreme Court's 1959 antitrust ruling that prohibited this type of joint board membership.

## WILLIAM KNUDSEN

When Sloan realized that a low-priced and better-made Chevrolet would be GM's main thrust to go after the Ford Company's Model-T, he needed a hands-on automobile manager who could follow this strategic marketing lead. The person to accomplish this was William Knudsen, who was already in place at the Chevrolet division. The ensuing Sloan-Knudsen collaboration would prove an immediate and profitable success. Further, it would demonstrate that Sloan's decentralized organizational system could turn around a marketing and sales problem.

He was born Signius Wilhelm Poul Knudsen in Denmark, emigrating to the United States in 1900 with every immigrant's dream of success in the new country. He was a giant of a man, standing six foot three and weighing over 200 pounds. By all reports, he could work other men into the ground, doing laborious chores longer than anyone else could. At 14, he was an apprentice machinist in a railroad shop.

Knudsen had natural mechanical abilities similar to Walter Chrysler. He was a person who could tinker with machinery to make it work or improve the design, and he possessed a natural affinity for on-the-job innovation. He moved easily from making bicycles to fashioning automobile parts. In addition, he had an instinct for mass-producing goods as inexpensively as possible. By 1913, he had caught the attention of Henry Ford, whose assembly-line manufacturing system seemed the ideal occupation for Knudsen. At Ford he was placed in charge of steel stampings.

Knudsen was very much his own man and chafed under the yoke of Ford's dictatorial leadership. At the Ford Motor Company in the decade between 1910 and 1920, there was only room for one dominant personality and that was Henry Ford, the perfect example of Louis XIV's Sun King *l'état c'est moi* mentality.

Sloan remembered the beginning of the fruitful Knudsen partnership in the first introduction: "Mott [former head of the Weston-Mott Company] recognized in Bill [Knudsen] a man who could do things, and believed he had the making of a man who could still do bigger things. 'How much shall I pay you, Mr. Knudsen?' 'Anything you like. I am not here to set a figure. I seek an opportunity.'"[14]

Sloan hired Knudsen originally for a position at United Motors in the accessory division of General Motors. Later, Knudsen was also given the task of working with Charles Kettering and his Research Division in the ill-fated air-cooled engine manufacture. When the project ended, and by then Sloan was GM's president, Knudsen was chosen to be the general manager of Chevrolet. As Sloan's biographer wrote of this appointment: "Sloan understood that Knudsen could produce and he meant to give to give him every opportunity to make Chevrolet perform. If General Motors was to become what Sloan believed possible, the industrial leader, Chevrolet would have to succeed."[15]

With Knudsen at the helm, Chevrolet exploded in sales as consumers validated Sloan's low-price, better-made car strategy. The years of the close collaboration reveal the success of Sloan's decision and Knudsen's stewardship.

**Chevrolet Yearly Sales (M)**

| | |
|------|-------|
| 1925 | 481 |
| 1926 | 692 |
| 1927 | 940 |
| 1928 | 1,118 |
| 1929 | 1,259 |

From 1925 to 1929, Chevrolet unit sales increased by 778,000 cars (a 162 percent gain) in an unprecedented success. Further, Chevrolet's share of total GM vehicle production (including trucks) rose from 26 percent of the GM total in the year 1918 to 70 percent in 1929. When Sloan published *My Years with General Motors*, using 1962 as his last year for company sales data, Chevrolet sold a record 2,555,000 cars, which represented 60.5 percent of total GM vehicle U.S. sales that year.

It is impossible to think what would have happened to General Motors had Pierre du Pont cancelled Chevrolet as a brand during the 1920–1921 company restructuring. The Chevy model remains historically the most profitable of all of Sloan's many profitable decisions.

Another measure of the Chevrolet K car's success was to examine the market totals for Ford and General Motors from 1923 to 1929. Forced to retool for the Model A, and closing its factories for months, Ford's share of the market tumbled. By 1926, General Motors had become the number-one car company in the world. By 1929, Ford regained a slight lead, which it retained in a steadily declining depression-era market through 1930. Then in 1931 GM retook the top spot, which it maintained from that year onward. Importantly, by 1933, the emerging Chrysler Company (also with a variety of cars) surpassed Ford in total sales for the first time.

(In 2003, GM, still the largest auto company in the world, generated a 28.3 percent U.S. market share, with Ford at 20.8 and Chrysler at 14.1. A more important statistic is that the American Big Three car companies totaled 63.2 percent of the U.S. market—or almost 37 percent less than the near 100 percent these auto giants had achieved before the proliferation of foreign cars sales via imports like Volkswagen and Toyota and, later, foreign company manufacturing in the U.S. like that of Honda in Ohio and Toyota in Kentucky.)

Knudsen knew his own managerial strengths and weaknesses and never hesitated to ask Sloan about sales and marketing problems. Eventually, Knudsen became executive vice-president and then president of General Motors.

In 1940, FDR lured Knudsen to come to Washington to manage the industrial war complex, one of the many GM executives tabbed for wartime duty. Sloan was disheartened to lose GM's capable president and warned Knudsen that Roosevelt (whom Sloan disliked) would first use his talent and then discard him. This proved true in 1942 when Knudsen was dumped as the head of Office of Production Management.

The staffing success at Chevrolet allowed Sloan to select capable people for other General Motors' positions of leadership from that division. The Chevrolet experience was considered the best managerial training at the company. After Knudsen's success at Chevrolet, Sloan realized that future GM leaders would come from this one division: "I wanted to spread the benefits of its [Chevrolet] management to the corporation as a whole by placing Chevrolet men in strategic positions."[16]

## CHARLES E. WILSON

The last person to be cited in-depth in Sloan's approach to staffing with the best people is Charles E. Wilson whom Sloan handpicked to be GM's president, succeeding Knudsen in 1940. Later, after leaving GM, Wilson served with distinction as secretary of defense in President Eisenhower's cabinet.

Wilson is best known for the misinterpretation of one of his statements that provoked a national outcry. He said in his 1953 testimony at the Senate confirmation hearing for the Defense cabinet post, "I thought what was good for the country was good for General Motors—and vice versa." But this was shortened and twisted by the media to "What's good for General Motors is good for the country." There was more than some verisimilitude in this statement, but it was reduced by an outraged media and by GM's critics in and out of the automobile industry to a claim of arrogant boasting.

Wilson earned a degree in electrical engineering at the Carnegie Institute of Technology in 1909. In his early career, he worked at Westinghouse Electric, developing automobile electrical equipment.

In 1919, he became chief engineer and sales manager of the GM-owned subsidiary Remy Electric, which changed its name in 1926 to become the famous Delco-Remy, manufacturers of starter motors, generators, and alternators.

At Delco-Remy, he caught Sloan's attention as a bright and conscientious manager, and 10 years later in 1929, Sloan moved him into the vice presidency of manufacturing at the Chevrolet division. It represented a resourceful move by Sloan: If Wilson could perform as well in automobile manufacture as in electrical components, then he would have a successful career in the management of the larger, General Motor's entity. Soon Wilson was appointed to GM's policy committee, another essential step up the corporate ladder.

Of interest is that Sloan, Knudsen, and Wilson had all started out in a nonautomobile manufacturing subsidiary of General Motors before moving into automobile production. As stated earlier, Sloan had no automobile experience before assuming the GM presidency in 1921. Sloan was more interested in efficient management by decentralization than the ability to understand the mechanics of an automobile.

When Knudsen abdicated the GM presidency to take on the war production duties in 1940, GM's policy committee set up a triumvirate to handle operations with Wilson as the new COO of GM. Behind the scenes, Du Pont Company management was lukewarm about Wilson's promotion and insisted that, with war possibly on the horizon, Sloan stay on as CEO, which he did for six more years, giving up the position in 1946.

General Motors provided more materiel to the war effort than any other U.S. corporation. Wilson converted the efficiently organized GM operation to production of tanks and trucks and other equipment. He was awarded the U.S. Medal of Merit in 1946, as much an acknowledgment of his leadership as a mark of respect to the men and women of General Motors who had contributed to the defense production effort. Wilson's demanding wartime effort was recorded for history by Peter Drucker: "As the company's chief operating officer, he [Wilson] had been in charge of the conversion to defense production...For more than two years [he] had never taken a day off, and rarely spent even a night away from the office."[17]

After the war, Wilson experienced a different kind of labor climate from the one Sloan experienced two and a half decades earlier as president and CEO at GM. The United Auto Workers—with the influential and dynamic Walter Reuther at the helm—went out on a 119-day strike in 1945–1946 and demonstrated it had real teeth. It wanted to be considered a partner with the automobile companies. The UAW succeeded in gaining most of its negotiation goals, including fully paid hospitalization and sick leave benefits.

Wilson was also concerned with the plight of GM's employees and the status of mass-production workers in the United States. In Peter Drucker, he found an ally: "We have to make the manual worker as effective as a citizen as he has become a producer. Let's find out what that means."[18]

Wilson set out to find out through an ingenious questioning of GM employees in a company contest titled, "My Job and Why I Like It." The company's workers wrote an astounding 200,000 essays. The results indicated that a satisfied workforce wanted more than merely salary; it wanted a feeling of job satisfaction. The employees needed to take satisfaction in the work they did. But the most intriguing finding was that pride at working at GM and pride in membership in the UAW were jointly independent.

Drucker questioned Wilson about GM's ongoing problem with unions. Wilson had a different perspective but he could have been speaking in Sloan's pragmatic voice: "The test of labor relations isn't rhetoric. The test is results."[19]

It was to Wilson that Sloan delegated the responsibility of determining a formula for payment increases to line workers at General Motors. This marked the beginning of the "annual improvement factor" at GM, which set the amount of fixed increase for these workers and was quite revolutionary in concept at the time.

In sum, Charles Wilson bridged the gap between the Sloan-Knudsen pre–World War II management style and the more modern approach that occurred after the war. He studied more deeply employee concerns than either of his predecessors, including profit sharing and the sound investment of employee pensions in the stock market. In this last effort, Wilson and GM had started to turn (in Peter Drucker's terms) "America's employees into America's capitalists."[20]

## THE STAFFING GENIUS WILLIAM BERNBACH

The conversion of the automobile industry brought about by Alfred Sloan's revolution in organization and management witnessed a similar transformation in the advertising industry through the genius of William Bernbach. In 1998, Bernbach was voted the most influential person in *Advertising Age*'s honor roll of twentieth century advertising executives.

Historically, most of advertising before Bernbach was a dull, mundane format of boring, talking heads. In the early days, to make ads memorable, ad agencies often utilized odd techniques, such as floating a man into a convertible car in the 1961 Hertz Rental Car commercial or the creation in 1953 of Alka Seltzer's animated Speedy character with his tablet body, tablet hat, and "effervescent" wand.

Bernbach was convinced the consumer was more intelligent and could fill in mentally and pictorially the understated message of an advertising campaign. He founded the Doyle, Dane, Bernbach (DDB) agency in 1949 with Maxwell Dane and Ned Doyle.

The classic DDB ad is the single-photograph soft sell of the Volkswagen Beetle, sitting under the provocative headline, "Think Small." (This 1959 ad was voted number one in *Advertising Age*'s best campaigns of the twentieth century.) Other memorable DDB advertising campaigns appeared for Polaroid with Lawrence Oliver and Louis Armstrong, the accommodating gorilla tester for American Tourister luggage, Jack Gilford's Cracker Jack "sharing" commercial, and "Mikey likes it!" for Life Cereal.

Bernbach proved that frank, clever, and evocative advertising could work and demonstrated this with the Avis "We Try Harder" campaign that increased the car rental's market share to 35 percent in 1966, up from only 11 percent in 1962. Bernbach and his DDB staff had spent three months with Avis personnel and recommended that the company revamp its emphasis on customer service.

From the outset, DDB set out to find art directors and copywriters who shared Bernbach's passion for advertising and who were willing to learn his creative style. The format was the single, uncluttered photograph, to direct the viewer's eye to the product or message.

The ad agency's quirky but effective ad and copy appealed to talented renegades who were willing to follow the creative founder's lead. From the day its doors opened, DDB attracted a staff of copywriting and art direction talent. The agency welcomed Helmut Krone, George Lois, Bob Gage, Phyllis Robinson, Mary Wells, Roy Grace, Julian Koenig, Marvin Hoeing, Bob Levinson, Ron Rosenfeld, Paula Green, and many others in an all-star lineup.

Many of these creative people would learn the Bernbach format and start their own agencies, further expanding the idiosyncratic distinctive DDB style. (e.g.; Wells, Rich and Green; Papert, Koenig and Lois; Rosenfeld, Sirowitz and Lawson).

As a manager, Bernbach projected a soft-spoken image and never revealed any emotion. He established himself as a creative guru to whom the creative staff brought their work, hoping for praise. He developed a sort of "A team" of the most talented and was constantly stroking these egos. The goal was to be called one of "Bill's boys" (females also).

Bernbach's attention was always on the advertising and whether or not it was on target. He would say, "It's good. It's very good but it's not out of the ballpark," and the creative team would go back until they found a better ad. Or he might ask for the cutting of an extra word or a line. His credo was, "It's always a mistake to make good advertising for a bad product."

Bernbach's charge was always to find the unique selling point that would have consequence to the consumer. On many occasions, it could be found when the creative and the account staffs spent time with the client to learn the business. One of the most memorable of these instances is when DDB art director Bert Steinhauser discovered by accident the Heinz ketchup viscosity test at the company's plant in Pittsburgh. This lead to the "slow" ketchup campaign that continued for many years and vaulted Heinz ahead of Hunt and Del Monte ketchups in market share. Today, essentially, thanks to DDB's visit to the client, Heinz is synonymous with ketchup, and no good restaurant sets out another brand.

## RESTAFFING AT FORD

### GM PEOPLE
When Henry Ford II assumed the leadership at Ford Motor Company in 1945, he realized the enormous task that lay before him. The war

years had generated company losses of almost $10 million monthly. His famous grandfather was ailing. There was also talk that if Ford Motors continued to decline, the federal government might have to bail out the company with millions of dollars in loans.

Henry Ford II (whom the media referred to as "Henry, the Deuce") recognized the problem at the company immediately: It needed a drastic overhaul of manufacturing policy and it needed new leadership. He had read Peter Drucker's seminal work *Concept of the Corporation* that described in detail how General Motors operated. (Drucker patted himself on the back when he said that the book became Ford's "official text."[21]) Henry Ford II was also keen on hiring executives in the GM managerial mold.

Ford II's first smart staffing appointment was to lure Ernest Breech who was chairman of GM's Bendix Aviation. At one time, he had been GM's assistant general treasurer and had later moved to the company's household division. He was considered primarily a financial expert but had demonstrated (at least to Sloan) highly capable managerial abilities. In performing so well in all his General Motors' assignments, he attracted the attention of Henry Ford II. He introduced General Motors' management and financial techniques into the new modern Ford organization.[22]

Henry Ford II was also aided by Alfred P. Sloan, Jr.'s behind-the-scenes encouragement to GM executives to take top jobs at Ford. Sloan also opened a back channel to Ford CEO Ernest Breech, naming for him the hidden talent at GM who might aid the Ford Motor Company in its recovery. This marked the second time that Sloan had aided a competitor, the first time being when he encouraged Walter Chrysler to start his own car company. Hiring from the competitor marked Ford's first major step to restaff the company with capable managers.

## THE WHIZ KIDS

In 1949, Henry Ford II embarked on a long-term plan to compete aggressively with General Motors; he hired 10 men from the Army Air Force's statistical group to work as a new team at Ford. They would be in charge of imposing order on the corporation and, importantly, finding innovations that would return the moribund company to its successful beginnings.

The 10 were called "whiz kids," and there is no example in history of such a numerous group hired to become collectively the new, effective leadership of a company. In effect, like a baseball team that suffered losses season after season, Henry Ford II traded or fired all the team's starting players and restocked the lineup with 10 new players, all untried but bubbling with enthusiasm and confidence.

The group was lead by Tex Thornton, who would go on to fame and failure at Litton Industries, Arjay Miller, a Ford president who would serve with distinction as Dean of the Stanford University Business School, and the most famous, Robert McNamara, who would become president of Ford Motor Company and later serve as secretary of defense to presidents John F. Kennedy and Lyndon Johnson.

The whiz kids' theory was that by crunching numbers they could find significant ways to cut costs and increase profits. The team's major success was the design and manufacture of the 1949 Ford, which went from design to production in only 19 months. The new successful model helped reestablish Ford as a competitor in the U.S. markets.

Eventually, through the efforts of the whiz kids (and not all their innovations were successful, including the ill-fated Edsel and the Mercury Turnpike Cruiser of 1957), Ford Motor Company rose to become the fourth largest corporation in the world. All credit for the turnaround goes to Henry Ford II, who realized what his grandfather did not, that managers were vitally needed in the new decentralized-centralized corporate structure pioneered by Alfred P. Sloan, Jr.

Henry Ford II made an additional brilliant staffing decision, appointing Lee Iacocca as Ford's general manager. Iacocca would design the new Mustang to sell in volume. Introduced in 1965, the sporty model sold an amazing 22,000 cars its first day and generated a million sales in its first two years. Iacocca's spectacular success did not prevent Henry Ford II from firing him as Ford's president in 1978, a dictatorial action more similar to his despotic grandfather than to the performance-based and even-handed leadership of Alfred P. Sloan, Jr.

## THE LESSONS OF CORRECT STAFFING

The earlier quote from Sloan bears repeating: "If we don't spend four hours on placing a man and placing him right, we'd spend four hundred hours on cleaning up after our mistake." It serves as the key to making good staffing decisions. Admittedly, filling a top position quickly is important, but adding more time and a larger pool of candidates also helps the staffing process.

Also of note is General Motors' 30-day rule, an interesting yardstick to ensure that the new hire is on the path toward a long career at the company.

## PROMOTE FROM WITHIN
Another good rule to follow is Sloan's promoting executives from within the company, finding the talent somewhere in GM's many divisions. If a company is large enough, it may also have a division like Chevrolet, which for reasons of volume and production, serves as the proving ground for the most capable executives.

The famous Carnegie Deli in New York City claims that one reason for its success is the standing decree that all promotions come from within the existing staff. Sandy Levine, the general manager for the past 12 years, has remarked often at business conferences that only current employees are familiar with the deli's unique "system." Proof of this good-working policy is that the average employee at the Carnegie Deli has worked there for 20 years and the turnover at the restaurant is practically zero.

## ELIMINATE INTERVIEWS IN LINE POSITIONS
One of the newest concepts in staffing for line positions is to eliminate the preliminary interview process by establishing an electronic application system. In essence, the system sets up a checklist that potential employees use to answer a set of questions for specific jobs.

The hospitality industry is starting to use on-site kiosks with employment computer stations. These allow candidates to look through the list of jobs available on a touch screen and then answer questions pertaining to past work experience and training. If the person has answered the questions satisfactorily, an interview appointment is made on the screen designating a time and place.

In companies with high turnover of line personnel, these new systems (soon to be online, also) cut down the internal time for human resources to find and interview prospective employees.

## BEYOND SKILL SETS FOR MANAGERS

To find the best candidates for executive positions, placement firms are starting to add "humanness" to their search and screening processes to find those persons who fit the specific corporate culture. Joie Smith of The Touchstone Partnership in Pennsylvania states, "Before I begin a managerial search, I spend time inside the company to assess the culture. It's an important step because anyone can find matching skill sets to the position, but I want to find that goodness of fit that matches the right person to the right culture." Even at the résumé stage, Smith studies the information, looking for indications that the candidate's background will also reveal signs of fit.

One of the many advantages to the "humanness" technique is that it reduces the number of candidates the placement firm introduces to the client. This also represents a savings to the client since it has to spend less time on final interviews.

## LEADERSHIP STYLES

Sloan's goal was to bring about managerial professionalism, to elevate corporate executives to the same high status of other trained professionals. He sought other like-minded experts (Donaldson Brown and John Raskob) who shared his commitment to a systematic and pragmatic approach in the running of a corporation.

Since those early days of Sloan's start at General Motors, the question of what kind of person makes the most effective business leader has been the subject of psychological and sociological studies. Each year, new books plumb the historical past to reveal the elements of the leadership genius of Marcus Aurelius, Napoleon, Robert E. Lee, etc. And many books detail the effective styles of the current crop of leaders (e.g., Jack Welch of GE).

Cogent leadership assessments all essentially break leaders into four groupings:

*Thinkers* Manage by assessing facts, data, and examining the past

*Intuitive leaders* Look at the big picture; are creative; conceptualize

*Feelers* Process information in accordance with its effect on
people

*Censors* Concerned with the here and now, quick solutions to
problems

The consensus is that the best managers combine the attributes of the thinker and censor. And these are the two main qualities of Alfred P. Sloan, Jr. In staffing, his one and only criteria was to find people like himself who performed.

CHAPTER

7

# COMPLEMENTARY AND ANCILLARY BUSINESSES

*W*hy new or ancillary business?...Sloan assesses GM's product line...GM's early acquisitions under William Durant...Sloan purchases other companies...GMAC, the financing gap that GM filled and not the banks...GM finds breakthrough in diesel locomotives...Sloan makes Frigidaire the market leader in home refrigeration...GM's brief flirtation with the aviation business...Gerber's surprisingly successful ancillary business...Kirk Kerkorian adapts MGM to new ventures...The managerial lessons of starting or acquiring ancillary or complementary businesses

ॐ ॐ

The attraction of expansion by merger or acquisition is similar to taking over an existing family unit instead of incurring the difficulties of beginning a new one. The ready-made business seems ripe for change and improvement. But the essential questions are whether to find a familiar business, look at opportunities outside the main company activity, or do nothing and concentrate on the business at hand.

The prospect is always tempting to try to increase corporate revenues by acquiring another company or purchasing an ongoing concern that may be similar to the main business. On some occasions, acquisitions have been in related or complementary industries that fit into the central or "core" business of the enterprise. But sometimes purchases are in unrelated industries that have no commercial association and are completely different from the core business.

In the past 20 years, the United States has been the setting for many multibillion-dollar mergers, the success of which is still unknown. What will be the outcome of the $2.4 billion Kinko acquisition by FedEx in 2004? How successful was the Chase and JP Morgan financial merger? Was it smart for the Disney Company to acquire the ABC television network? Was it a good business fit and also a good investment for Daimler-Benz to take over the Chrysler Corporation?

For every successful Pepsi-Frito Lay merger that elicits applause from Wall Street, there is a Time Warner and America Online financial catastrophe. Although, in truth, the investing community originally praised Time Warner for its daring vision of a communications future with AOL acting as the leading profit center tap the potential riches of the Internet. Recent history demonstrates successes and failures of companies in their efforts to merge or acquire other businesses.

What is the right approach for a manager to take toward ancillary or complementary business acquisitions? Perhaps part of the answer—a cautionary one—lies in Alfred P. Sloan, Jr.'s history at General Motors.

## SLOAN'S PHILOSOPHY

The facts are straightforward: During Alfred P. Sloan, Jr.'s tenure as president and CEO of General Motors he *did not* purchase another domestic company *outside* the fields of automotive, aviation, appliance, and locomotives until 1953, when he purchased the Euclid Road Machinery Company. The company's main acquisitions were automotive and overseas: Opel in Germany, Vauxhall in Great Britain, and Holden in Australia.

When it came to acquiring ancillary businesses, Sloan expressed the General Motors' response: "We have never made anything except 'durable products' and they have always, with minor exceptions, been connected with motors."[1]

Within the broad definition of "durable products," General Motors embarked upon successful ventures in nonautomobile industries without veering too far off the automobile component. The key example is the Frigidaire Company, which seemed an unlikely business to be operated profitably by this automotive giant. This appliance company was in place when Sloan became president in 1921. (General Motors spun off Frigidaire to White Industries in 1979, when GM decided not to remain active in the appliance business.)

Certainly, part of the reasons for Sloan's disinterest in mergers and acquisitions must remain the overwhelming task of running five distinct car divisions, a truck division, overseas operations, plus finance, research, and insurance companies.

As General Motors increased sales and profits annually and its size and stature grew, Sloan and his board were always looking over their shoulders at possible federal antitrust action against them as one of the largest corporations in the world.

Sloan's rationale for continuing in the ancillary businesses—diesel electric locomotives, appliances, and aviation—was twofold: GM already operated these diverse companies, and these other industries were in their infancy, making new products with new technology yet untested in the marketplace. The technology offered GM an opportunity for profit and expansion despite the fact that these ancillary businesses were not in the GM core business. In essence, Sloan perceived GM had as much opportunity to succeed in the new technology as any other U.S. company.

(An ironic sidebar of the decision for GM to pursue aviation companies was the naive belief in the 1920s that a small, family-owned airplane would become a serious consumer transportation challenge to the automobile industry. The thought was that Americans would become a one-car, one-plane-in-the-same-garage family!)

In the final analysis, Sloan was wary of going outside of the core business to look for any other type of mergers. He wrote, "There have always been limits to our product diversification."[2]

## GENERAL MOTORS EARLY BUSINESSES

William Durant can be considered one of the fathers of vertical integration in the history of the U.S. corporate world. It was his foresight that brought diverse accessory and component companies into the GM fold through outright purchase. He had the insight to realize that automotive companies would require the unique skills of other manufacturing disciplines outside general automotive manufacturing work. Acquisition represented the most efficient and expeditious method to bring these other skills to the company.

It is important to recall that Durant, who had first collaborated with David Buick in 1903 to build a horseless carriage, was one of the first executives to imagine unlimited opportunity in the then-fledgling automobile industry. In 1908, U.S. car sales totaled a mere 65,000, selling into a restricted market consisting of mostly wealthy people who enjoyed taking the flivver out for a day's drive. Buick was the number-one U.S. brand, selling 8,487 cars compared to 6,181 Fords.

Sloan praised Durant's exceptional and unique vision for those early years when he wrote: "Mr. Durant looked forward to a one-million car year to come—for which he was regarded as a promoter of wildcat ideas."[3]

By 1914, a scant six years, the industry manufactured about 500,000 automobiles of which GM (Buick, Cadillac, Oldsmobile, and Oakland [Pontiac]) produced 146,000 cars or 29 percent of the market. Buick's 90,925 cars represented 62 percent of total GM production.

Between 1908 and 1910, Durant acquired 25 companies for GM; 11 automobile, 2 electrolamp manufacturers, and 12 accessory and auto part producers. This was the beginning of the future of GM's vertical integration and multibranding strategy of a variety of cars for a variety of tastes. In 1908, a Buick prospectus alluded to the economies of "integrated production," referring to the company's tactical geographical placement in an array of Detroit-area manufacturing plants that made axles, springs, castings, etc., all conveniently located near the Buick plant for on-time deliveries.

(Nomenclature trivia: French explorer Antoine Cadillac named the land west of Lake St. Clair *le detroit* [the strait] which, when the French pronunciation was Americanized, became the name of the Motor City.)

## REASONS FOR DURANT'S DIVERSIFICATION

William Durant's consistent pattern of purchasing companies was rooted less in his grand concept for an integrated General Motors than an uncertainty as to what the future would bring for the automotive industry. Those earlier car-making years in the United States represented a true maverick mentality when every tinkerer in America experimented with producing a different kind of horseless carriage. For each individual person's name recognizable today—Buick, Olds, Nash, Chrysler, Ford, Dodge—there are many hundreds of old make and models names lost to automotive history.

There was the firm belief that the sudden and dramatic success of the gasoline-powered automobile could be supplanted quickly by some new technology that would render some manufacturing methods of the automotive industry obsolete. Until the 1930s, the Big Three were always looking over their shoulders with apprehension at potential technological breakthroughs, which would alter an important aspect of engine size or chassis design.

Every turn-of-the-century manufacturer was experimenting with different makes of self-starter motors, beam headlights, two- and four-wheel axles, brake systems, gear transmissions, and the like. No one in Detroit knew whose invention or improvement would prove to be the most efficient, the least costly, and the most profitable. For Durant the gamble would be narrowed by having an extensive group of different companies with different technologies on hand and owned by GM.

Sloan pinpointed Durant's reasoning for the expansion at GM: "The second pattern was diversification, calculated it seems, to cover the many possibilities of the engineering future of the automobile, in search of a high average result instead of an all-or-none proposition."[4]

The second reason Sloan identified for Durant deliberately building up an array of ancillary manufacturers was to increase integration. A motor car comprised many different parts, an "anatomy" as Sloan characterized it. Durant needed to "dress up" the various parts of the car. Early in his GM stewardship came:

Northway Motor and Manufacturing—motors
Champion Ignition—spark plugs

Jackson-Church-Wilcox—parts
Weston-Mott—wheels and axles
McLaughlin Motor Car—carriage maker

Durant first found and then invested in Champion Ignition by seeding the start-up money to race car driver Albert Champion. The company became, eventually, the manufacturer of the nationally known and profitable AC-Delco Spark Plugs.

After he had been ousted for the first time from the presidency of General Motors in 1910, Durant bought, with his own money, a small car company that he named Chevrolet after the race car driver Louis Chevrolet. Durant built a nationwide Chevrolet organization in just four years, making a low-priced, light car with great consumer appeal. He used personal stock in the profitable Chevrolet company to regain a majority hold on General Motors' stock, this time with the financial assistance of Pierre du Pont and the Du Pont Company. Then in 1918, Durant brought Chevrolet into the GM group. By 1919, it was the highest-selling GM-made car and has held that rank ever since.

(The 75th anniversary issue of *The Chevrolet Story* in 1986 offered two descriptions of the origin of the familiar Chevrolet bowtie logo. William Durant maintained that he spotted some similar design on a wallpaper inside a Paris Hotel in 1913. Later, his wife asserted that Durant saw a comparable shaped company logo in an advertisement inside a Virginia newspaper. To support her account, a historian researched old, southern newspapers, finding a Georgia coal company that printed its name in the familiar bowtie logo shape.)

In 1916, when Durant was again in control of General Motors, he continued the pursuit of integration by purchasing additional companies. This second term of Durant's presidency witnessed some of his most inspired achievements. He acquired:

Hyatt Roller Bearing—ball bearings
Samson Sieve Grip Tractor—tractors
Guardian Frigerator—refrigerators
New Departure Manufacturing—ball bearings
Remy Electric—electrical equipment
Dayton Engineering Laboratories (DELCO)—electrical systems

In 1919, while Durant was still president, he began a formal association with the talented Fisher brothers, who were renowned for the workmanship of automotive bodies. GM purchased 60 percent of Fisher manufacturing, and it would later acquire 100 percent of the company. The Body by Fisher description would become an important part of GM's advertising campaign in the introduction of the annual model.

As history would show, Durant's many purchases provided General Motors with diverse technical know-how in the 1910–1920 period, a formative decade in automotive manufacturing. More important than the products or companies he acquired were the executives who came into GM through these acquisitions. These men would make available their formidable managerial skills and engineering talent to take the company into world dominance. The list of names reads like a who's who of American automotive all stars: Chrysler, Kettering, Fisher, Nash, and Sloan. Least remembered is that William C. Durant was solely responsible for their entrance into General Motors.

## SLOAN'S FIRST GM ACQUISITIONS

After Alfred Sloan was made president and CEO of United Motors in 1916, he embarked upon his first search for accessory and component companies. The first purchases were Harrison Radiator and Klaxon, the manufacturer of car horns.

(Electric horns for automobiles appeared in 1908 at Lowell-McConnell Manufacturing. The head of that company named the horn Klaxon from the Greek verb *klaxo:* to shriek. So popular was this uniquely sounding product that within a few years at dangerous U.S. roadside curves and hazards, signs warned the motorist to "Sound your Klaxon.")

Equally important, Sloan started the United Motors Service company, a new entity, and one of the first automotive companies to offer postsale parts and service. The organization established stations in 20 cities with additional dealers in smaller areas of the country. This company was the forerunner of General Motors' Mr. Goodwrench postsale service.

By the time Sloan took over the GM presidency in 1921, the ancillary companies were in place for the efficient supplying of parts to the lineup of the five automobile divisions. He would first concentrate on the core "durable products," the cars and trucks, before he turned to increasing sales of GM's other already-acquired businesses in refrigeration, aviation, and diesel locomotives.

## THE GMAC HISTORY AT GENERAL MOTORS

One significant GM ancillary business development remained for Sloan to expand upon and improve, Jacob Raskob's 1919 groundbreaking General Motors Acceptance Corporation (GMAC). This wholly owned finance division elicited one of Sloan's infrequent introspections when he wrote: "A stranger to the history of the automobile business might wonder how it happens that General Motors owns one of the most important financial institutions in the United States, through which the corporation is engaged in consumer financing."[5]

For General Motors, through spectacular years with dominance of market share and also through leaner years with dwindling sales and influence, its GMAC division always generated significant profits, providing one of the highest returns on investment within the entire corporation. For many years GMAC revenues represented between 16 and 18 percent of the nation's annual total vehicle financing.

Sloan captured the reason why this uncommon opportunity arose at General Motors:

Mass production brought with it the need for a broad approach to consumer financing, which the banks did not then take kindly to. They neglected...to meet the need.[6]

Before GMAC, the American consumer could buy on a time-payment plan items like furniture, sewing machines (the Singer model), and, of course, housing mortgages. In 1915, the first automobiles offered on the installment plan came from the Willys-Overland Company. Sloan agreed to become a director of the Guaranty Securities Company, the financial agent of the Willys cars out of his friendship with John Willys.

The consumer in the 1920s could also take advantage of borrowing from what were known as Morris Banks, the first kind of financial institutions created expressly to offer loans to poorer citizens. The Morris Banks did not require collateral but did need two cosigners. For a while, these were the sole lenders of credit to America's lower-income classes. These banks disappeared after commercial banks started to offer consumer loans in the mid-1920s.

## SLOAN REVITALIZES GMAC

In 1919 GMAC filled the vacuum of credit financing created by the nation's banks, which did not foresee a profitable market in financing automobiles. One of many reasons for the banks' lack of interest was the fluctuating national economy with its boom or bust years. Banks feared—rightly, so—that in economic downturns the number of potential car defaults could be considerable. The banking community was not interested in becoming a vast network of used car dealerships.

Sloan took an atypical backhanded jab at the staid banking system, which he and other industrialists perceived remained overly reactionary and locked into a puritanical view of never loaning money for "pleasure."

> They [the banks] believed that the extension of consumer credit to the average man was too great a risk. . .believing apparently that whatever fostered consumption must discourage thrift.[7]

Raskob realized that GM had to assist its vast dealer network with some kind of credit financing. In essence, it was the thrust of his genius that an automobile manufacturer could also become a lending institution. GMAC succeeded because in 1919 there existed no federal law on the books prohibiting this unique kind of corporate credit financing and because the banking industry perceived that GMAC would not become a significant player in the issuing of credit.

The automobile dealer network had traditionally sold cars only for cash. This system prospered when car ownership remained primarily a rich person's market but, thanks to Henry Ford's Model-T produced for the masses, many more average-income citizens began to purchase cars. After World War I, when the nation experienced a short-term financial boom, dealers had to reexamine how to stock up on inventories and also extend credit. The question was how to finance this burgeoning segment of first-time car buyers.

General Motors could not prosper unless it moved the volume of cars manufactured annually to the dealerships and through to the consumer. The answer proved to be GMAC with its initial down payment followed by credit financing at reasonable rates through the GM dealerships.

Working with Raskob, Sloan needed to reorganize the lending apparatus: "In the beginning, we had two primary motives, to establish the validity of the system (GMAC), and to crusade for reasonable rates for the customer."[8]

In characteristic Sloan managerial style, he relied on a factual study of credit, a GM-commissioned analysis published in 1927 by Professor E. R. A. Seligman head of the Economics Department at Columbia University. The seminal, two-volume work, *The Economics of Installment Selling,* altered forever how debt in the United States was calculated. Seligman employed different terminology to transform the negative connotation of debt and credit ("consumptive") to more positive acceptance ("productive debt" and "productive credit").

The study generated more open-mindedness for installment buying. Sloan paraphrased the crux of the work: "It [debt] not only advances the time of demand but by interaction with the economy actually increases purchasing power."[9]

For GM, increased purchasing power through GMAC represented an additional, positive step for the company. It also offered another benefit to the consumer, which the competition, in this case, every other American car manufacturer, did not also extend. For many buyers, the only option was a General Motors car because of the availability of financing.

Even later in the 1950s, when GM was threatened with government intervention, the company held to the firm stance that its GMAC financing division did not prohibit the consumer from seeking credit elsewhere from banks or other lending institutions. The government's restraint of trade issues faded away, and GMAC continued to finance new-car purchases. Sloan clearly saw the mutual benefit: "The advantages GMAC offers to General Motors is a sympathetic relationship, equitable to the consumer."[10]

The historic GMAC statistics are staggering: Since 1919, in 41 nations, it has extended $1.3 trillion in credit financing to the purchase of approximately 160 million vehicles. Its earning power has been the envy of global financial institutions. By 1985 the division had earned its first $1 billion, and by 2003 it had topped over $2.8 billion in earnings.

Today, it is a bona fide financial entity with mortgage lending and other financial services like relocation, insurance, and even a GMAC Bank.

## SLOAN TACKLES OTHER ANCILLARY BUSINESSES

By the late 1920s, Sloan could begin to concentrate on the nonautomotive aspects of General Motors in the areas of diesel locomotives, household appliances, and aviation. All of these businesses, which William Durant had originally purchased, rested outside of the car and truck divisions. For Sloan, these assorted companies represented a conundrum and a challenge: "We had, of course, some natural interest in diversification, which might afford us a hedge against any decline in automobile sales."[11]

Sloan recognized that the three nonautomotive divisions succeeded because the staffs, especially research personnel within the companies, were convinced of the sales potential of the new knowhow. These companies were involved in new techniques that heralded different technologies that would be markedly different from existing competition.

Sloan was agreeable to gambling on the future with the new. He was also confident that the decentralized organization system he had put into place at GM for cars and trucks could work successfully in other nonauto businesses. In essence, the first test laboratories for his revolutionary corporate system became the GM ancillary companies under his aegis.

## DIESEL LOCOMOTIVES

In the 1930s, railroads in the United States meant only one type of engine: steam. Yet, within 10 years, diesel was the dominant type of locomotive, and to the shock of the American railroad community, the leading diesel manufacturer was the General Motors Corporation.

The switch from steam to diesel resulted in significant dollar savings to the railroad industry. Sloan gave two reasons for GM's ascendancy to the leadership position: "The first was simply that we were more tenacious in our efforts to produce lightweight, high-speed diesel engines. . . . The second reason was that we brought to the locomotive industry some of manufacturing, engineering and marketing concepts of the automobile industry."[12]

Steam had been the power source of choice for the American railroad system since 1827 when John Stevens had demonstrated its capabilities in Hoboken, New Jersey. In 1830, Peter Cooper manufactured the first American-built steam locomotive, the famous Tom Thumb engine. Diesels ultimately overtook steam because of the latter's expensive raw materials and also the expensive labor-intensive maintenance costs.

General Motors, not locked into any romantic steam railroad manufacturing past, proceeded to treat locomotives in the same manner as car design and new technology. Again, it was research genius Charles Kettering who spearheaded the drive for diesel technology. Sloan made available a capitalized program that provided research space, personnel, investment, and, most importantly, Sloan's confident backing.

In 1929, after Kettering had succeeded with some new diesel concepts, GM purchased two companies: Winston Engine and Electro-Motive Engineering both in Cleveland, which provided diesel-making facilities. The new acquisitions also provided Sloan with some backup technology in gas-electric car manufacturing, a possible hedge against the uncertainty of the decline in the 1929 automobile market. In effect, Sloan was doing what Durant had done years before, finding new companies with new technologies and keeping them on the GM back burner—just in case.

For years, Kettering's new diesel model represented an experimental concept without commercial sales. However, U.S. railroad companies were looking for drastic solutions to the upwardly spiraling material and labor costs of steam locomotive operation. GM's two-cycle engine caught the attention of Ralph Budd, president of the Burlington railroad line who investigated the prototype engine at the 1933 Chicago Century of Progress Exposition where the engine powered the Chevrolet assembly plant exhibit.

After another year of improvements, in 1934 the GM diesel engine, housed in a streamlined locomotive that Ralph Budd named the *Zephyr*, raced along the tracks in the now legendary "dawn-to-dusk" Denver to Chicago run. The elegantly styled *Zephyr* traveled the 1,015 miles in an astounding 13 hours, 5 minutes, averaging 76.6 miles per hour and breaking the world's long-distance railroad record.

The engine's success prompted Kettering to request additional funds for experimentation with a diesel-powered locomotive. The following dialogue reveals the confidence that both Kettering and Sloan had found for their research projects:

> I inquired how much money he would need.
> Mr. Kettering said he thought it might take as much as $500,000.
> I told him that...he could not give us a locomotive on such a comparatively modest sum.
> "I know," he replied amiably, "but I figure if we spend that much, you'll come up with the rest."
> He got his money.[13]

By the time Sloan published his second autobiography in 1963, GM's Electro-Motive Division had sold over 25,000 diesel locomotives throughout the world.

## FRIGIDAIRE

The development and successful sales of the Frigidaire appliances is another part of the managerial brilliance of Alfred P. Sloan, Jr. It also demonstrates his calculated gamble on research to provide answers to product problems that had previously hindered significant consumer sales.

Durant had purchased the Guardian Frigerator Company with his own money in 1918, despite the fact that between 1916 and 1918, the company sold a paltry 34 units. He renamed the company Frigidaire to emphasize its main benefit as an iceless refrigerator.

Sloan explained what he had been told about the GM's president's reason for this unusual purchase: "Durant was concerned about the prospect of the automobile business being declared unessential to our World War I mobilization effort, and he was looking for an 'essential' business."[14]

GM's initial efforts to mass produce the original model proved unsuccessful; the Frigidaire appliance was perceived as a luxury item and generated disappointing sales. The company absorbed significant losses, totaling about $2.5 million in 1921.

Internally, there was an increasing move to get rid of the unprofitable appliance company whose product and sales methods were so different from the crux of GM's business. But fortuitous external events prevailed; the two separate Domestic Engineering and Dayton Metal Products acquisitions (later, forming DELCO) had been working on refrigeration technology in 1918, ironically also, as a hedge business to the end of the World War I and its armament sales. This new refrigeration technology was targeted for some use in the appliance business.

Sloan studied the Frigidaire problem and sensed that it might be given one last chance with a new input from the research and marketing teams acquired to form DELCO. Initially, Sloan made another savvy decision by moving the Frigidaire manufacturing to Dayton where it was removed from the Detroit potentially meddlesome automotive community.

Sloan's charge was to mass-produce—to standardize an improved model, anticipating that as volume increased, the retail price would decline to allow average-income families to purchase the refrigerator. But first came the successful research: "We realized that the whole future of Frigidaire depended on our ability to crack several research problems, and to produce a machine that would operate safely, economically, and dependably."[15]

After incurring a few more years of losses, by 1924, Frigidaire generated a small profit. The increase in annual production demonstrated the success of the new sales and research teams, with the number of units climbing from 2,100 in 1922 to 63,500 by 1925. The researchers in Dayton had solved most of the design, safety, and cold-making problems that had dogged other refrigerator manufacturers.

The public responded with enthusiasm for the redesigned and more efficient refrigerator with the catchy name. By 1927, stylistically, the Frigidaire went from a clunky wood cabinet, oversized brine tank, and water-cooled compressor to an attractive porcelain cabinet with asphalt, cork sealing, and an air-cooled, two-cylinder compressor. From 1922's 834-pound monster retailing at $714, GM's research staff dropped the weight to 362 pounds and the price to $468. Sloan crowed a little when he wrote: "During the 1916–1928 period no other manufacturer or organization made any appreciable contribution to the refrigeration business."[16]

It was true; the other refrigerator companies did not have either the research objective or the financial backing of a corporation as successful as General Motors.

The early history of Frigidaire had one more prominent story to tell: Fumes from all makes of refrigerators caused serious home health hazards. Someone had to discover a new chemical method to eliminate these risks. Sloan and Kettering outlined five primary and secondary points that had to be met before GM would consider a new chemical for home use.

By 1929, after experimenting on fluorinated hydrocarbons, the chemists at Frigidaire concluded that a safe compound named Freon-12 met all of the Sloan-Kettering refrigerant points. The new technology removed the last safety obstacle to a home refrigerator. In characteristic altruism, Sloan insisted that the Freon-12 formula be offered to all of GM's competitors so that every American home would be safe with refrigerators manufactured by all American companies.

Frigidaire went on to produce the first room air-conditioner and food freezer. By 1956, it had sold its twentieth million product, and nine years later in 1965 it sold its fiftieth million.

But by 1979, even after Frigidaire product line expansions during the 1940s and 1950s to washers, dryers, ovens, etc., other competitors like Westinghouse, Kelvinator, Amana, and, particularly General Electric, had seized control of the consumer appliance market. These appliances represented their core businesses, and General Motors did not want to spend the money to compete, deciding that year to sell the Frigidaire name and product line to White Consolidated Industries.

Over the years, and after many hundreds of thousands of refrigerators, it was Frigidaire that gave its name to the often-used American abbreviation—the fridge.

## BENDIX AVIATION

Aviation was the final part of the General Motors nonautomotive ancillary businesses. Although the association was for a brief time—and without the noticeable, public commercial successes like the diesel locomotive or Frigidaire—it represents a short but intriguing GM chapter. Even Sloan considered the relationship of extraordinary interest: "It will, I suspect, come as a surprise to many readers that General Motors long ago made a major effort to enter the commercial aviation field."[17]

The surprise to his readers in 1963 was that some of the most famous names in international aviation history could trace their beginnings to some association with General Motors. These numbered: Bendix Aviation, North American Aviation, Trans World Airlines, and Eastern Airlines.

The company's initial forays into the aviation business came in 1929 with investments into Bendix Aviation (29 percent) and also the Fokker Aircraft Corporation (40 percent). The reason, as stated before, was to protect GM against sudden competition from the development of a "flivver" plane, a concept that sounds ridiculous today: a light, small airplane for everyday use. It is important to recall that in 1929 there was no massive national highway system crisscrossing the continental United States. In addition, there was plenty of empty land outside all cities that could accommodate small airports. For example, as late as 1990, a person could fly into a major metropolis like Kansas City and land in a rural area, not in crowded suburban housing sprawl.

General Motors consolidated its divergent holdings into one company called North American Aviation. Its main and significant contribution was to set up a systematic production and financial system similar to its automobile operation. The new company secured some important military orders and manufactured planes and engines during World War II. However, GM did not add significant innovations in the engineering or technical field of aviation.

At the end of World War II, Sloan began to rethink GM's participation in the airline industry. In a fact-finding report, with clarity and vision, Sloan outlined the existing prospects in the nation's airline industry. He separated the opportunities into three markets: military, commercial, and air transport. For each one, he indicated the pros and cons, grasping that airline manufacturing could never offer the profit nor the potential of a standardized, consumer-made durable product. He concluded: "The corporation should not contemplate airplanes in either the military or transport areas. [But t]he corporation should develop as complete a position in the manufacture of accessories as its capacity...make[s] possible."[18]

In 1948, General Motors disposed of its interest in North American Aviation and Bendix. This ended the company's flirtation with aviation.

## GERBER'S ANCILLARY BUSINESS

Gerber has been synonymous with baby food since 1928, when a few strained varieties were first sold nationally by the Fremont Canning Company of Fremont, Michigan, owned by the Gerber family. Years later it would open an ancillary business that had nothing to with babies but everything to do with the parents of these babies.

Over the years, Gerber achieved a near monopoly of baby food with market share near or above 70 percent. (Today, Beechnut has about 20 to 25 percent, Heinz Baby Food and some small, organic producers comprise the rest.) In the past 77 years, Gerber has faced challenges from more than 75 different baby food competitors but the result—much like the soup category dominated by Campbell's— is that baby food in America belongs to Gerber.

For 40 years, the company adhered to its uniquely memorable slogan "Babies are our business—Our only business." It evolved quickly into a brand name mothers could trust, publicizing that it opened a research facility dedicated solely to infant nutrition. The public began to write to the company for advice, and in 1938 it received 800,000 questions. Today, the Gerber Research Center is the largest private research institution devoted exclusively to infant nutrition, and the company remains the most trusted American name in the feeding of babies.

Over time, to generate greater revenues, Gerber took many steps within the core business of baby food preparation. It increased the number of its offerings to include more than 190 different varieties. It also ventured overseas, currently selling in more than 80 countries and in 18 languages. As the number of Hispanic-Americans and Latino-American families increased in the United States, the company introduced its tropical line of popular baby foods in regional fruits and vegetables from Central and South America.

(Of historic interest is that Gerber was one of the first U.S. package-good companies to stock its own product in supermarkets, much like local bakery deliveries of breads, cake, and rolls. Because of the proliferation of baby food varieties—and the small margin of profit on these low-priced items—the chains finally rebelled against paying their own clerks to stock the complete line. The answer was square metal baskets on the shelf, each one holding one variety of baby food in loose array. These bins have proliferated into other loose items such as small, travel items like toothpaste, shaving cream, shampoo, etc.)

Keeping again within the baby business image, in 1960, Gerber began marketing 350 different brands of NUK plastic baby products manufactured in Germany and sold throughout the world. U.S. consumers responded positively to the Gerber-NUK line of bottles and other baby accessories.

Gerber had instituted a successful policy of contacting new parents through direct-response mailings, offering cents-off coupons for all of its products and nutritional information. The data were generated through new-birth lists supplied by pediatricians, nurses, and hospitals. In effect, Gerber had already established an efficient system of reaching its target market before the baby's birth and immediately after.

By the mid-1960s, the company realized that it had almost tapped out baby-oriented products. It might have researched its own line of baby clothing but this would have been a radically dissimilar retail market with distrbution systems different from the supermarket chains where most of its product was sold.

The question became, what ancillary business could the company find that could capitalize its historic good name and not dilute the equity in the brand? The answer surprised the consumer and the investment community. It was life insurance.

Gerber understood that there are few highly motivated times when people are willing to buy short-term and long-term life insurance. The birth of a baby, especially, the first child, is one of those motivated times. Parents confront their new obligations and, perhaps, the possible effect of their own mortality on the family.

In 1967, the company formed the Gerber Life Insurance Company as a subsidiary to sell infant and adult life insurance through direct-response. In essence, Gerber already had a working pipeline into the market from its prenatal list-gathering. It started to include life insurance pamphlets with the other prenatal and postnatal information.

The company's insurance print advertisements and direct-response pieces always utilized the Gerber baby logo. These promotions emphasized that this was a company—albeit in a new business—that American families had trusted in the past and could trust in the future.

Currently, Gerber Life has more than $25 billion in life insurance in force, insuring more than two million people. It has received an "A," or Excellent rating (third of thirteen rankings), from A. M. Best, an impartial insurance rating firm.

Gerber had carved out a niche in the life insurance business that no other insurance company had filled. This was similar to General Motors' Frigidaire business, where the company had an equal opportunity to succeed since no other corporation had an edge in technology. For Gerber, no other insurer specifically targeted new parents and new parents only.


## MGM—CASINOS AND BEYOND CASINOS

MGM, the movie studio that could boast that at one time it had almost as many stars as found in the heavens, was best known for its marvelous musicals of the 1940s and 1950s. In that postwar period, it released the classics *Meet Me in St. Louis*, *Singin' in the Rain*, and *The Band Wagon*. All MGM movies were introduced by the familiar Leo the Lion roaring mascot and the Latin inscription *Ars Gratia Artis* (Art for Art's Sake). The initials and the lion made this movie studio a recognizable American icon as familiar as the GE logo.

In 1969, Kirk Kerkorian, who had made his millions from hotels in Las Vegas, purchased MGM Studios and sold off most of its Culver City, California, back-lot real estate and movie memorabilia, including Dorothy's ruby slippers from *The Wizard of Oz*. In 1973, he opened the first MGM Grand hotel in Las Vegas and, by 1979, stated that MGM should be considered first and foremost a hotel company.

By 1993, the company finished building the MGM Grand, its spectacular Las Vegas showpiece. The revitalized and new hotel offered 5,005 rooms, making it the then-largest hotel in the world. Inside, the decor capitalized on the studio's movie-making history, using *Wizard of Oz* themes and characters, highlighted by the Emerald City Casino.

The company, which was called Tracinda after Kerkorian's two daughters, had made the successful transition from movie maker to casino owner, taking to Las Vegas its history and, most importantly, the three letter MGM initials that signified family entertainment. Admittedly, the movie and television studios Disney and Universal with their successful ride and theme parks had paved the way for the acceptance of elaborate movie studio site extensions.

MGM decided its profitable future was in the casino business and not rolling the dice making television and motion pictures. During Kerkorian's ownership, MGM Studios had not remained competitive in the movie business, turning out many middling pictures and just a few hits, like *Thelma and Louise*, *Barbershop*, and *Legally Blonde*.

Kerkorian tried to sell the MGM Studio name and its former properties but these attempts proved unsuccessful—once to Ted Turner in 1986, and the second fiasco to Giancarlo Parretti, an Italian financier who defaulted on loans in 1992. Kerkorian was stuck with the company and enlarged its capacity by purchasing other studio properties. Yet, within the Hollywood movie community, MGM could no longer attract top talent to make megahit movies. Finally, in 2004, Sony Pictures Unit made a successful bid for the MGM Studio name and company. Kerkorian, after a so-so 25-year motion picture run, cashed in his chips.

He continued his Las Vegas expansion, utilizing the MGM initials as ongoing brand equity. In 2000, he purchased hotel magnate Steve Wynn's Mirage Resorts, including the elegant Bellagio hotel. The new entity is called MGM-Mirage, and it remains one of the largest suppliers of rooms in Las Vegas with six hotels. Recently, it added four more hotel sites through the purchase of Mandelay Bay Properties also in Las Vegas.

The final piece in the MGM ancillary business saga was reported in December 2004, when the MGM-Mirage Company announced plans to build a gigantic residential condominium and hotel complex on 66 acres on the Las Vegas strip. Currently, the work-in-progress name is City Center, and it will be the largest, privately financed developmental project in the United States. But to sell the many thousands of condos and to attract the best shops and restaurants, a good bet is that the company may use again the MGM logo in front of the project's name and maybe a drawing of Leo the lion roaring as in movie days of the past.

## THE LESSONS OF FINDING ANCILLARY AND COMPLEMENTARY BUSINESSES

There are many proponents of the school of thought that advises not going outside the core company competency to look for ancillary or complementary businesses. This holds true if the company's established name will add little or no value to a product or service that is demonstrably different from its own.

The consumer realizes that when Daimler places its name in front of Chrysler, an acquisition in the same industry, that the Chrysler name benefits from the quality German company modifier. What if any impact will Procter & Gamble's name do plus or minus in the pending Gillette acquisition?

Also, what to make of the new FedEx-Kinko merger? Will the workers inside the locations be trained in the efficient FedEx method that has excelled at the singular task of expediting package delivery? Kinko's offers a variety of home-office type services and the unanswered question is whether there are will be any more benefits to Kinko's users in addition to a greater number of convenient FedEx locations? Or will FedEx install a new and improved customer-service mentality?

## THE CORE COMPETENCY DILEMMA

There exist possible dangers for those companies that find or start ancillary businesses outside of their core business operation. These risks include unfamiliar business cultures, different distribution systems, a new and dissimilar customer base, profit margins, and lack of empirical knowledge to succeed in a new market or industry.

An example of a bad choice in ancillary business occurred at a large-sized PBS television station that had been successful in

transforming into books many of the cultural and historic documentaries that it had produced and aired. This kind of new and significant revenue-generating business model was suggested by
BMR Associations, media consultants in northern California, as a
method for public stations (later also for niche-interest cable stations like the History Channel) to reap additional revenues from
printing books arising from their in-station productions aired
throughout the United States.

This one PBS station decided that after having been successful
year after year with on-air book sales, that it would open its own
retail bookstore in the large city in which it was based. The station's
familiar call letters enjoyed high awareness, and local consumer
research indicated that the public held the station and its work in
great esteem.

On paper, the concept seemed viable; the station would promote
its own book series, the books spun off from documentaries of other
PBS network stations, and also, complementary books, similar in
content to the varied topics. In addition, the store would also feature
many of the PBS children's series books from *Sesame Street, Tele-
tubbies,* and other programs.

The retail store proved a costly failure; it was not an idea whose
time had come. The PBS station assumed that because it had succeeded in the mail-back fulfillment of book orders it would also be
successful in retailing books, but the wholesale and retail disciplines
were vastly different. Although it hired an experienced book retailer,
it did not have a business plan of how to succeed with its limited
book offerings, not taking into account that many of these PBS-based
books could also be purchased online and also at the chain book-
stores, often at a lower sales price than found in the PBS store.

Ultimately, the store closed without a note of protest from the
book-buying public. The station had embarked on what seemed like
a potentially profitable venture. It had gone too far beyond its core
media and programming business.

## BUSINESS COMPLEMENTING THE CORE
An uncomplicated method for finding a complementary business
within the main business dynamic is to question existing clients. If a
company enjoys a good working relationship with a client marked by

a frank dialogue, the customer might offer information about a competitor or supplier that indicates dissatisfaction.

For years, Leebo Printing in New York had specialized in printing the highest quality, four-color letterheads, booklets, and brochures for the cosmetics industry also based in Manhattan. It proved to be a very competitive business with many local and national presses vying for the business of Revlon and Chanel and other cosmetic houses based in Manhattan.

To find additional or complementary business, the president of Leebo started asking customers about their other types of printing purchases. After many conversations, listening to clients citing satisfaction with printers doing other, less sophisticated types of projects, he finally heard one major and repetitive complaint: many printing companies did not want to bid on or did not do well the laborious and unglamorous thin folded package inserts found in each cosmetic box.

The package inserts required thin paper and a special folding process to reduce them sufficiently to fit into cosmetics boxes. The Leebo president understood why other printers did not seek this arduous and highly detailed kind of business. But he and his associates studied the problem until they had mastered the intricate detail. Leebo bid for one new package insert job with an existing client as a trial to gauge the difficulty and profitability.

The result is that today Leebo specializes in package insert printing. And, by owning this niche, it has continued to do repeat business annually with its cosmetics clients on the higher end. The new business would never have materialized had the Leebo president not inquired about the work of other printers and learned complaints about competitors.

This inquiry step is an easy one for managers to take, especially if they can plan to visit clients on occasion with the main salesperson who calls on the business. The modus operandi of questioning requires no extensive survey work, merely talking on an informal basis and listening for information.

## THE ANCILLARY BUSINESS FOUND WITHIN THE CORE
For some companies that seek new products or wish to create an ancillary business, often the answer can be found by looking inside

the company. A good beginning is to take inventory of what products or services are offered and to assess if these can be expanded or redesigned to appeal to new markets. On occasion, some out-of-the-box or reverse thinking can provide an original concept.

A case in point is Conway Data of Norcross, Georgia, publisher of *Site Selection* magazine, the original magazine in the real-estate and development field founded in 1954. In the mid 1990s, a new Conway Data chief operational officer assessed the state of the company's business and saw declining advertising revenues in an over-crowded field of several similar magazines, also targeting the finite corporate development industry.

The COO studied the problem, wondering what additional products or service he could bring to the 50,000 U.S. magazine subscription base to generate new revenues. After spending a week considering a range of ideas beyond advertising, like forums and seminars, he and his staff had not found any dynamic concept.

As he began to study the statistical details of the subscribers, he saw that Conway Data had gathered facts about the specific industries, their standard industrial classification (SIC) codes, annual revenues, and other executive information. This caused him to reverse the main thrust of the new-business search. He was no longer interested in the prospect of marketing a new service to these executives *but rather* the reverse: Who would be interested in presenting themselves to this specialized list?

Who, using Conway Data and its *Site Selection* magazine as net-workers, would pay for access to the 50,000 development executives?

Once the COO had turned around the thinking process, he began to consider who could become possible clients for a new business. The one conclusion was European economic development agencies. European provinces and cities were constantly searching for new ways to present their economic histories and infrastructure to high-ranking executives at American corporations that might seek to establish an office or to build a factory within the European Union.

The first step was to pretest the theory by contacting some of the larger European agencies and writing a feasibility study. The COO, buoyed by initial positive feedback, created a new business called the World Economic Development Service (WEDS). He wanted it based in Europe and hired an experienced international businessperson in Rome. He also contracted the services of Freeman Global, a New York–based company knowledgeable about the overseas development needs of U.S. companies.

WEDS's first customer was the city of Trieste, Italy, a scientific community that was seeking expansion of its medical and scientific base. The project was a 12-page, four-color booklet about the benefits of doing business in Trieste. The booklet was inserted into *Site Selection* magazine, it was also mailed with a cover letter to a narrowed, target list of U.S. scientific and medical companies, and a phone call followed to inquire about possible interest in Trieste.

Over time, WEDS succeeded in finding other European development agencies that saw the benefit of the targeted project. Eventually, the COO added on the final and remunerative piece to the ancillary but in-the-core business: He offered an appointment-making capability for European agencies to come to the United States and take meetings with interested and prescreened American companies. These appointments were scheduled and arranged, and a WEDS executive accompanied the Europeans on their American trip.

Here was a savvy new business concept that arose from assessing the data within Conway Data and then finding an intriguing new and different business. After some restructuring at Conway Data, WEDS was discontinued and Freeman Global continued the international appointment-making business, servicing Spanish and German development agencies.

## ANCILLARY BUSINESS FROM COPYING OTHERS

Sometimes a new business idea is no further away than examining a successful ancillary business of another company, not necessarily a competitor. Copying or imitating an idea affords the advantage of studying a successful concept from a distance without having to incur significant upfront investment.

One of the most successful quasi-similar businesses is General Electric's GE Capital, which replicates the General Motors GMAC financing model to produce spectacular earnings. Begun in 1932 as the General Electric Contract Corporation, the original idea was to assist GE customers finance appliance purchases, a duplication of the GM auto-financing concept.

After World War II, General Electric Credit Corporation loaned money and dealt in commercial paper and consumer financing. It changed its name to GE Capital in 1987 to reflect that it was a major provider of business financial products. In 2002, it was reorganized into four separate divisions; Commercial Finance, Consumer Finance, Equipment Service, and Capital. In 2004, it generated an outstanding $500 billion in revenues in 47 countries worldwide.

To start an ancillary business that follows a model from another successful company, the old saw advises, "To get in one step ahead of the sheep."

## ANCILLARY BUSINESSES—FINAL WORD

What every company wants is to bring out a new product that has been as successful as Apple's iPod, a complementary, new business that is sufficiently within the core of its computer-based background. The consumer had no difficulty accepting that Apple's technology could deliver the music-playing platform.

Sloan had inherited the nonautomotive businesses and probably would have divested the locomotive, refrigeration, and aviation companies in the GM fold if other people he trusted within the company (Kettering most of all) had not thought otherwise. In addition, he always pointed out that these ancillary enterprises were in their infancy and GM had as much chance of success as other competition.

For Sloan, the yardstick for any business was if "no profit can be satisfactorily obtained, the enterprise should be abandoned." This dictum kept General Motors on a course to concentrate on its core business, automobile manufacturing. And it allowed General Motors to generate profits until two of the ancillary businesses—refrigeration and aviation—became more difficult to operate, at which time they were sold off, also at a profit to the company.

C  H  A  P  T  E  R

# THE DECENTRALIZED ORGANIZATION AND FINANCIAL CONTROLS

*T*he organizational system before Sloan...Sloan's "Organization Plan" of 1919...The beginnings of decentralization at GM...The Sloan plan in practice...Sloan's two main principles...Sloan's five organization objectives...Decentralization in action...Financial controls and the executive committee...The Smithsonian: Model of effective decentralization...The managerial lessons of effective decentralization

ഛ൦ ൦ൎ

It is essential to remember that business corporations, and the manner in which they were established historically, have followed a pattern that had survived for centuries. The traces of the system can be found in the organization of Greek and Roman armies or in the effective managing of personnel within a gigantic institution like the Catholic Church. Hierarchies of status formed the recognizable pyramid of unmitigated power at the apex and service or servitude in great numbers at the bottom.

To examine the political system of ancient Egypt, one of the first successful large organizational social structures in the civilized world, is to observe the early seeds of today's modern corporation. In the Egyptian chain of command the Pharaoh stood at the top, many layers of priests with great powers came next, followed by an informed managerial class of civil servants that controlled the secular lives of citizens, and finally the everyday people or workers.

In all organizations, past and present, two elements are required for great accomplishment; leadership and policy. A society or an institution can be blessed with great leadership, but without a corresponding working system, the leader's value may be minimized. Similarly, a system cannot work to its maximum potential without the vision and guiding wisdom of a savvy leader. For General Motors, Alfred P. Sloan, Jr., would become the leader *and* the system.

When Pierre du Pont assumed the presidency of General Motors in 1920, he formed a revised executive committee, which included vice-president Alfred P. Sloan, Jr., and three other executives. The new group replaced an inefficient committee made up of division managers, who now found themselves in a lesser role, serving as merely advisors to the executive committee. As Sloan wrote: "These changes, through an emergency nature, coincided with a sweeping reorganization of General Motors, going to the roots of industrial philosophy."[1]

The "sweeping reorganization" that would change General Motors' fortunes forever would also have a profound influence on the global business community. The changes would come about almost in their entirety from a document Sloan wrote in 1919 when he suffered under the autocratic rule of GM's president William Durant. The written work was called appropriately "Organization Study." Years later when he penned his autobiography, Sloan was conscious of its impact: "Since this plan has become the foundation of management policy—an expression of the basic principles of 'decentralization' that govern its organization—it is said thereby to have had some influence on large-scale industrial enterprise in the United States."[2]

The main tenet of Sloan's transformation of General Motors was that the organization should move from the centralized concept of the one man, one rule to the more democratic, decentralized system of shared responsibility and specific accountability. Peter Drucker summed up the problem: "General Motors could not function as a centralized organization in which all decisions are made at the top, and in which the divisional managers are but little more than plant superintendents."[3]

## HOW SLOAN CONCEIVED OF THE "ORGANIZATION STUDY"

Sloan pointed out two specific areas where the ideas for the organization plan *did not* come: prior military examples and, as many supposed, from the forward thinking Du Pont Company. The latter had embarked on many modern concepts of the corporation during its early-twentieth-century reorganization. But Sloan debunked the notion that when Du Pont executives had moved over to GM, these people (Pierre du Pont, Raskob, Brown) had influenced his thinking: "The two plans did not share their particulars, but only the management philosophy of decentralization."[4]

In fact, although reorganization ideas might have been roiling his brain for years, it was when he headed up United Motors Company that the first notions of a decentralized plan occurred to him. United Motors was made up of 12 separate companies, each one manufacturing a different component, united by nothing more than the fact that it was owned by General Motors and did business in the automobile accessory segment.

One of the first steps Sloan took as president of United Motors was to consolidate repair and service into one, new nationwide organization under the United Motors Service Corporation name. The move seems logical today, to have one service entity represent the divisions, and thereby access all the efficiencies of location, personnel, marketing, and advertising. It was easier and more organized to have one service center under one name than to mount repair stations under the many disparate component companies.

But the United Motors' division heads (all former small-company presidents like Sloan and also accustomed to complete independence) rebelled against the idea. Sloan had to prevail: "The divisions naturally resisted but I persuaded them of the need for it, and for the first time I learned something about getting decentralized management to yield some of its functions for the common good."[5]

Later at General Motors, Sloan would continue the modus operandi of convincing inflexible staff to cede divisional goals for the good of the corporation.

Making each United Motors division responsible for its own profit-making represented another significant crystallizing principle in Sloan's plan. As its president, he was interested in the profit and loss of each company and installed a standard system of accounting for the divisions to follow. With this new financial system, Sloan could see in black and white the many facts about cost of payroll, overhead, raw material purchase, rents, and other charges. Now he could subtract these overhead charges from revenues to determine each division's true profitability.

Armed with these new sets of facts, Sloan could spot trouble areas within each division in terms of out-of-line costs or other out-of-the-ordinary variables. He could accurately assess each division's contribution to the profit and loss of United Motors.

In 1918, when General Motors' expansion rolled United Motors into the main corporation and Sloan as vice-president, William Durant had no interest to continue Sloan's profit-and-loss divisional fact finding. This proved troublesome to Sloan: "I would no longer be able to determine the rate of return on investment. This would necessarily mean that I would lose some degree of managerial control over my area of operations."[6]

Unhappily, he found himself back to the subordinate position as when he first started at Hyatt Roller Bearing; someone else was in control of the decision making and, in his opinion, doing a poor job: "I knew that I operated a profit-making group, and I wished to continue to be able to demonstrate the performance rather than to have my operating results swallowed up in the extra bookkeeping profits."[7]

Under William Durant's all-divisions in the mix, every entity at General Motors would be stirred into one big corporate melting pot with no precise or accountable system to identify who in the company was profitable and who was not.

Monetary reward was not Sloan's motivation for wanting to keep divisional profit and loss separate and distinct. He was well-compensated at General Motors and also well-liked by Will Durant. Additionally, he held a large stock position, stemming from converting his shares of Hyatt Roller Bearing into General Motors' stock. If GM's share price rose because of Durant's aptitude in convincing Wall Street of the positive efforts of General Motors, then Sloan would reap huge paper profits.

Sloan was in a double bind, he was the head of United Motors and also, as vice-president of GM, a member of the Durant's executive committee. In essence, he was reporting to himself, and as the executive committee member he wanted to know objectively the specific effectiveness of each division. Because he believed: "It was irrational for the general officers of the corporation not to know where to place the money to best advantage."[8]

And more galling to Sloan was the fact that other members of GM's executive committee were solely interested in promoting their own division's agenda.

## A MAN, A PLAN, AN ORGANIZATION

At General Motors, Sloan was doubly frustrated by the lack of accountability of the divisions and also annoyed by the suboptimization of other executive committee members who favored their own agendas. He decided that to try to remedy the situation he would write his recommendations for change, addressed to William Durant. Even though by 1919 the Du Pont Company had installed some of their own experts in the corporation, president William Durant remained the controlling power.

Durant threw Sloan a bone when he allowed the vice-president to chair a committee on interdivisional relations. Sloan was eager to have his thoughts be known and toiled away for a year on an analysis of how to improve the organization. Finally, in December of 1919 he submitted the report. It will be helpful to summarize the key points:

- The purpose of an enterprise [GM division] is to earn a return on capital.

- If no profit can be satisfactorily obtained, the enterprise should be abandoned.

- A business that is profitable should be expanded in the marketplace.

- Interdivisional sales should be on a cost-plus basis to permit a fair profit.

In net, Sloan promulgated that rate of return should constitute the sole financial variable to determine the measure of a division or business. But he also perceived the benefits of the rate of return on decentralized, divisional operations:

- Moral is increased because each division is eager to define and augment its contribution to the corporation.

- It requires correct statistical analysis, which will determine the true comparison between the net return of the division's invested capital.

- It facilitates the placement of strategic capital for investment where it is best needed.

As Sloan wrote, "This was the first written statement of the broad principles of financial control in General Motors."[9]

## COMMUNICATING THE TWO MAIN PRINCIPLES

Sloan must have experienced conflicting feelings about the "Organization Study." On one hand, it carefully outlined needed changes for General Motors, and on the other hand, it was being presented to William Durant who had never demonstrated any interest in reshaping the GM corporation with tighter controls. Further, Durant, in the dictatorial mold of Henry Ford, enjoyed the similar authoritarian power broker status of being the sole decision maker at the company.

Sloan found another alternative to communicate his opinion, he circulated the "Organization Study" throughout the executive staff at General Motors, an end-run around Durant. Modestly, he referred to its wide popular acceptance as being like a "best seller," and he printed the report in quantity. The response was overwhelmingly favorable: At last someone in General Motors had composed a blueprint plan for remedying the company's financial and organizational chaos.

Then, in September 1920, he took the one action that would change history, he sent the "Organization Study" to the newly appointed General Motors chairman, Pierre du Pont. It was not an uncalculated risk, William Durant's star was falling as GM was mired in financial problems, and it seemed that the Du Pont Company was ascendant in managing the company.

In his autobiography *My Years with General Motors,* Sloan purposely waited to impart the two principles of his "Organization Study" until *after* he had introduced Pierre du Pont onto the stage. It seems to represent a subconscious attempt to indicate that this marks the historical and chronological point in the narrative, the pivotal moment in the turnaround of GM and also his career. The principles included this statement:

> The responsibility attached to the chief executive of each operation shall in no way be limited. Each such organization headed by its chief executive shall be complete in every necessary function and enable[d] to exercise its full initiative and logical development. Certain central organization functions are absolutely essential to the logical development and proper control of the Corporation's activities.[10]

Here was the culmination of years of Sloan's thinking of how a corporation could function with divisional authority and still report to a central authority.

## THE FIVE OBJECTIVES

Then Sloan embellished the two principles with five primary objectives:

1.  To determine definitely the functioning of the various divisions constituting the Corporation's activities, not only in relation to one another, but in relation to the central organization.
2.  To determine the status of the central organization and to coordinate the operation of that central organization with the Corporation as a whole.
3.  To centralize the control of all the executive functions of the Corporation in the president as its chief executive officer.
4.  To limit as far as practical the number of executives reporting directly to the president.
5.  To provide means within each executive branch whereby all other branches are represented in an advisory way.[11]

Sloan's prose was never light, and he referred to these lengthy objectives as a "big chew." Yet in these five points can be seen the basic foundation of the modern and efficient corporate system. Divisional heads would be in control of many areas, but not all, and these other matters would be run by the GM president, who also would have wide discretionary powers. In essence, it resembled a democratic process not unlike the U.S. political system, with defined authority and checks and balances.

In the final analysis, Sloan, acting as an iconoclast, had recommended the end of the dictatorial, one-person rule of a William Durant or a Henry Ford. Sloan could claim years later that: "The principles of organization in the study thus initiated for the modern General Motors the trend toward a happy medium in industrial organization between the extremes of pure centralization and pure decentralization."[12]

There was one final piece to Sloan's recommendations to achieve the "happy medium," a newly drawn organizational chart that reflected the scope of his judgment on reforming the company along decentralized lines. This clear-cut plan is another example that demonstrates his logic and ability to utilize structure to illuminate theory. The heavy prose style in the "Organization Study" was simplified to crystal clear simplicity in one glance at the well-thought-out and well-structured chart.

The January 1921 chart consisted of almost 110 separate organizational and functional boxes. Executives who were heads of one of the GM divisions (all listed under the midranking "operations staff" level), could see with clarity where they stood in the hierarchy of the reorganized corporation. Gone was their separate control over finances, real estate, research, and design. And conspicuously redrawn was reporting directly to the executive committee.

Within the 1921 chart, each specifically named corporate entity of cars, trucks, and automobile components, could see that it stood in its own distinct box. The divisions could also realize that they would rise and fall as a result of their own autonomy. Along with the indisputable fact that all organizational roads led to the president of the corporation, was the subtle concept that even a division as important as Chevrolet was just another member within the wider scope of the larger entity called General Motors.

It would take the rest of the decade of the 1920s for Alfred P. Sloan, acting in capacity as General Motors' president, to weld all the divisions into a smooth-running corporation. The result would see the efficient marriage of centralized authority and decentralized management working in tandem to a great and successful purpose.

Peter Drucker would write in 1943 of the company's historic reformation:

> Hence General Motors has become an *essay in federalism*—on the whole, an exceedingly successful one. It attempts to combine the greatest corporate unity with the greatest divisional autonomy and responsibility; it aims at realizing unity through local self-goverment.[13]

## THE EXECUTIVE COMMITTEE FOLLOWS THE PLAN

In 1921, the new executive committee set out immediately to try to breathe life into the moribund company. The members were Pierre du Pont, Sloan, John Raskob, and J. Amory Haskell. Sloan cited an interesting fact about these four: not one had automotive experience. (Sloan, "I was still underdeveloped in car operation."[14])

The year before in 1920, General Motors' sales had risen to an all-time high of 393,075 vehicles. Then in 1921, owing to the sudden decrease in car demand as the wartime boom ended, sales dropped precipitously to a paltry 214,799, a stunning decline of 178,275 vehicles or a decline of 46 percent. Net sales revenues correspondingly decreased in the same period by $262,833 million, also a 46 percent drop.

There would be reorganization hits and misses for the executive committee during 1921 as the company found itself in serious financial and inventory difficulties. With GM gasping for life and with William Durant evicted from all corporate and board titles, the decision-making authority rested in the executive committee.

It is plausible that *not* possessing any knowledge of car production, these four men were able to look at General Motors in a way that strictly automotive experts might not have done.

This committee was unburdened with auto-making experience and embarked on revolutionary solutions that proved ultimately beneficial for the corporation. In essence, the group did not focus exclusively on just selling more automobiles, but on solving the overall and critical problems related to long-term success of a manufacturing operation in the automotive business.

(This group of four represented, perhaps for the last time in America, that the most upper-echelon executives at any of the Big Three car companies would *not be* savvy and experienced in the automobile business. Over the next 60 years, for example, Charles Wilson, Lee Iacocca, and Jurgen Schrempp would produce impressive résumés of past automobile experience to assume the top car-company jobs.)

The operation of this executive committee demonstrated the smooth workings of a dedicated group. Sloan was proud to report that the committee met 101 times in formal sessions to solve the topical problems of 1921. The members decided to visit all of General Motors' plants and offices to gauge firsthand the depth of the problem. But what was wrong with the corporation was clear to Sloan: "We recognized that General Motors had no explicit policy as to the line of cars to be produced, and that was the next order of business."[15]

## THE FIRST ATTEMPTS AT DECENTRALIZATION

Alfred P. Sloan, Jr., grasped the fact that the General Motors divisions and the executives who ran these divisions would dissent from following the new federal decentralization that he had recommended in the "Organization Study." It would represent a classic example of the unwillingness of people to part with power previously held to hand over to a newly established central authority. Historic examples of reunification in nation building—Bismarck in Germany or Garibaldi in Italy—reveal similar reluctances of smaller provinces who feared being swallowed up by the new and larger entity.

In addition, many of the executives within the five GM car companies had climbed the ladder from mechanics to shop foreman to division staff positions. In this new decentralized system, the members of the executive committee that was communicating the organizational changes were considered numbers men based in New York City who had no empirical familiarity with the building of automobiles. Pierre du Pont and Sloan did not have the natural "feel" for cars like the state of Michigan's own William Durant. The question was asked: What did these Easterners (and all but Raskob with college degrees) know about the nuts and bolts of the car business?

Sloan set out to meet the people in the General Motors organization, recognizing that he had to put a face on the executive committee (at a time when he was still vice-president in charge of operation). He knew that by listening to the gripes and suggestions, many automobile-related, he would learn new information about the organization and the people who worked in it.

(There were so many back and forth trips from New York to Detroit that Sloan slept inside the General Motors building. He could work the long hours for which he was known and retire for the night not far from his office.)

As Sloan traversed the country speaking to the executives at the car divisions and the component companies, time and again these people must have questioned what the new organization chart meant for their departments. Although many might have previously applauded the "Organization Study" when it was words on paper, suddenly seeing that changes were in the offering must have raised numerous questions and doubts.

It was Sloan's task to take the organization chart and point out the short-term advantages that decentralization would bring to the divisions. His line of reasoning proceeded logically by pointing out that now the divisions would be measured individually, without being thrown into the common mix. Further, he demonstrated the cost saving and the efficiency achieved by eliminating the duplication of similar responsibilities within the divisions that would now be handled by specialized departments for all divisions (i.e., real estate, legal, etc.).

But most of all, Sloan had to bend these executives to his purpose, to his long-term objective that the corporation (no matter what business it was in) had to be profitable and sustaining. And the strategy for this goal was decentralization: "Divisional management must be both autonomous and directed; central management must at the same time give effective, unifying leadership and be confined to regulation and advice."[16]

The short-term benefits to Sloan's decentralization plan produced new thinking among the executives who staffed the various

General Motors divisions. The form that engendered autonomy would narrow the many decisions into a defined focus for the department heads. In addition, divisional executives knew that their coworkers at other divisions were involved in the same kinds of self-governing decision making. But these executives also knew that Sloan was in charge of many aspects of their business. As Peter Drucker wrote: "At General Motors, top management at the central office sets the price ranges within which each automobile division's products have to fall, and thus controls the competition between the major units of the company."[17]

But Sloan had more surprises in store for the divisional managers, he promoted them out of the division and into more senior positions in other departments. The sales manager who succeeded at Buick was not pigeonholed as a "Buick" person but would find advancement in another GM car make. The federal decentralization established a wide system for finding talent and allowing junior executives the opportunity to perform. Much of their performance skills evolved because they knew exactly what defined areas of decision would mark their careers, and they did not have to worry about many areas of responsibility occupied by the central organization.

## AMASSING INFORMATION FOR FINANCIAL CONTROLS

Cleverly, Sloan would use financial facts to continue to persuade the doubting Thomases at the divisions. But first he and the executive committee had to define what kind of controls would be implemented in a company that had never been operated under the tight scrutiny of statistical data: "Our modern financial policies, like those in the organization, came out of the ruins of 1920."[18]

When Sloan was president of United Motors, he had instituted a new system of accounting practices designed to provide more accurate financial reporting. Under the auspices of the new executive committee, the group of four made it their mandate to implement a new financial system for all of General Motors' divisions. Sloan's objective was to assess the financial picture of each department so that he could continue to push his decentralization plan. He wrote: "My responsibility involved the application of financial methods, for finance could not exist in a vacuum but had to be integrated with operations."[19]

His goal was twofold: to restrain the divisions from their past independent history of profligate spending and to centralize operating controls. In the latter case, Sloan wanted to make sure that the corporation, and not the separate divisions, would control the purse strings.

The individual steps taken to reign in financial controls marked one of the first attempts within a corporation to classify the various tasks tied into all of its expenditures.

Although most of these controls are commonplace today, it is important to review how they affected General Motors.

## APPROPRIATIONS FOR CAPITAL SPENDING

The company wrote a manual that assigned a system for the prioritization of spending by the corporation. In addition, it permitted the divisions to spend smaller amounts without having to request sums from the finance committee.

## CASH CONTROL

Before the institution of a controlled policy, the divisions managed their own cash receipts, depositing these in divisional accounts. If General Motors had to pay dividends, taxes, etc., it had to go back to the divisions for contributions. The new outcome eliminated these separate accounts by consolidating cash control as a central corporate function. The result was an immediate rise in the corporation's supply of credit, better banking relationships, and also an increase in earnings through investing in short-term and safe financial securities.

## INVENTORY CONTROL

Of all the newly implemented regulations, inventory control proved the most significant to the corporation. Before Sloan, the divisional general managers negotiated individually with suppliers. No thought was given to whether sales would generate enough short-term revenues to cover the costs of the material. Under Sloan's direction, central inventory management was instituted, again taking control from the divisions. Immediately in 1921, the huge inventory was reduced by more than half, and, in two short years, the turnover of inventory was doubled to four times a year.

## PRODUCTION CONTROL
General Motors began a four-month forecasting estimate of the expected number of vehicles it would sell. Production schedules became mandatory from the divisions before Sloan would sign off on the funds to continue manufacturing. The gap in the projections arose from a lack of accurate prediction in retail sales. This problem would plague Sloan for years after because of the two conflicting opinions on how many cars would be sold. Sloan characterized the reasons for the wide differences in projections coming from: "...two kinds of persons in General Motors. One kind is the sales manager with his natural enthusiasm, optimism. The other is the statistical person who makes analyses objectively."[20]

## CONCEPT OF STANDARD VOLUME
The final step in the financial control system was designed to measure the long-term results of the company's return on investment. The new measurement established benchmarks and attempted to reconcile the variables (volume, costs, prices, and rate of return on capital) into a predictive formula.

From 1923, when Sloan became president, to 1925, he and the finance committee worked tirelessly to transform the giant corporation into a cohesive whole. Over time, as Sloan's system succeeded at GM, even the "Durant men" realized that the revitalized and restructured organization was now the dominant U.S. automobile manufacturer.

The divisions had had to relinquish independence in many areas, especially financial, but the result of the federal decentralization would help the corporation generate record sales, revenues, and most important, profits. Sloan could report with a measure of pride that: "The need for financial controls grew out of crises. Controls were brought in to ensure that crises did not occur. Central office management was able to know whether the decentralized management was working out well or poorly."[21]

In sum, the newly configured General Motors would set the stage for the two-tiered track of corporate success: the emergence of a strong central authority exercising widespread control of costs and finances and decentralized divisions shifting to key areas of autonomy. The result would be that every division could be measured, and its contribution assessed.

It was clear to Sloan what he had created when he wrote in 1941 about the decision to choose decentralization: "The first step was to determine whether we would operate under a centralized or decentralized form of administration. Decentralization was analogous to free enterprise. Centralization, to regimentation. We decided for free enterprise."[22]

## THE SMITHSONIAN INSTITUTION— SUCCESSFUL DECENTRALIZATION

The effectiveness of decentralization in the good working of an organization can be demonstrated by the Smithsonian Institution. This famous American organization operates in a similar fashion to Sloan's General Motors with its own highly efficient central committee and the mainly autonomous operations of its numerous museums and research centers.

There are many parallel examples to GM of the Smithsonian's discrete divisions involved in relationships directly with the public or with suppliers and not reporting all the time to the central functional executive, in this case the Smithsonian's highest ranking officer, the secretary.

In essence, the Smithsonian can be considered principally in museum operations, but this is a underestimation of what the great historic institution does and what it accomplishes. It is made up of 18 different museums or galleries, the National Zoological Park in Washington, D.C., seven research centers, and the Smithsonian Business Ventures unit, which includes magazines, mail-order catalog, product development, entertainment, etc.

(The fact is that the Smithsonian attracts more visitors than the Louvre in Paris and the British Museum in London combined. The new Air and Space building near Dulles Airport is the largest enclosed room in the world.)

With so many diverse offerings for visitors, the Smithsonian can function efficiently only as a motivated and highly decentralized operation. The museums, galleries, and zoo range in attendance from as low as 22,000 for the Anacostia Museum for African American History and Culture to the 4.9 million visitations to the National Air and Space Museum.

All of the Smithsonian's various divisions report to one of four main operational units: the chief operating officer, the under secretary of art, the under secretary of science, and, finally, to the CEO of the Business Ventures unit. These four individuals in turn report directly to the secretary, forming a sort of executive committee to decide major policy and operating issues.

A little known fact about the Smithsonian is that 80 percent of its 6,300 full-time workers are government employees. These employees are subject to the same pay grades, health benefits, etc., as the U.S. military or other full-time federal careerists. And their specific job descriptions—for example, art restorer or taxidermist—are as strictly defined and codified as every other federal position. The other 20 percent of the staff are known as "trust fund" employees with comparable salaries and benefits. This two-tiered system of employment allows the Smithsonian a certain measure of independence from the government since all of its employees are not under federal guidelines.

The operating budget is $600 million to administrate this massive complex with 70 percent coming from the federal government in appropriations, grants, and contracts. The balance of the operating budget comes from soliciting the private sector through individual and corporate member programs. Contributions can be general to the institution, specific to a museum or a research center, or even designated for a singular, special exhibit or research project.

Fund-raising is carried out under the Smithsonian banner name and also by the divisions themselves, particularly, the museums and the national zoo, which all field in-house money-generating campaigns. Many of the departments also have their own membership programs that produce specifically targeted revenues.

In terms of decentralization, each museum, research center, and the zoo operates as a separate and distinct division with its own director, staff, and many autonomous functions. For special, nonrecurring exhibits, the museums produce these shows independently and also mount advertising campaigns without central approval. But the campaigns must be done in line with certain standard guidelines.

The central administration primarily monitors the performance of the museums by examining annual visitation figures. But these numbers do not represent the totality of the assessment. The central office gauges other important variables, including visitor responses, survey data, and interestingly, outside peer reviews from other curators and museum professionals.

The staff hiring is left almost entirely to the divisions with the exception of the key positions of museum director or the head of fund-raising, which are high-ranking positions controlled by the central management.

Similar to Sloan's successful corporate campaign to publicize General Motors as a single entity, the *Smithsonian Magazine* with two million subscriptions helps achieve this concept of the one, central administrator. The magazine covers topics on American culture, art, music, natural history, and modern-day society.

The Smithsonian takes branding its own name one step further to ensure that the public remembers who operates the many branches; online it places its name over the individual museum and galleries. The name also appears before the seven research facilities. In addition, a flaring sun in white or yellow serves as an effective logo (like GE's script) for all areas of the Smithsonian.

## THE LESSONS OF DECENTRALIZATION AND CENTRALIZATION

The format that Alfred P. Sloan, Jr., administered first at General Motors works, for the most part, in large, multidivisional corporations or organizations. Yet, even in smaller entities, the essence of Sloan's plan of autonomy for many divisions reporting to a central authority is still the most efficient method of management. It does away with the dictator theory of management, which proved so unsuccessful under Henry Ford's reign.

It forces an organization to define the slots within the organization, and the responsibilities of the people who will fill those slots. In this way, the goal is always performance, where the individual division or department enjoys many freedoms to achieve goals without the constant interference of an overlord with too much authority.

## USE COMMITTEES

One of the hallmarks of Sloan's organization plan was the establish-ment of and reliance on specialized committees to study problems and to recommend changes. He was able to staff these committees with experts to maximize their output. He referred to this method as grouping together "common relationships."

In addition, one of the overlooked examples of Sloan's innovative brilliance was the establishment of new committees as the business changed over time. His "Dealers' Council" marks just one of the many new committees that started and succeeded.

The key is to avoid the old saw that a camel is just a horse designed by a committee.

## CONTROL THE PURSE STRINGS

Another important piece of the decentralization plan is for the autonomous divisions (and or committees) to report to one, central authority for spending purposes. This accomplishes two important things: It states that not all important decisions will be taken by the division without outside control, and it makes the divisions more cost conscious, knowing they have to present budgets to a financial authority.

# DEALERS AND DISTRIBUTION

*T*he history of automobile dealerships...Sloan goes into the field to meet the dealers...GM implements new dealership agreements...Sloan retools dealer geographical penetration...Offering allowances to move the old models...Sloan establishes financial controls for the dealer network...GM invests in the dealerships...GM's new method of dealer communication...Sloan agrees to arbitration to settle dealer disputes...Cell phone dealerships...The managerial lessons of company and dealer relationships

Alfred P. Sloan, Jr., knew that an effective distribution network was vital for General Motors to succeed in the marketplace. However, in the beginning of his stewardship in 1923, it proved to be a somewhat nettlesome business because power over the dealers (although franchised exclusively to GM) remained outside of his grand scheme for decentralization with an internal process for central control.

The variance between manufacturer and dealer that bothered Sloan, as it had concerned other automobile manufacturers with similar dealership agreements, was that the car manufacturer had to rely upon franchised organizations independent of the parent company for both the retail sales to, and the direct interaction with, the public. As the practically minded Sloan stated:

> The franchise of distribution makes sense only if you have a group of sound, prosperous dealers as business associates. I have never been interested in business relationships that are not of benefit to all concerned.[1]

In General Motors' efficient system, the company would spend time and capital trying to codify the variables that resulted in the selection of the best dealers. The original concept of choosing a prominent businessman in the community might have been the best method to find a dealer when the automobile was new and needed a local and reliable person with a first-rate reputation. But Sloan decided that this outmoded method needed some modernized improvement if the dealers were to be part of his transformation of the entire General Motors organization: "I was able to see the historic change that was underway. . . that the economic position of the dealers was becoming less satisfactory than it had been, and our franchises were in less demand."[2]

Over time, for those people who would be interested in securing an automobile franchise, but especially acquiring one from General Motors, where a dealership for one of the five models was tantamount to almost a guaranteed lifetime of wealth and status, car companies looked for more than just financial stability and town or village importance. The Big Three car companies sought dealers who could provide fully integrated sales and service operations, with strong emphasis on the service aspect.

What Sloan identified from the start was the dichotomy of having a producer manufacture an automobile without the input of the eventual sales force, the dealer. Here was the essence of trust, the dealer would put its faith in General Motors to style, produce, and nationally advertise vehicles that would appeal to the consumer. In turn, General Motors would rely upon the local dealers to market, sell, advertise locally and regionally, and offer postsales service. Sloan said: "The significance of the dealer in automobile distribution is two-fold. First, as in many industries, the dealer makes the direct personal contact with the customer; he makes and closes the deal that sells the car."[3]

In the final analysis, a marketing mind as busy as Sloan's would not let the antiquated dealer system he inherited from William Durant continue without some serious tinkering. The most substantial result was his decision that the parent company should not nor would not leave the direct selling—and all that it entailed on the local level—to self-ruling dealerships to do whatever they wanted. Sloan decided General Motors would not only offer significant assistance by expanding the form of the existing dealer financing (GMAC), but also by finding the best and most efficient method for the dealers to represent GM. In essence, Sloan searched for best dealer-practice procedures that could be replicated productively from one dealership to the next.

The goal in Sloan's dealership restructuring was "...to distribute cars on a sound and economic basis for all concerned."[4]

(Where is the least opportune place to own a Big Three Car dealership in the United States? It's in the same city as the company's world headquarters. The "Bob Ford" Ford dealership—so named because it was initially owned by Henry Ford's brother—is located across the street from Ford's Dearborn, Michigan, headquarters. The dealership receives unsolicited telephone calls from high-ranking Ford executives who, while driving to work, might spot a stray, windblown piece of paper in front of the dealership or notify the dealer's staff if anything else looks out of place.)

## THE DEALERS RESEARCH FEEDBACK

Before he would implement any sweeping changes, Sloan insisted upon gathering the facts. This involved visits to the dealers throughout the United States and doing qualitative research with one-on-one questions between Sloan and the GM franchise owners.

Sloan had to deal with over 13,000 GM car dealers, discovering that each one was an entrepreneur with divergent opinions on how the cars should be sold and advertised. The dealers were in the front lines of selling and servicing GM's cars. He was circumspect about their importance to the corporation: "Although in the 1920s we had made some great advances in getting the facts about General Motors' economic position, we did not then have the facts regarding the economic position of our dealers."[5]

When the demand for new automobiles increased in the mid 1920s—especially, the rapid rise of General Motors' car sales—along with a concurrent rise in a burgeoning used car market, U.S. automobile manufacturers witnessed changes in dealing with their distribution network. Sloan characterized this significant dealer shift as going from easy selling to hard selling.

The fact-driven Sloan knew that the answers he would need to transform the inefficiencies of the past rested with the dealers in the field. On the road he went to find out the facts. Here again, Sloan would not rely on either anecdotal information or hunches. He wanted to make sure that the opinions and concerns of GM's far-flung national dealerships were similar to the problems of the local Michigan-based and midwestern-area franchise owners. Sloan did what few presidents of Big Board–traded companies of his day or later ever did: "I fitted up a private railroad car as an office and in the company of several associates went into almost every city in the United States, visiting from five to ten dealers a day."[6]

When Sloan met with these dealers, he took copious notes, jotting down their criticisms and suggestions. These frank exchanges allowed Sloan to understand the nature and needs of the dealer network. In addition, the dealers must have sensed that Sloan would accept criticism and dissent with an open mind. And they were right; Sloan was solely interested in their frank opinions.

When he returned to the head office, he read all of the dealers' notes and then, in 1927, decided to implement a new dealer arrangement, realizing finally, that the two entities shared common goals and interests. He never would have reached these conclusions had he not gathered the facts in the field and face-to-face.

## SLOAN'S NEW DEALERSHIP AGREEMENTS

After Sloan had collected the facts, he studied the dealer-company problem looking for an equitable solution for both parties. His travels around the country had changed his mind about the franchise owners, whom he now appreciated were as eager to succeed as the parent company. He had been impressed by their sincerity and truthfulness.

What both parties needed was a fair way to achieve that mutual benefit. He regarded the franchise system as the best way and wrote:

> But what are the alternatives [to the current method]? There are
> only two that I know of; either manufacturer-owned, manager-
> operated dealerships, or the selling of cars by everyone and anyone.
> I look askance at either of these changes. I believe the franchise sys-
> tem, is the best one for manufacturers, dealers, and consumers.[7]

Basically, Sloan isolated the inherent and classic problem that had
always existed between the car manufacturer and the dealer network.
In the past, automobile companies made as many vehicles as possible
and then insisted that the dealer take possession of vehicles without
any consideration for the nation's economic situation. The production
reasoning for this method was obvious to Sloan: "The quicker merchandise moved from the raw material to the ultimate consumer...the
more efficient and more stable the industry becomes."[8]

Thus, simply stated was the historic paradigm of manufacturer
and franchised supplier, the latter locked in a chattel arrangement
with one automobile manufacturer and without the freedom to sell
multiple car models from other companies. Sloan saw the intrinsic
unfairness of a system that allowed the manufacturer to dictate sales
totals to the dealer.

Eliminating this tyrannical process marked the first step in
rethinking the agreement. Sloan noted that the end to the past's
authoritarian sales totals would mark: "...a new approach to pro-
ducer-dealer relations in General Motors, based upon the recognition
of the community of interest."[9] In the future, General Motors would
no longer dump hundreds of vehicles onto dealers' lots without some
mutual understanding, but he allowed leeway in the sole instance
where GM was closing out a model and needed to reduce inventory
for a new model. Dealers would have to cooperate in running these
models through their franchises.

## RETHINKING DEALER AREA PENETRATION

Another question that Sloan set about to solve immediately was one of
how many dealerships should exist in a geographical area. In addition,

what were the statistical variables to determine whether a town or village could support its own dealership. To Sloan the dual aim was straightforward: ". . .to penetrate the market as effectively as possible, and since in the end this had to be carried out by our dealers, it was necessary to have the appropriate number."[10]

To find the answer, General Motors embarked on economic research, studying population, income, past dealer performance if applicable, and current business cycles. This study was revolutionary for its time, but Sloan, as usual, wanted to see the big, factual picture before he amended General Motors' policy, especially, in the delicate area of dealerships.

In smaller regional areas, GM could examine past dealer sales and determine how goals had been met. In the larger populated urban areas, the problem proved more complex. GM compiled population data on a neighborhood basis and judged potential on a limited geographic area.

(For years, the Big Three insisted on single franchises only, barring the ownership of two car models even within the same automobile company. But European car manufacturers decided it was easier to find an existing car dealership than start a new one, and they successfully broke the single car dealership custom. The result, for example, was that Pal Buick became a Pal Buick and Volvo dealership. Although the Big Three were unhappy with this new arrangement, called "duals," legally they could not take prohibitory action, and many more duals proliferated around the country.)

## THE LAST YEAR'S MODEL ALLOWANCE

Sloan ingratiated himself and General Motors to the dealers by executing a new arrangement to move old models through to the customer before the appearance of the more desired, new models. It marked the first occasion in the automobile industry for these "year end sales."

In the past arrangement, dealers had to liquidate old models at their own expense to make way for the arrival of the new models to which they were contractually tied by annual sales projections. The old policy worked to the dealers' advantage if the GM model was attractive and their original estimate was correct on the number of cars they could move through to customers. But if a model proved less appealing, then the dealer had to take a season-end financial loss.

Under Sloan's insistence, GM started to offer allowances to dealers on their remaining inventories. There was a statistical formula to decide the amount. The reduction of the old model to a zero sum of cars was never the objective since Sloan understood that some old models had to be on hand at the showroom in the month when the new models arrived.

## ESTABLISHING FINANCIAL CONTROLS FOR THE DEALERS

Sloan still remained discontent with the overall General Motors and dealer contractual accords. He found an inequality of management skills among the dealers. Some were successful while others were not making a decent return on capital despite selling in large volumes. The dealers' hodgepodge methods of finances and selling, every dealership an independent and autonomous entity, caused Sloan anxiety. He called the dealer network the "weakest link" in the General Motors' raw material to customer chain, and he wrote: "I feel a great deal of uncertainty as to the operating system of the dealer organization as a whole."[11]

The question was how to change it effectively and quickly? How to stamp Sloan's innovative genius on the independent dealer network?

Time and time again, Alfred P. Sloan, Jr., demonstrated an intelligence in solving complex problems, often by employing proven methods that had worked well for him and General Motors in the past. The inventive solution to how best to manage and organize the vast and disparate dealer network of more than 13,000 separate U.S. franchises rested in the finding and the analysis of facts. After the national dealer data had been gathered, then Sloan would find some efficient way to modify the workings of the dealer network to the betterment of both parties.

Because Sloan headed up Hyatt Roller Bearing for some years, he had garnered firsthand experience with operating a small business, and it made him more sensitive to the plight of the dealers. Instinctively, Sloan knew that introducing some sort of financial control would prove the key to the innovative dealer system. In one sense, he aspired to replicate the executive committee's centralized control over the franchise owners in a manner similar to the committee's financial control over GM's divisions. But since the dealerships were independent from the parent corporation, GM could only recommend changes; it could not force its will upon the dealers.

Sloan decided that General Motors had to assess the dealership's financial systems internally. He recognized that GM as a large organization with sophisticated systems and procedures could find the financial personnel within the company and the time to compile a major dealer report. Here was another stoke of his genius, GM would incur the costs involved in a research project and then share these findings with the dealer network at no cost to the franchise owners.

Never a penny pincher when it came to potential improvements, Sloan was willing to pay for the dealer research with supplementary GM corporate funds. He regarded the study as investment spending. The money expended would, he estimated, establish an accounting system that would enable GM to gauge accurately—through financial dealer statements sent back regularly to the company—how each dealership was performing. The financial data would trigger alarms about poorer functioning dealerships and give GM some lead time to correct problems or, in drastic situations, to consider closing down the dealership: "If I could wave a magic wand over our dealer organization with the result that every dealer would have a proper accounting system...I would be willing to pay for that accomplishment."[12]

The new system was an auditing process set up in 1927 and called Motors Accounting Company. Sloan sent a missionary staff into the field to install and sell the benefit of the new financial system. The research was a statistical sampling operation of 1,300 dealers, approximately 10 percent of total dealerships, and representing 30 percent of unit sales. The result as Sloan stated: "...was a big an expensive effort but it enabled each division of General Motors and the central office to look through the whole distribution system."[13]

When the first audit sampling was completed, GM published the results for all the dealers to read. In this manner, franchises could compare their sales and accounting data with the group averages of other GM dealerships. In net, GM dealer benchmarks were established for the first time by the parent company. Information, previously unrecorded, now became a standard operating procedure. Sloan had put the dealerships on notice that General Motors had now instituted franchise performance norms.

## INVESTING IN THE DEALERSHIPS

Two quandaries remained in Sloan's amelioration of the dealer relationship: The first, how to reduce dealer turnover and support capable and savvy dealers who lacked the necessary capital for expansion? And the second, how to amend and improve the General Motors and dealership contractual agreement?

The answer to the first problem was the formation of another GM-operated entity called the Motors Holding Division. This department's objective was to supply capital to franchise owners in exchange for shares of their dealerships. Sloan bragged about this new investment concept: "When we got past the experimental stage, we realized that this was one of the best ideas we ever had in the distribution field."[14]

The objective of Motors Holding was to find and then fund the best potential managers to run and own a General Motors dealership. This investigative process might have been the nation's first systemized franchise owner search. It represented a further example of Sloan's reliance on as many facts as he could gather before making a decision, even though choosing dealers involved many other subjective and nonquantifiable judgments.

General Motors provided seed capital, management techniques, and ongoing assistance and advice with but one goal: to make the dealer profitable. Sloan's objective was to train the dealer in the most efficient methods as revealed by studying successful GM franchises. The ultimate goal was for the dealers to become so successful that they could buy the GM-owned shares and then be the sole owners of their businesses. However, the dealers evinced a certain reluctance to part from the parent company. Sloan cited: "...the assistance provided by Motors Holding was so highly valued that the dealers often resisted purchasing the last shares of Motors Holding's investment."[15]

By becoming stakeholders in the individual dealerships via stock purchase, General Motors was able to increase its familiarity with the total automobile retail operation. In effect, through Motors Holding, Sloan was able to sit inside the location with dealers, developing a first-hand understanding of the problems of running a dealership. He called this new understanding, "...a clearer and more sympathetic knowledge of the dealers' problems."[16] Ever the pragmatist, Sloan emphasized that the significance of the Motors Holding experience was in the knowledge of maintaining the adequate amount of dealer capitalization.

Interestingly, Sloan referred to the Motors Holding Company program as making "character loans." He saw clearly that risk capital had to be supplied to the entrepreneur franchise owner, the small businessmen who made up the heart and economic soul of America. And he could pat himself on the back when both Ford Motor Company (1950) and the Chrysler Company (1954) implemented similar dealer lending plans. Never one to compliment himself, he relied upon an associate, Herbert M. Gould, a former manager of Motors Holding to say: "When your competitors follow you, that's the medal in the business."[17]

## THE NEW DEALER COMMUNICATION

The final part of Sloan's adjustment of the dealership relationship represented the intersecting of two of his chief operating principles: generating facts and encouraging dissent. Sloan had stated that he was "never interested in business relationships that were not of benefit to all concerned." He needed to find that better way for GM and the dealers to communicate. He knew that there were many problems of broad, corporationwide policy that required closer contact and information leading to some definite cooperative actions.[18]

The innovative solution to this problem of communication was the formation of the General Motors Dealer Council. At the historic juncture in 1934 of GM history, Sloan saw a mutual benefit by inviting dealers into company headquarters for discussions. The first attempt saw 48 dealers (later, Sloan invited other dealers so new and different voices would be heard) divided into four panels of 12 dealers each. GM executives, including Sloan, sat in on the individual panels. The purpose was clear: "The first job of the council was the long practice of working out the general policies for improved dealer relations. Our meetings dealt with policy and not the administration of policy."[19]

The crux of the meetings was to hammer out the dealer selling agreement, the document that determined the specific conditions in the automobile industry that existed between the parent company and the franchise owners. Difficult topics were brought to light and debated. These included the length of the contract agreement, number of days given before cancellation for nonperformance, allocation of number of vehicles, number of maximum dealerships in a defined area, and importantly, the rights of dealers to pass on franchises to their family in case of death.

By inviting dealers into discussions, Sloan sent a strong message that GM and its distributors were all working together for a harmonious goal: profit for all parties. Sloan was magnanimous in praise of the council when he said in a 1937 talk to the members: "I have been particularly impressed with the broad approach to these problems. . . . I am encouraged by the practically unanimous desire to solve these problems from the standpoint of fundamental soundness."[20]

(The dealers demonstrated their sincere appreciation to Sloan by presenting him with a check for $1,525,000, designated for cancer research at the Alfred P. Sloan, Jr., Foundation. Years later, this group became known as the General Motors Dealer Appreciation Fund for Cancer and Medical Research and continued its generous donations.)

## THE LAST DEALER STEP: ARBITRATION

Sloan had set in place an effective dealer arrangement to handle problems during the turbulent depression years to the war years when General Motors' sales declined significantly and some smaller dealerships went out of business. He had employed the principles of democratic representation, and all sides had a chance to air their opinions and suggestions.

In the early 1960s, General Motors took the final step in the dealer-company understanding by the appointment of an outside arbiter, a retired judge, to listen to possible dealer appeals regarding decisions relating to their contractual General Motors agreement.

Over the years of his leadership, Sloan had elevated the dealers to active participants in the General Motors Corporation. He had given them data, loans, advice, and finally, a council of their own. No decisions about their status became arbitrary or personal; the facts, most of these financial, determined outcomes with the parent company.

Management guru Peter Drucker would praise the General Motors dealer system that Sloan had formulated as exceptional and innovative. He stated that the general principles by which General Motors had solved the problem—federalism and the resolution of conflicts in harmony—"might well provide a model for a job that is still to be done in other branches of America's economy."[21]

## CELL PHONE DEALERSHIP STORES

Wireless companies have been forced to open, staff, and operate cell phone retail stores as necessary dealership systems to sell phone plans to a confused customer base. The widespread proliferation of these stores in malls and city locations has proved to be an essential method for generating additional users and increasing market share.

Initially, the reason to staff and stock these retail outlets grew out of the need to help guide prospective customers through the often mystifying maze of cell phone choices and cell phone plans. With so many different choices for phones and plans, many customers required the one-on-one dialogue that only a personal store visit to a dealership could provide.

The full-page advertisements for the retail stores, from Sprint, Verizon, T-Mobile, Cingular, and others, all trumpet a headline about a particular company plan, but what catches the consumer's eye is mainly the deal offered for the cell phones. The cell phone hardware serves as the siren song to lure the potential customer into the store. The key words in the ad copy are "Free" or "Save $" for the cell phone and not the headlines that offer, for example, "Add a line for $9.99" or "No unfair overages." To the future user or plan switcher, these monthly plans are baffling enumerations of the number of lines, number of minutes allowed, and then seemingly subjective prices per month for the service.

Further, the dealership stores allow the user to pick from among many cell phone brands and then to test phones for ease, portability, and also to check the various inner-workings. Some customers use these sessions as prepurchase practice and instruction periods to master the puzzling details on how to use all the phone's hidden tone and messaging benefits.

In addition, there are also many discount retail cell phone dealership stores that offer many plans from many different companies and also sell a variety of cell phone brands. These stores fill the gaps of the major carriers like Sprint and Cingular and receive a commission for selling a company's plan.

The consumer dynamic of seeing the advertisement and then visiting the store to take advantage of the specific deal can turn into a modified bait and switch if the consumer is a cell phone neophyte and unsure of what kind of phone and what kind of plan. But to paraphrase Sloan's statement on the reasons for purchasing an automobile, "Today the type of cell phone is a most important factor in wireless communication because every one knows the phone will work."

## NEW DEALINGS WITH AUTOMOBILE DEALERS

In the 1980s, automobile consumer research revealed a fact that every American already knew: Consumers across the country abhorred the process of negotiation for new and used vehicles at their neighborhood dealerships. The dealers and their sales employees were considered rip-off artists, venal price gougers who generated gigantic (and unwarranted) profits from a gullible public that had no freedom of choice in car purchasing.

The dealers took no steps, no counterargument to deter this opinion, false though it was. Stand up comics, cartoons, movies, and television shows all alluded to the horrible experience of Americans visiting their local car dealership. The new car purchase became an uncomfortable national rite, a painful ceremony that fostered ill-will toward the dealership, its employees, and the automotive companies that allowed this off-putting process to continue.

The actual operational facts were different; dealerships generated modest profit margins of between 5 and 10 percent, a low profit margin considering the large capital outlay and extensive inventory needed to show and stock cars. The truth that no one publicized was that dealers made more substantial profit from finance and insurance and also from postsale parts and service than from selling cars

How had these national negative feelings developed about car dealerships? And what was the root cause?

The answer had nothing to do with dealers and everything to do with the Big Three U.S. car companies, which, after World War II, franchised so many new dealerships that, in many places of the country, the marketplace was oversaturated. In the northeast and midwest, with their large and contiguous populations, same make dealerships seemingly popped up in town after neighboring town. The expansion occurred less in the southwest and west. But the modus operandi of the new car hassle continued nationwide.

With so many dealerships competing for business from the same local population universe, dealers had to scrape for every cent of profit. The results were cost-conscious operations that tried to make a decent profit per car because it was not possible to generate a large volume with so many nearby competitors from all car companies and all models. This in turn caused constant negotiating for price as dealers struggled to make a profit.

Into this picture stepped the Japanese automakers who studied the oversaturation by the Big Three American car makers. The Japanese understood the annoyance bargaining engendered among Americans buying cars. Toyota, Nissan, and Honda decided to transform the buying experience by making newly purchased automobiles a fixed price, no discounting process. The customer knew what the price was and paid it. In effect, said the Japanese, a car is not unlike an article of clothing or an appliance from a department store, it has a fixed price and there is no negotiation in the sale.

Further, the Japanese decided to create larger sales territories for their franchise owners so that dealerships would not be vying for the same customers in the same area. The dealerships were spread out to avoid manufacturer cannibalization. With plenty of room to work, the Japanese car franchise owners could concentrate on sales and service without the double bind of bothersome negotiations and also the competition from other dealers close to the location. (Today in the United States there are about 5,000 Chevrolet dealerships and only 1,100 for Toyota.)

Over time, Americans came to understand what constituted the fixed price of a car the dealer paid the manufacturer for both foreign and domestic manufacturers. The Internet supplied sticker price information, including the car maker's invoice cost to the dealerships, the dealer prep charge, and the shipping cost to transport the vehicles to the dealership. Consumers could decide whether or not they wanted to hassle with the dealer or not.

## THE MEGADEALERSHIPS

Some years ago, investment bankers looking for the next wave of new profits from existing businesses turned their eyes toward the staid and unchanged American automobile franchise operation. What especially interested Wall Street was the anomalous fact that an automobile dealer who sold 100 cars annually paid the same price to the manufacturer as the dealer who sold 1,000. There was no volume purchase discount built into the sales price of domestic or foreign automobile companies.

(The one exception to the same price for everyone rule are the rental car fleets that are offered a discount by the U.S. car makers. Hertz and Avis purchase thousands of new cars, often the same model, annually. The car manufacturers argue that these automobiles are not for initial new car sale and therefore do not impede dealer sales.)

The innovative idea developed that megadealerships could sell a significantly greater number of cars and then demand a sizable discount from car companies. By receiving discounts, the megadealer could then offer cars at a lower price to the consumer. Over time, volume sales would offset the lower profit margins. The objective was to create a Wal-Mart–style lower-priced car dealership.

This radical idea led to the start of Auto Nation, United Auto Group, Sonic, and other supersized auto dealerships. These new megacompanies issued stock, but the results have been mixed as far as Wall Street is concerned.

The reason for middling sales is that the megadealerships have not yet attracted customers in such great numbers to be able to put pressure on the car manufacturers for a possible volume discount. Further, the manufacturers have started to limit the number of consolidated dealerships in a territory in an attempt to curtail one dealer from dominating the market. The superdealerships have arrived but so far they do not offer substantial savings in purchase.

## THE LESSONS OF DEALERSHIP IMPROVEMENT

Most companies do not have discrete dealerships in the manner of automobile or insurance companies, relying instead on distribution systems. However, some of the suggestions for dealer improvement can also apply to current channels of distribution.

### GO INTO THE FIELD

After Sloan's extensive nationwide railroad visits to GM's dealer network, he had a better factual understanding of who the dealers were, their needs, and specifically, their problems. He was able to fashion a new system because of the one-on-one interaction with the franchise owners that he met in the field.

As a matter of standard practice, many companies send representatives into the field—usually, incognito—to produce empirical information after interfacing with the dealer or distribution staff to simulate real-world customer visits. These unannounced drop-ins pinpoint problem areas in how potential clients are treated.

### GATHER AND SHARE DEALER INFORMATION

Another successful practice is to gather feedback via dealer telephone surveys or by conducting one-on-one qualitative interviews in the field. The key is to share this information with the entire dealer network. Some dealers or distributors outperform others, and it will be helpful to share the systems that succeeded.

Too frequently, companies complain about their dealership or distribution networks without making ongoing efforts to understand the particular problems of hiring, inventory systems, and sales. A company that shares proven methods and systems helps the dealers remain in business.

Sloan was honest in reporting that because the automobile manufacturers were undercapitalized in the early days of the automobile, they had no choice but to approve the franchise system as the only way to sell their cars. More advantageous to the car makers would have been owning and servicing the franchises themselves. But he also understood the reliance of the manufacturer on the dealer network when he wrote:

> . . . in 1927 started a new approach to the purchaser-dealer relations at General Motors, based upon the recognition of the community of interest between the corporation and the dealers and of the interdependence of our interests. [22]

# 10

# THE CORPORATE IMAGE: ADVERTISING AND PUBLIC RELATIONS

*S loan realizes the need to publicize the parent corporation...Sloan and GM discover Bruce Barton, advertising genius...Barton begins GM's institutional advertising campaign...The campaign begins with excellent internal results...Pontiac name first introduced, using the GM corporate advertising...The corporate campaign moves into the other GM divisions...The results of Sloan's institutional campaign...The General Electric corporate campaign parallels GM with Bruce Barton...Nike, the success of "Just Do It!"...Ford stages a comeback with memorable advertising...MasterCard, the ultimate success...The managerial lessons for corporate advertising*

෴ ෴

After Alfred P. Sloan, Jr., had succeeded in establishing his system for the inner workings of the organization with the formation of the executive, purchase, and finance committees, he started the institutional advertising committee. This step would result in one of the most successful institutional advertising campaigns in American history.

Before it began advertising in 1922, General Motors was practically an unknown and undefined corporate name. In less than a decade, the company became one of the most respected and trusted names in the United States, an icon of dependability as symbolic of the nation's virtues and strength as the American eagle.

During the 1920 decade that witnessed the birth of the new consumerism with sweeping national prosperity, GM hoped to tap into the dynamic American spirit by positioning itself as the car company of the highest achievement. The ad campaign's objective would be to transform the disparate automobile divisions into one, recognizable and approved entity—General Motors. Sloan recognized the problem: "The next significant step toward co-ordination was in the area of advertising. I had had some consumer studies made in 1922, and we found that people throughout the United States, except at the corner of Wall and Broad Streets, didn't know anything about General Motors."[1]

The modus operandi was typical Sloan: first, to define the problem (no advertising awareness on a corporate level); second, to commission a study to investigate the depth of the problem (Did consumers know about GM? And, if yes, what did they think about the company?); and finally, to find a solution.

In the 1920s, publicizing the parent company was not a novel advertising idea to corporate America. Some of the country's larger companies like the Pullman Car Company and AT&T had mounted "do good" institutional advertising campaigns.

Among the memorable goodwill campaigns were a series of print ads from the Metropolitan Life Insurance Company that were informational health- or hearth-oriented. One featured a drawing of an elderly man sitting forlornly on a bed under the headline "Home or Homes?" The copy went on to describe the lonely conditions of old people living in squalor.

Of note also is that at the bottom of the ad under the words Metropolitan Life, came the tagline, "Biggest in the world. More assets. More policy holders. More insurance in force. More new insurance each year." Really, quite a mouthful, even 80 years ago, and a stark contrast to the company's current and concise tagline, "Have you met life today?"

## SLOAN FINDS BRUCE BARTON

The brilliance of Sloan's many managerial decisions are shaped like perfectly wrought pyramids with the bottom and wider sections indicating the breadth of his thinking, upward a level to the research studies, and then narrowing to the small triangle on the top that can be considered the person chosen to execute the policy. Kettering rested atop of the research pyramid; Raskob and Brown sat at the apex of the finance triangle; and Knudsen was at the pinnacle of Chevrolet manufacturing. Harley Earl was on top of the styling pyramid.

What Sloan needed to find was the most capable and talented person to undertake the corporate advertising campaign for the company. Again, his selection demonstrated his skill for choosing intuitively the individual who could succeed with the undertaking. He decided upon a brilliant wordsmith, an Amherst College–educated, self-confident son of a clergyman, named Bruce Barton. Barton was the cofounder in 1919 of the advertising agency BDO, derived from the first initials of the surnames of Bruce Barton, Roy Durstine, and Alex Osborn. (George Batten would add his name in 1928 to make it into the famous BBDO agency.)

Barton began his meteoric rise to advertising fame by insisting on the exactitude of language to instill products and companies with positive, human characteristics. His first copy assignment revealed his genius for catching the reader's attention. P. P. Collier's published *The Harvard Classics,* an all-inclusive anthology of 50 important historic literary and philosophical works (such as *The Aeneid*, *Don Quixote*, volumes of English and American poetry, etc.). But sales remained below the publisher's expectation until Barton wrote an advertisement with the startling headline: "This Is Marie Antoinette Riding to Her Death." The copy informed the reader of the useful value of being familiar with the well-known classics of literature. The ad generated sales of 400,000 sets of the literary series.

Later during World War I, Barton wrote the famous Salvation Army slogan, "A Man May Be Down, But He Is Never Out." The culmination of his wartime work was to pen an attention-getting Victory Loan campaign targeted at New Yorkers. The ad (which must have caught Sloan's attention since he lived in Manhattan) was called "I Am New York and This Is My Creed," and it conferred on the giant metropolis its own personality. David Farber writes: "[Barton's] advertisements were meant to ennoble New Yorkers by leading them to appreciate what a high-minded city they lived in, which, in turn would prompt their buying war bonds."[2]

In the back of Sloan's mind must have been the thought that if well-written and literate advertising copy could create a warm and distinct persona for New York City, then it was possible to accomplish a similar, positive outcome for the General Motors Corporation.

Barton always exuded self-assurance and positive enthusiasm without ever revealing any huckster or hustler side. He genuinely believed in himself and in his work. His goal would be eventually to change General Motors into a symbol of the American family by transforming GM into something personal and human. Over his lifetime, he coined many memorable quotes: "If you can give your child only one gift, let it be enthusiasm," and "In good times, people want to advertise; in bad times, they have to."

So it was to Barton and his agency that Sloan turned to in 1922 to breathe new life into the General Motors corporate image. Sloan's biographer wrote: "The Barton Sloan knew was a bundle of enthusiasm, can-do certainty, and effervescent creativity.[3]

These were the precise qualities that Sloan searched for in a person who would establish the General Motors name.

## THE GENERAL MOTORS INSTITUTIONAL CAMPAIGN

In 1922, General Motors generated a significantly lower share of the automobile market than Ford Motor Company. The corporation consisted of five disparate passenger car divisions, a truck division, and more than a dozen accessory and component companies. It had little or no public image, hindered by the consumer's lack of knowledge that one company controlled the manufacturer of familiarly recognizable brand-named cars (Buick, Cadillac, Oldsmobile) that had stood alone and independent for years.

A second problem that BDO had to overcome was that GM's auto companies and its subsidiaries did not feel that they belonged to a central, corporate unit. Under William Durant, the car companies had acted as self-governing entities and, at first, they resented Sloan's decree of decentralization. Still, by 1923, there was a visible lack of coordination between the divisions.

Further, General Motors' headquarters was in Manhattan, which must have seemed like a "foreign" power making the decisions for the companies whose plants and culture were rooted in the industrial midwest. There also could have been some resentment toward the wealthy and patrician Pierre du Pont, the interim president, and later to his M.I.T.–educated, eastern-born-and-bred successor.

Everyone in the automobile business knew that Alfred P. Sloan, Jr., was a component's expert and subsidiaries' manager, not someone who had climbed the executive ladder of Michigan car manufacturing with years of axle grease on his hands. After all, no one had driven in a "Sloan" vehicle in the manner of an Olds, Dodge, or Chrysler.

In essence, Barton's difficult task was twofold: to create a positive corporate campaign for General Motors in front of the public and also a campaign that would engender enthusiasm and pride of workmanship among the GM employees. Barton had many meetings with Sloan in Manhattan and also accompanied him frequently by rail to Detroit. There Barton and his staff interviewed many GM employees to determine morale and to generate a feeling about the workers' attitudes toward the company.

In an unusual sequence, BDO decided first to pursue a campaign internally within General Motors before moving forward with its institutional public advertisements. BDO printed brochures, distributing these throughout the corporation to division managers.

The GM car dealerships were given jumbo-sized posters, which they displayed prominently in showroom windows. The literature described a great American company making strides through better workmanship and more efficient productivity. The internal handouts also featured articles about the forthcoming consumer ads that would talk about General Motors in terms of a unified "family."

BDO solicited the workforce for positive General Motors' stories to embellish its corporate theme of family, a metaphor for the corporation and the consumer. This digging around the company for actual, real-world consumer experiences was novel for its time. The goal was to find exciting cases of GM automobile car performance and of American lives that were altered for the better as a result of driving a GM car.

The first two-page advertisement consisted of a drawing of George Washington astride his horse, majestically overlooking a rustic and prosperous idyllic American landscape. The title to the story was "Making the Nation a Neighborhood." Washington embarks on a journey through the new nation to advocate national unity (GM corporate as family) of purpose as opposed to 13 disparate state goals (the many divisions of GM). The copy began, "George Washington saw clearly and far ahead. He saw Distance was the enemy which menaced the republic most."

In the upper-right-hand corner was a Chevrolet in front of a modern house. The storyline combined the greatness of the father of the country with the dependability of Chevrolet automobiles made by General Motors. Chevy's familiar bowtie logo appeared at the end of the copy.

Of key importance was the name General Motors in all-capital letters, running along the bottom of the ad with each word appearing on a separate page. The corporation's name represented about 15 percent of the total length of the ad. In size, the General Motors' name stood about three times larger than the Chevrolet logo, an indication to the reader that General Motors was the essential name to remember.

The ad marked also a significant break with the past because "Corporation" had been dropped from the advertisement. The name General Motors standing alone, presented a friendlier name and image.

Other two-page ads continued on the same theme. One showed a family on their way to a picnic and waiting for a train. The headline stated, "*Now* This Family Can Have Its Own Car." To emphasize the negative aspect of waiting, a sullen boy is seated on the ground, obviously despondent that he has to pass the time waiting. A companion ad depicted another family already eating at a picnic table. This ad unreservedly solved the waiting problem of the other family; its headline offered the good news that: "The Whole Family Enjoys Life Much More. Because It Owned a General Motors Car."

The family theme continued after BDO started to receive first-person accounts from GM employees and letters from customers about their GM automobile experience. Some described vivid accounts of a GM automobile coming to the rescue or working in an emergency.

Sifting through this considerable stack, BDO produced warm ads that depicted GM vehicles performing an altruistic or heroic deed. In one ad, a country doctor saves the life of a dying child thanks to a GM car. The headline read "That the Doctor May Arrive in Time." In the upper-left-hand corner was a car plowing through a severe storm and the entire right-hand page depicted a beautiful drawing of the doctor, the little girl asleep in bed, and the grateful mother beaming at the physician. The copy began, "There came an urgent call at night."

No sentiment was left untouched. One of the first-person ads told of a journey by a clergyman. This ad, which was titled "Through the Eyes of Faith," began, "Out of hundreds of letters from pastors and priests, let us quote only one." The story told of the pastor's newly found ability to minister to remote communities thanks to his General Motors automobile.

The success of the family theme worked both with the consumer and within the corporation. These kinds of ads would later be renamed "goodwill" advertising, a term used for a broad institutional campaign to influence public perception. The primary objective, at least in GM's case, was not to sell automobiles. The soft "sell" was to generate universal goodwill, and the external and internal campaigns accomplished this institutional goal.

## THE GENERAL MOTORS CAR FAMILY AD CAMPAIGNS

Alfred P. Sloan, Jr., stated that General Motors should offer "A car for every price and purpose." With the increasing national prosperity of the 1920s and the realization that the automobile buyer wanted more than an open-air, black Model-T Ford, GM had to distinguish among the main differences between its five car divisions. It had to make the public aware of the divisional variances in style, engine size, and chassis among its offerings.

Sloan instructed General Motors' research section to measure the success of the campaign titled "Facts about a Famous Family" because this top banner appeared on many of the ads. The department's preliminary findings indicated that the public responded positively. This lead Sloan to the conclusion that the company could introduce its new car line, emphasizing that it came from "the GM family."

Initially, GM and BDO decided to piggyback the divisional advertisements onto the institutional "Family" campaign. Barton decided that if the corporation itself could be assigned a singular "benefit," (e.g., thoughtful, caring, patriotic, and reliable), then each individual car should also have its own unique attribute.

For example, an Oldsmobile ad retold the story of a cross-country race in 1905, when two Oldsmobiles raced from New York City to Portland, Oregon. The headline blared, "What Oldsmobile Brou ght to General Motors." The race winner called "Old Scout" made the trip in 45 days. Old Scout's transcontinental voyage—much like the Conestoga wagon pioneers who headed out west on the Oregon Trail in the 1840s—trumpeted the energetic American family spirit of a successful General Motors product. The copy reinforced the unification of car and company; thus Oldsmobile brought to General Motors the courage of the pioneer.

### THE "FAMILY" CAMPAIGN FOR THE OAKLAND/PONTIAC

During the mid 1920s, Sloan decided that to fill in the gaps between the company's car divisions he needed a mass-produced, smooth running, lower-priced six-cylinder car in a closed body. But he realized that it should not be a low-price Chevrolet since the new car offered a more powerful engine than a standard Chevy four cylinder and also other, better, styling benefits. The general manager of the Oakland division requested permission to manufacture this new car and sell it as a subclass model in his division.

The ad for Oakland in 1922 simply said "The Company behind the Oakland" and described General Motors. In all the ads, the General Motors name was written in bold across the bottom of the pages.

Four years later, in 1926, General Motors decided to introduce the Oakland's companion car under the name "Pontiac" after the Michigan city in which it was built. The name also conjured up memories of the great Indian chief of the Ottawa tribe who had banded together four Indian nations into a powerful confederation that, ironically, attacked Detroit.

The first Pontiac model introduced was called "Chief of the Sixes," a six-cylinder car that was launched at the 1926 New York City

Auto Show. This began Pontiac's association with the history of the famous chief that would broaden to include a stylized head of an Indian as the logo. Further, keeping with GM's utilizing Americana to tell its family story, Chief Pontiac's name could also represent another symbol of American history similar to Oldsmobile's Old Scout.

The advertisement introducing the first Pontiac touted the car as "reflecting 17 years of General Motors experience." The new model was a big success, and many perceived that the General Motors imprimatur had abetted the introduction by citing that it came from an established and now recognized American car company. The Oakland name was permanently dropped in 1932; after that year Pontiac would be the only name of this division.

Sales of Oakland cars jumped from 44,642 in 1925 to 133,604 in 1926—the largest percentage gain of GM's five divisions. The next year in 1927, its second year as Oakland-Pontiac, it rose again to 188,168. Finally, in 1928 it overtook Buick for second place among the five divisions, selling 244,584 cars. In three years, the Oakland-Pontiac models had increased an astounding 200,000 cars, much of the spectacular gain coming from its new closed-body chassis but also because it was successfully promoted through the General Motors "Family" ad and its individual model campaigns.

## THE "FAMILY" CAMPAIGN FOR OTHER DIVISIONS

Sloan was so confident by the acceptance of the family theme that he authorized its use for Frigidaire. In 1927, an ad proudly stated: "The Only Electric Refrigerator Made and Guaranteed by General Motors." And, in another unusual, two-page ad, the headline read: "The Car in the Kitchen." The drawing on the left showed people taking food out of the Frigidaire, while the opposite page depicted a woman welcoming a male guest whose GM car was parked in front of the open door. The copy read, "General Motors early recognized that the market for electric refrigerators was as great as that for automobiles." Again, the large General Motors name split the two-page spread.

Using the "Facts about a Famous Family" top banner, GM created separate ads for its Research Laboratories. One headline read "Day and Night in Dayton" and related the fact that GM automobiles were being driven 24 hours a day to assess any faults in the operating and mechanical systems.

Even Body by Fisher merited its own ad, a beautiful rendition of a Fifth Avenue woman in a torrential downpour standing under the large, safe umbrella held aloft by the fashionable building's liveried doorman. The headline said, "Like Sterling on Silver." The analogy was that the Fisher Body's closed-car design would protect passengers with the same waterproof assurance of the dedicated doorman. The famous Fisher French coach logo appeared in a small square.

(The Fisher Brothers adopted the elegant coach design logo from the Napoleonic era to denote a link back in time to handcrafted chassis workmanship. The emblem actually combined two different coaches: the one used at Napoleon's coronation and the other for his nuptials to Marie Louise of Austria.)

## THE RESULTS OF GM'S INSTITUTIONAL ADVERTISING

The year 1923 began General Motors' rapid ascendancy to the top position in U.S. automobile manufacture. The two most important reasons were Alfred P. Sloan, Jr.'s decision to offer a wide range of cars in appealing models and prices coupled with Henry Ford's unwillingness to alter his one-model, one-color car. But a third reason for GM's success can be attributed to the innovative institutional family-theme advertising that Bruce Barton and BDO created for the corporation and for the individual divisions.

By the end of the decade of the Roaring Twenties, Americans had established a new and positive image of General Motors. Sloan's overall goal for corporate unification through centralization had succeeded additionally in the field of advertising. The goodwill institutional campaign demonstrated the effectiveness of a well-thought-out and well-executed campaign. All Americans could relate to the subtle messages in the BDO American-family stories.

Somewhat overlooked has been the importance of the transformation of the workforce within General Motors. The binding of disparate divisions into a cohesive entity facilitated Sloan and his management's ability to generate confidence with each new manufacturing and marketing decision. Sloan said: "You started on a course with a policy and things not foreseen fell into place."[4]

The wonderful "things not foreseen" at General Motors would be the company's acknowledgment that Alfred P. Sloan, Jr., demonstrated time and again a managerial intelligence unmatched in the corporate world of American business. It was good to be on a successful team lead by such a talented president and innovator.

## GENERAL ELECTRIC: THE PARALLEL INSTITUTIONAL AD CAMPAIGN

The similarities between General Motors and General Electric down through the past century are many and varied; the connection of their first names, the well-known two-letter, GM and GE identification initials, and also the market dominance within their fields. Both also started profitable financing divisions (GMAC and GE Capital) that have continued to pump money into the corporations. The list could be enlarged, perhaps designating GE's former CEO, Jack Welch, the most recent heir apparent to Alfred P. Sloan, Jr.'s mantel of American corporate managerial brilliance.

But there is another story to tell of General Electric's decision in the 1920s to embark on an institutional advertising campaign that joined the nation's two big corporations together at the same advertising agency at the same time, where both would have goodwill institutional campaigns undertaken and planned by Bruce Barton and BDO.

Historically, General Electric in the 1920s was known principally as a manufacturer of heavy industrial electrical equipment (turbines and motors). Its light bulbs (called lamps back then) and electric fans represented the few products marketed directly to the public. Logically, selling mainly to a range of amorphous state utilities and different railroads, the company had no need to pursue any public relations campaign for the consumer market. What people remembered about General Electric—if recalling any fact at all—was that Thomas Edison started the company, incorporated in 1892.

In 1922, two executives, Owen Young and Gerard Swope, took over the leadership of the company from the stewardship of CEO Charles Coffin, a conservative businessman from the old school. Young was a Boston University–trained lawyer whose early specialty was mediation and negotiation. He helped create the Radio Corporation of America (RCA). Swope was an M.I.T. classmate of

Sloan, who had served as an executive at Western Electric, a GE subsidiary.

(Later in life, both Sloan and Swope were members of an advisory board at their M.I.T. alma mater that supervised the teaching of a course called "Engineering Administration," which covered finance, accounting, law, marketing, and other business-oriented subjects to the techies at M.I.T.)

Owens and Swope had a different and progressive vision of the new age of consumerism. One of their first tasks was to improve the public's perception of General Electric and also to meld into one entity the dissimilar and far-spread manufacturing subsidiaries. In the latter case, GE had many wholly owned businesses that sold products under their own brand or company names, many without reference to or benefit from General Electric, its historic Edison beginnings, or its valuable two-letter script logo trademark.

Swope had a short-range plan for the company to start to produce more consumer electric products. He could see that the decade of the 1920s before him would represent new prosperity, and he wanted General Electric to be in a position to meet the burgeoning demand for radios, lamps, toasters, and other household appliances. The company could retool for its consumer push, but it needed to create a positive image in the public's eye.

Bruce Barton assessed the GE problem, which appeared on the surface similar to that of General Motors. Both companies had not created positive or definite images at the public level. In fact, both suffered from appearances of big businesses run by Wall Street trusts with little consideration for the average American worker. Both experienced poor or low employee morale, and both companies needed to unite their many divisions into one cohesive unit.

Barton decided that what was good for General Motors would be also good for General Electric, an institutional advertising campaign that would advance a grand corporate purpose and a reason for being. Essential to the external campaign's objective was to heighten the prominence of the distinctive logo so that it appeared in every General Electric ad. Importantly, the decision had been made that the initials "GE" would appear more welcoming than the cold "General Electric Company." Again, similar to General Motors' "corporation" ending; GE's "company" was considered a negative term that hindered establishing a positive and warmly personalized public image.

One of the first BDO ads showed the GE circular script logo on top of the page in a notably large size. The headline said simply, "The Initials of a Friend." The first paragraph lead stated, "You will find these letters on many tools by which electricity works." Two short paragraphs later, the copy ended with, "Hence the letters G-E are more than a trademark. They are an emblem of service—the initials of a friend." What Barton had achieved shaping a positive attitude for General Motors with "family," he would do for General Electric with "friend."

At the same time the initials were receiving such prominence in all the advertisements, they were stamped on all the products of the subsidiary companies. The GE script logo became ubiquitous. Barton and the ad agency printed the advertisements for the newsletters published by GE's various divisions. The meaning was clear; you may think you work for the Edison Lamp Company but your real employer is General Electric. Barton advised GE to make "its own organization advertising conscious."

(The origins of the GE initials logo are lost in history. The archive section of the Schenectady Museum in New York—GE's home city—affirms that the logo first appeared in 1898 as a medallion on a cordless fan, although the designer's name is unknown. But some historians state that a similar logo was used centuries ago by a Chinese warlord as a battle insignia.)

In effect, the GM and GE campaigns could have been switched with little change in copy or headline. George Washington's trip to unite the GM nation could have also represented GE's subsidiaries that, at the beginning, resented losing autonomous control over their marketing and advertising. "Friend" and "family" are interchangeable to these giant corporations.

But there was one significant difference between the external advertising that Barton created for the two companies. Owens and Swope shared a pronounced social conscience that neither Sloan nor his GM board possessed. Swope had served for a year as head of the famous Jane Addams's Hull House settlement programs in Chicago. Owens had served on the post–World War I committee to determine German reparations. The two men also had sincere concerns for worker safety and the development of employee programs.

Some of these revolutionary social ideas became components of Franklin Delano Roosevelt's New Deal programs.

Bruce Barton was up to this task of social reform. Using the same dramatic drawing style from the General Motors' doctor on call or clergyman ads, he created a one-page ad with the provocative headline: "Any Woman Who Does Anything Which a Little Electric Motor Can Do Is Working for 3¢ an Hour!" The woman stoops over a wash tub, her despondent shadow displayed three times larger in dire black against the wall. The copy states: "There are few bleak tasks in the home that electricity cannot do something about." America could save its wives and mothers with electricity and time-saving appliances made by General Electric.

Both GE's internal and external campaigns were judged successes. Throughout the 1920s, General Electric would launch new consumer products like refrigerators and radios, adhering to Swope's vision that the future of the company rested in the growing consumer good area. All GE products would be stamped with the now recognizable logo. The advertisements had united a company into a cohesive unit. The result over the next 80 years would be a continuation of the institutional advertising goal of goodwill and more engendering of a positive public attitude.

One of the most successful corporate goodwill campaigns has been General Electric's campaign "We bring good things to life."

## NIKE—JUST DO IT!

Often times, a company that markets and sells a variety of related kinds of brands can find a broad advertising message that generates an overall benefit to the entire corporation. This kind of advertising is quasi-institutional because its primary objective is to increase sales; goodwill is not the goal.

Since its inauspicious beginnings in 1962, Nike (named after the Greek goddess of victory) has become the leader in sports gear, establishing a dominant name in track and basketball footwear, the latter, thanks to its past association with the former Chicago Bulls' megastar Michael Jordan. The brand became synonymous with sports, and it built up loyalty among the primary target group, consisting of young males aged 13 to 18, the largest sneaker-purchasing segment.

The familiar Swoosh logo has come to symbolize innovation and a love of sport achievement. A teenager may never attain the stardom of a professional basketball player, but wearing those Air Jordans and making a shot in the playground that's "all net," connects, for just an instant, the boy with the hero. And both wear Nike shoes.

(The Nike Swoosh logo was created by Oregon college student Carolyn Davidson in 1971. She was paid a $35 fee. She said that the linear curved design was inspired by a wing of the goddess Nike. In 1983, she received a diamond ring set in the Swoosh design and also company stock in appreciation for the exceptionally memorable logo.)

Nike has created a profitable crossover corporate advertising and public relations campaign that successfully incorporated all its various divisions into one, centralized theme—the memorable "Just do it" commercials that began in 1988. In addition to using specific sports magazines to advertise its individual or specialized brands (i.e., track or basketball shoes), the Nike campaign created a compelling and unforgettable sports umbrella theme into which all of its various current and future divisions would fit.

Even when the company advertised a specific sport—like soccer (with the "Secret Tournament" commercial directed by ex-Monty Python movie maker Terry Gilliam) that depicted 24 of the world's greatest professional soccer scorers—the positive reaction to the "Just do it" tagline carried over into the Nike brand name and its other products.

When Nike decided to enter into the golf market, including balls, clubs, footwear, and apparel, it decided to combine its previous two merchandising successes—megastar endorsement and the "Just do it" campaign—to promote the golf line. The idea was to jump start the extension of the brand name via an entry into a new golf market, one in which it had no previous history. The first product was a golf ball in 1999, and by 2004, the company had a 6.6 percent share of the $500 million golf-ball market.

The results of hiring Tiger Woods, coupled with "Just do it," translated into a successful new golf product introduction, at least in creating awareness. Virtually overnight, Nike established credibility as a manufacturer of golf products, a sport in which history and tradition have always been important variables.

In the final analysis, the "Just do it" theme allows Nike to increase sales within existing markets or to open new ones without having to create expensively original advertising campaigns for each new product or new line launch. In 2003, the company's revenue product mix indicated 56 percent for footwear, 29 percent for apparel, equipment at 6 percent, and other products at 9 percent. It is clear that for Nike to grow, more sales must be generated from the nonfootwear divisions. Within this minority revenue grouping, whether new equipment acquisition, footwear line introduction, or even any other ancillary business, Nike can continue to use its "Just do it" theme.

## FORD REBOUNDS WITH INSTITUTIONAL ADVERTISING

Ford Motor Company's fortunes took a sharp decline during the depression when the company fell into third place among the Big Three car manufacturers. Ford had never recovered from the 1920s organizational turnaround at General Motors and Alfred P. Sloan, Jr.'s decision-making brilliance. Up to and including World War II, Ford's operation (except for an efficient dealership sales network) seemed passé and out of tune with the newer methods of General Motors' decentralized management in every aspect of automobile production.

In the early 1940s, within the close-knit auto industry community in Detroit and on Wall Street, expectations grew that when the seasoned and industry knowledgeable Edsel Ford took over from his aging father, the Ford Company would start the process of needed change. Hopes were that after modification, Ford Motors would emerge once again as a competitor to GM and Chrysler. But sadly, Edsel Ford died in 1943. By this time, Henry Ford's paranoia and mistrust of his executives had reached a feverish peak; he had even hired a private police force to spy on the executive staff. Peter Drucker summed up Henry Ford's destructive managerial attitude: "Fundamental to Henry Ford's misrule was a systematic, deliberate, and conscious attempt *to run the billion-dollar business without managers*."[5]

By 1943, at Edsel Ford's untimely death, Henry Ford was 80 years old and incapable of operating the corporation on a day-to-day basis. He had to turn to his eldest grandson, Henry Ford II, a 27-year-old who possessed no significant managerial experience and no previous advertising expertise.

The result of the new Ford Motor Company approach saw Ford creating a series of memorable institutional ads. In effect, once Ford realized the benefit of corporate advertising for all its divisions (Ford Motor Company had acquired the Lincoln as a luxury car at auction in 1922 and added the Mercury line in the mid-1930s), it found the same capable advertising talent as GM. Ironically, since most of Ford Motor Company's many campaigns occurred after World War II, today people remember the Ford ad classics, but hardly anyone, except automobile history buffs, recalls General Motors' "Family" campaign in the 1920s.

Ford's first memorable institutional ad occurred during World War II with "There's a Ford in Your Future." This was a clever attempt from the J. Walter Thompson advertising agency to try to maintain some loyalty during a period when few Fords were manufactured and no one could buy the advertised product. The campaign spoke about a better tomorrow, a future of renewed national prosperity. One ad depicted a crystal ball with two men talking under the headline: "Talk about Style—It's Got It." The tagline was "There's a Ford in your future," with the Ford name written in the company's familiar script logo.

For the competitive truck division, the company ran the "America's Truck—Built Ford Tough" campaign that linked the durability of the truck line to the manufacture of all Ford automobile products. The word *tough* in automobile circles was owned by the Ford Motor Company thanks to this campaign.

The commercial that followed was the "Have You Driven a Ford Lately?" This was a well-thought-out campaign targeted at car consumers who had not considered Ford in their purchase decisions or former Ford owners who had switched to other makes. The campaign at least made some people pause and wonder why they had not looked at a Ford or Lincoln/Mercury car.

Then Ford Motor Company created the campaign "Quality Is Job One" in the wake of the successful invasion of Japanese cars that many Americans and consumer groups perceived were better-made and safer. Of note is that the company employed the services of its own factory employees in the commercials and did not use actors playing workers' roles. Internally, the workforce responded positively to these "quality" ads that featured people from the company. There was also the subtle hint that the jobs of these on-screen, hardworking, quality-driven Americans would be possibly jeopardized or lost forever to foreign imports.

One Ford Motor Company institutional campaign, "There Goes Another Satisfied Ford Driver," is best remembered by the many MBAs who studied the case in a marketing or advertising course at business school. The reasons behind the campaign, its message, and how and where it was executed remain a classic case study of psychology affecting postpurchase behavior.

The "Satisfied" campaign came about from applying Professor Leon Festinger's 1940s theory of "cognitive dissonance" to automobile purchase behavior. *Cognitive dissonance* is the theory that people will seek consistency and reassurance from their beliefs and avoid those theories or beliefs that contradict their own. In Festinger's study he indicated that buyers of Fords tended to read Ford advertisements exclusively, excluding from sight Chevrolet or Plymouth ads—even when all ads appeared in the same magazine.

In the mid-1960s, research at the Ford Motor Company revealed that new owners of Ford cars would actively look for other Ford automobiles on driving trips. If they spotted many similar Ford models, this confirmed that they had made the correct purchase decision in buying a Ford. An absence of similar Ford makes and models—or sighting too many Chevrolets—created the "dissonance" of having made the wrong car purchase choice.

Ford Motor Company and its ad agency solved the random hit-and-miss problem of the number of Ford cars seen daily on the road by using billboard outdoor advertising. The billboards blared the happy message, "There Goes Another Satisfied Ford Driver." Ford owners who saw the ads were now relieved of the anxiety of having made a wrong and expensive purchase decision. They would be more prone to praise the car to friends and associates via positive word of mouth.

Two of the other Ford Motor Company notable institutional ads were the 1930s "Watch the Ford Go By" and, later, in 1968 "Ford Has a

Better Idea," which put the light bulb graphic to excellent use. Ford continues to use institutional advertising today to considerable success.

(An institutional campaign that the Ford Motor Company never ran might have been called "Fast Getaway." During the early 1930s, the powerful Ford V-8 was the car of choice for the nation's many infamous bank robbers. A letter to Henry Ford, supposedly from Clyde Barrow—the handwriting was never authenticated—in 1934 praised the model for its speed and reliability.)

## MASTERCARD'S "PRICELESS" CAMPAIGN

In 1997, MasterCard launched a new series of commercials titled "Priceless." This campaign represented average Americans in everyday settings, using their credit card for unselfish purposes by rewarding friends and family. The tagline stated, "There are some things money can't buy. For everything else, there's MasterCard."

Importantly, since MasterCard has no product or line of products other than its credit card, the advertising is considered consumer-oriented and not institutional. MasterCard and its competitors want to generate more users of their cards and also increase usage among the existing cardholder base. Apart from different interest rates and payment options set by participating banks or specific issuing institutions, there is really no difference (other than accruing points or miles) between using MasterCard over VISA or the American Express Card.

The success of the "Priceless" campaign (rolled out globally in 97 countries and in 47 languages) not only increased MasterCard's profit performance, but it also produced a serendipitous benefit: it generated resounding goodwill among the company's workforce. In effect, by translating the benefit of a credit card purchase from self or selfishness to a thoughtful and considerate deed of pleasing others, the campaign moved beyond spending money (bad) to wondrous, favorable deeds (good).

In the "me too" sameness of credit card usage and advertising, MasterCard's current corporate campaign has cut through unremembered ad clutter to achieve a distinct and positive identity. The upbeat attitude of consumers toward the warm and fuzzy advertising succeeded in establishing a new image for the card.

From its launch in October of 1997, MasterCard's "Priceless" campaign has evolved to become a case study in successful global advertising, having earned every major creative award in the industry and more than 100 individual awards. "Priceless" has helped build MasterCard's business, and the campaign is routinely heralded as one of the most successful campaigns ever created.

The success of this campaign in instilling pride within the workforce at MasterCard paralleled the positive accomplishment that occurred at General Motors after the "Family" advertising campaign ran in the early 1920s. Many advertisers realized as Sloan did that worker morale can be influenced by variables greater than company profits.

## THE LESSONS OF INSTITUTIONAL ADVERTISING

Institutional or corporate advertising differs from product or service advertising since its primary goal is to generate a positive opinion among the public and also among leading opinion leaders. In the broadest sense, institutional advertising's objective is to craft goodwill by citing the company's praiseworthy mission or dignified undertaking.

### GOODWILL AT A LOW COST

Most smaller companies or organizations do not have advertising budgets that allow for money to be siphoned away from targeting the client or consumer and used for an institutional campaign. It may seem hackneyed to see the annual procession of company photographs in magazine ads or television commercials that feature a large crowd of smiling employees, mouthing the headline: "We Want Your Business." But the ancillary goal of this obvious and much clichéd announcement is establishing a shared feeling of commonality among the staff.

### BAD TIMING FOR INSTITUTIONAL ADVERTISING

In the current climate of corporate malfeasance (Enron) or internal public dispute (Disney), American companies have received bad press. The bottom line is that a climate of negativity is never a good time to embark on a goodwill institutional campaign.

The public, bombarded, by a steady stream of harmful corporate news, will probably remain unreceptive to any major institutional campaign. The goodwill message will either not be able to penetrate the clutter of negative corporate or organizational stories or, if it does, will bring about skepticism.

One new concept is for corporations to use the Internet for longer (i.e., 90 seconds) goodwill commercials for one-on-one interaction with the public. With more than 40 percent of American online users equipped with broadband hook ups, the possibility exists of reaching some people some of the time.

(Major U.S. corporations have found another way to "publicize" their institutions by having baseball stadiums named after them, a form of local goodwill. Currently, there is Bank One for the Arizona Diamondbacks, U.S. Cellular Field, the home of the Chicago White Sox, and Pacific Bell Park for the San Francisco Giants to name but a few. Nextel sponsoring the NASCAR winner's series is another example. For many years in European football (soccer), global corporations have used the top teams' jerseys to advertise logos. To date, American professional sports have vetoed this type of advertisement.)

### LAST WORD

It is important to remember that even institutional advertising with its goodwill intentions is really selling. As famous advertising legend David Ogilvy said, "Every advertisement should be thought of as a contribution to the complex symbol which is the brand image." Sloan understood that to succeed in the new consumer marketplace he had to transform GM from a lineup of five distinct and unallied car models into one maxibrand called General Motors.

Once Bruce Barton's celebrated campaign began, the American public accepted that a new corporate entity existed in the nation. It was Sloan's charge to meet the expectations of that entity with quality products. GM's spectacular 50 percent share of the domestic marketplace that lasted until Sloan's death was proof positive of his ability to meet and exceed those expectations.

# 11

# DOING THE RIGHT THING:
# THE SLOAN WAY

I
N **ALFRED P. SLOAN, JR.**'S first autobiography, *Adventures of a White Collar Man,* written in 1941, he included a 1940 photograph of the 25-millionth General Motors automobile rolling off the assembly line. On the reverse side is a photograph of Sloan with William Crapo Durant on stage at the celebratory dinner to mark the historic occasion of the record-setting GM car.

Durant clutches Sloan's hand in heartfelt and grateful appreciation as his successor strides toward the microphone to introduce the man Sloan once said "had unusual vision, courage, daring, imagination, and foresight." Twenty years after Durant had been forcibly ousted from the GM presidency by the Du Pont Company shareholders, Alfred P. Sloan, Jr., wanted everyone in the room that night and everyone in the Detroit automobile community to remember that General Motors owed an enormous debt to William Durant.

It was an act of generosity and class to bring back into the public eye the 69-year-old founder of the car company he had named. The ill-fated Durant had lost another fortune in the stock market crash of 1929, and by 1941, he was reduced to dabbling in bowling alleys. Sloan wrote: "The most worthwhile part of it (the celebration) was the opportunity of our entire organization to pay tribute to W.C. Durant, who had the original conception of General Motors, and who was our first leader."[1]

Sloan had always been forthright in his criticism of Durant's mercurial dictatorship at General Motors, but he had never been mean-spirited. He had never gloated over Durant's ouster, never wrote a word of conditional probability along the lines of "If William Durant had listened to me, he would not have...etc."

Another example of Sloan's evenhandedness occurred when management expert Peter Drucker in the early 1940s had been asked by General Motors to prepare an in-depth study on the internal management structure within the company. The result was the watershed book *Concept of the Corporation* published in 1946. This marked the first appraisal of the inner workings ever of a large U.S. corporation and was later used by Henry Ford, III, and the Japanese industrialists after World War II as a blueprint of how to organize and staff large commercial enterprises. (In Japan and Europe the term *decentralization* changed to mean "divisionalization.")

Sloan was not an advocate of allowing any outsider to witness and report on the governance of General Motors. Upon first meeting with Drucker, he let his feelings be known to the newly hired consultant: "You have probably heard, Mr. Drucker, that I didn't initiate your study. I saw no point in it. My associates overruled me. It is therefore my duty to make sure that you can do the best job you are capable of. Come and see me any time I can be of help."[2]

Sloan was good to his word, often inviting Drucker into his office to ask if he had questions on the procedures he had witnessed. When Drucker's book was published in 1946, it was an instant success and created a huge hullabaloo in the corporate world, especially at GM where it was seen as being overly critical of the company and its culture. But Sloan brushed off the book (and its importance) as though it were nothing but a stray and unwanted piece of lint. He did not criticize Drucker's work; he ignored it.

Sloan recognized that Drucker possessed a fine analytical mind even though the consultant had come up with conclusions different from what Sloan believed to be the truth about GM. Sloan asked Drucker's opinion's often on his second, more important and more revealing autobiography and also placed Drucker's name as a candidate for a professorship at the M.I.T. School of Administration, which Sloan endowed.

The act of bringing back William Durant and the act of treating Peter Drucker with politeness and respect were the right things to do. Doing the right thing was a firm guiding principle that Alfred P. Sloan, Jr., followed throughout his years at General Motors.

## SLOAN'S LEGACY

The managerial and leadership brilliance of Alfred P. Sloan, Jr., seems today somewhat antiquarian, because so many of his innovative "firsts" have become standard procedures within corporate America, and his disciplines and practices are taught in some form or another at graduate business schools or in undergraduate business courses. Sloan's basic principles have stood the test of time and remain the basic building blocks of effective managerial leadership in organizations large or small.

The factual proof of his genius is demonstrated by looking at the last page of his second, more detailed autobiography, *My Years with General Motors*. Here is a unit tally of General Motors' vehicle sales from 1909 to 1962. Examining 1923, the grand total for that year for the five car divisions, GMC trucks, and the overseas sales was 798,555. By 1962, the last year he used sales figures for the book, the total number of GM units had risen to 5,238,601—a net gain of 4,440,046 vehicles.

Most significant, the Chevrolet model, which Sloan had championed as the main competitive strategy to go head on with Ford's Model-T, had increased in sales from 454,386 cars in 1923 to 2,555,081 in 1962. It had become the largest-selling U.S. make. Moreover, it had become the first GM car many American families purchased and who then, as their incomes rose, moved up to a more expensive Oldsmobile, Buick, or Pontiac, in accordance with Sloan's plan for "a car for every price and purpose."

In every numerical column on that page, the upsurge in sales units had been considerable. Most noticeably was the 747,154 cars manufactured overseas in 1962 (in four countries: Germany, Great Britain, Australia, and Brazil), which had started with the acquisition of Vauxhall and then Adam Opel AG in 1930 and which cumulatively, represented 14 percent of total GM car sales that year. These overseas automobiles represented new markets that Sloan had established with manufacturing plants abroad.

The facts—Sloan's favorite variable—showed GM's overwhelming success in every division and in every area: market share, profits, and sales volume. In 40 years, General Motors had transformed itself from the distant second place car manufacturer with a low market share behind the Ford Motor Company to become the largest automobile manufacturer in the world. In addition, it had also prospered with its GMAC financing unit and Frigidaire divisions.

(By 1964, two years before Sloan died, U.S. automobile production dropped to 7.9 million units. That year, the Japanese manufactured 482,000 cars, which accounted for only 3 percent of total worldwide production. The Japanese were not then an important player in the world's market, and there is no mention of their car brands in Sloan's second autobiography, published in 1963. These totals would change 20 years later when, in 1984, Japanese automakers would manufacture more vehicles than any other country in the world and hold a 30 percent share of the U.S. auto market.)

## ALFRED P. SLOAN, JR.: LESSONS IN MANAGEMENT AND LEADERSHIP

General Motors significant accomplishments after 1923 came about as a result of Alfred. P. Sloan Jr.'s managerial leadership as president and as CEO. He stated what he considered was the goal of his stewardship at the company: "Those charged with great industrial responsibility must become industrial statesmen."[3]

Sloan demonstrated his statesmanship by making himself available for interviews with the national and regional media during his long tenure at General Motors. He was aware that, as the head of the largest automobile manufacturer in the world, the American public wanted to know what GM was doing and what it planned to do in the future.

In addition, Sloan gave speech after speech at automobile organizations and associations, like the National Association of Manufacturers or internally at the General Motors Dealer Council. He understood that his was the face and the voice of the corporation.

One of the most memorable of Sloan's many public appearances, occurred in 1932 when he appeared before the U.S. House of Representatives' Committee on Labor:

> Congressman Welsh: "What is the saturation point in the automotive industry?"
>
> Alfred P. Sloan, Jr.: "I wish you could tell me. I would like to know."
>
> Congressman Welsh: "What determines sales?"
>
> Alfred P. Sloan, Jr.: "Purchasing power."
>
> Congressman Welsh: "Then you would have an automobile for every person in the United States, is that it?"
>
> Alfred P. Sloan, Jr.: "_Two_ for every person!"

## BUSINESS INNOVATIONS AND POLITICS

During Sloan's tenure at GM, he instituted stock options as a form of executive compensation for the managerial staff of the divisions. This marked the shift within the American corporate system from a one person (or family) ownership society to a shareholder society where much of the stock was owned by the professional managers who ran the company.

Sloan was a lifelong Republican and displayed a keen interest in politics as it affected the macro- and microeconomics of the automobile business. Conspicuously, he always tried to steer General Motors on a neutral path so that it never appeared to take sides in any political debate. He perceived that it was intrinsically wrong for a corporation to ally itself with one political party or candidate or one provocative cause.

His biographer summed up one aspect that made Alfred P. Sloan, Jr., an excellent manager: ". . . to put aside almost all the issues that did not affect GM's profitability is part of what made him so extraordinarily good at his job."[4]

Even the last words of his second biography echo a theme of continuation and regeneration, "Then work of creating goes on."[5]

The final lessons of Alfred P. Sloan, Jr., for today's managers and leaders are that his practical and sound systems "go on." Testaments to his outstanding General Motors' business career success are the four private foundations that bear his name. These offer education, medical care, culture, business learning, and automobile history to the American public.

The Alfred P. Sloan, Jr., Foundation in New York City, which increases its income substantially every year, is regarded as one of the premier not-for-profit organizations in the country, supporting a wide group of deserving institutions and projects.

## THE ULTIMATE SLOAN

Howard Gardner, the well-respected psychologist and author, awarded Alfred P. Sloan, Jr., a special place as the only businessman in his important book *Leading Minds, An Anatomy of Leadership*. In writing about great leaders of history like Margaret Mead, General George C. Marshall, and Robert Maynard Hutchins, Gardner referred back in time to the development of "estates," the many historical and divergent sectors of public life. He praised Alfred P. Sloan, Jr., as "a leader of the contemporary 'estate' of the corporation."[6]

Sloan, almost single handedly, created the corporate estate. He fashioned it, redesigned it, and made the corporation the dominant capitalistic organization in the world. In effect, to paraphrase his famous remark: Every man, woman, and child, including generations yet to be born, owes a debt of gratitude to Alfred P. Sloan, Jr., of General Motors.

# NOTES

## CHAPTER 1

[1] Alfred P. Sloan, Jr., *My Years with General Motors*, New York: Doubleday Currency, 1990 (1963), 4.

[2] Alfred P. Sloan, Jr., *Adventures of a White-Collar Man*, New York: Doubleday, Doran & Co., 1941, 132.

[3] Sloan, *My Years with General Motors*, 317.

[4] Peter F. Drucker, *Adventures of a Bystander*, New York: Harper Collins, 1991 (1978), 285.

[5] Sloan, *My Years with General Motors,* 52.

[6] Sloan, *Adventures of a White-Collar Man*, 193.

## CHAPTER 2

[1] Sloan, *Adventures of a White-Collar Man*, 107.

[2] Ibid., 16.

[3] Ibid., 103.

[4] Ibid., 114.

[5] Ibid., 106.

[6] Ibid., 140.

[7] Sloan, *My Years with General Motors*, 80.

[8] Ibid., 89.

[9] Drucker, *Adventures of a Bystander*, 279.

[10] Sloan, *My Years with General Motors*, 99-100.

[11] Drucker, *Adventures of a Bystander*, 283.

[12] Ibid., 283.

[13] Ibid., 282.

## CHAPTER 3

[1] Sloan, *My Years with General Motors*, 150.

[2] Ibid., 67.

[3] Ibid., 60.

[4] Ibid., 147.

[5] Ibid., 154.

[6] Ibid., 154.

[7] Ibid., 162.

[8] Ibid., 272.

[9] Sloan, *Adventures of a White-Collar Man,* 184.

[10] Sloan, *My Years with General Motors*, 269.

[11] Ibid., 271.

[12] David R. Farber, *Sloan Rules*, Chicago: University of Chicago Press, 2002,101.

[13] Sloan, *My Years with General Motors*, 238.

[14] Sloan, *Adventures of a White-Collar Man*, 183.

[15] Ibid., 183.

[16] Ibid., 53.

## CHAPTER 4

[1] Sloan, *Adventures of a White-Collar Man*, 140.

[2] Drucker, *Adventures of a Bystander*, 104.

[3] Farber, *Sloan Rules*, 13.

[4] Ibid., 33.

[5] Sloan, *Adventures of a White-Collar Man*, 132.

[6] Sloan, *My Years with General Motors*, 60.

[7] Ibid., 62.

[8] Ibid., 64.

[9] Ibid., 98.

[10] Ibid., 118.

[11] Ibid., 141.

[12] Ibid., 129.

[13] Peter F. Drucker, *The Practice of Management*, New York: Harper Business, 1986 (1954), 230.

[14] Ibid., 133.

## CHAPTER 5

[1] Sloan, *My Years with General Motors*, 314.
[2] Ibid., 317.
[3] Ibid., 318.
[4] Ibid., 319.
[5] Ibid., 320.
[6] Ibid., 324.
[7] Sloan, *Adventures of a White-Collar Man*, 203.
[8] Sloan, *My Years with General Motors*, 324.
[9] Ibid., 328.
[10] Ibid., 313.

## CHAPTER 6

[1] Drucker, *Adventures of a Bystander*, 281.
[2] Ibid., 281.
[3] Ibid., 281.
[4] Ibid., 281.
[5] Ibid., 281.
[6] Ibid., 282.
[7] Sloan, *My Years with General Motors*, viii.
[8] Ibid., 44.
[9] Farber, *Sloan Rules*, 120.
[10] Sloan, *My Years with General Motors*, 118.
[11] Ibid., 127.
[12] Drucker, *Adventures of a Bystander*, 263.
[13] Ibid., 264.
[14] Sloan, *Adventures of a White-Collar Man*, 138.
[15] Farber, *Sloan Rules*, 97.
[16] Sloan, *My Years with General Motors*, 170.
[17] Drucker, *Adventures of a Bystander*, 272.
[18] Ibid., 275.
[19] Ibid., 275.
[20] Ibid., 278.

[21] Ibid., 267.

[22] Sloan, *My Years with General Motors*, 367.


## CHAPTER 7

[1] Sloan, *My Years with General Motors*, 340.

[2] Ibid., 340.

[3] Ibid., 4.

[4] Ibid., 6.

[5] Ibid., 302.

[6] Ibid., 302.

[7] Ibid., 304.

[8] Ibid., 306.

[9] Ibid., 306.

[10] Ibid., 310.

[11] Ibid., 341.

[12] Ibid., 342.

[13] Ibid., 350.

[14] Ibid., 354.

[15] Ibid., 357.

[16] Ibid., 358.

[17] Ibid., 362.

[18] Ibid., 373.


## CHAPTER 8

[1] Sloan, *My Years with General Motors*, 45.

[2] Ibid., 56.

[3] Peter F. Drucker, *Concept of the Corporation*, Somerset, NJ: Transaction Publishers, 1993 (1946), 45.

[4] Sloan, *My Years with General Motors*, 46.

[5] Ibid., 47.

[6] Ibid., 48.

[7] Ibid., 48.

[8] Ibid., 48.

[9] Ibid., 50.

[10] Ibid., 53.

[11] Ibid., 53–54.

[12] Ibid., 55.

[13] Drucker, *Concept of the Corporation*, 46.

[14] Sloan, *My Years with General Motors*, 56.

[15] Ibid., 56.

[16] Drucker, *Concept of the Corporation*, 45.

[17] Drucker, *The Practice of Management*, 222.

[18] Sloan, *My Years with General Motors*, 116.

[19] Ibid., 117.

[20] Ibid., 133–134.

[21] Ibid., 148.

[22] Sloan, *Adventures of a White-Collar Man*, 134.

## CHAPTER 9

[1] Sloan, *My Years with General Motors*, 280.

[2] Ibid., 281.

[3] Ibid., 280.

[4] Ibid., 283.

[5] Ibid., 286.

[6] Ibid., 283.

[7] Ibid., 301.

[8] Ibid., 284.

[9] Ibid., 284.

[10] Ibid., 284.

[11] Ibid., 287.

[12] Ibid., 287.

[13] Ibid., 288.

[14] Ibid., 288.

[15] Ibid., 289.

[16] Ibid., 290.

[17] Ibid., 290.

[18] Ibid., 291.

[19] Ibid., 291.

[20] Ibid., 292.

[21] Drucker, *Concept of the Corporation*, 114.

[22] Sloan, *My Years with General Motors*, 284

## CHAPTER 10

[1] Sloan, *My Years with General Motors*, 104.

[2] Farber, *Sloan Rules*, 71.

[3] Ibid., 70.

[4] Sloan, *My Years with General Motors*, 165.

[5] Drucker, *The Practice of Management*, 114.

## CHAPTER 11

[1] Sloan, *Adventures of a White-Collar Man*, 128.

[2] Drucker, *Adventures of a Bystander*, 279.

[3] Sloan, *Adventures of a White-Collar Man*, 145.

[4] Farber, *Sloan Rules*, 248.

[5] Sloan, *My Years with General Motors*, 444.

[6] Howard Gardner, *Leading Minds*, New York: Basic Books, 1995, 132.

# BIBLIOGRAPHY

Drucker, P. *Adventures of a Bystander.* New York: Harper Collins, 1991 (1978).

———. *Concept of the Corporation.* Somerset, NJ: Transaction Publishers, 1993 (1946).

———. *The Practice of Management.* New York: Harper Business, 1986 (1954).

Farber, D. *Sloan Rules, Alfred P. Sloan and the Triumph of General Motors.* Chicago: University of Chicago Press, 2002.

Gardner, H., with the collaboration of Emma Laskin. *Leading Minds, An Anatomy of Leadership.* New York: Basic Books, 1995.

Slater, R. *Jack Welsh and the GE Way: Management Insights and Leadership Secrets of the Legendary CEO.* New York: McGraw-Hill, 1999.

Sloan, A.P., in collaboration with Boyden Sparkes. *Adventures of a White-Collar Man.* New York: Doubleday, Doran & Co., 1941.

———. *My Years with General Motors.* New York: Doubleday Currency, 1990 (1963).

# Index

## ABOUT THE AUTHOR

**Allyn Freeman** is a writer, business consultant, and the coauthor of six successful business books. He holds BA from Brown University, a BFT from Thunderbird, The American Graduate School of International Management, and an MBA from Columbia University Business School. Over the past 20 years he has worked in qualitative research and management, consulting for numerous Fortune 500 companies, including AT&T, Coca-Cola, Ford Motor, and American Express. Currently, Freeman operates Freeman Global, a seasonal consulting business.